The Missing Book of Possibilities

And Other Lost Gods

Gary E. Belschner

Text Copyright 2013 Gary E. Belschner

Graphic drawings by Gary E. Belschner.

Editor, Barbara Fandrich

Other books by Gary E. Belschner:

River Jim World Class Piscator (fisherman) 2010

Dedication

This is my second book. It also must be dedicated to the women who share my life. My wife, Rosemarie, is still putting up with me and is centermost in my life. Jenny, has given us the most perfect granddaughter in the world, Rosalie Danger, who also hits my dedication list. Rachel is a soon-to-be nurse and will be a gift to that profession. My mother, Gloria, is still kicking at ninety this year, and is still a feisty, independent woman. They all bring me joy in this complicated existence. GB

A special thanks to several friends and family that helped me with early editing and storyline suggestions. First, to my brilliant wife, Rose, for her twelve pages of suggestions. She was, as usual, spot on. To my good friend, Bradley Taft, who filtered through his truly Christian heart. My brother, Jay, and his excellent wife, Shelly, helped, as did my daughter, Rachel, and friends, Barb Miller and Norma Yant. Others tried, and for that I thank you. Jeff House and Nathan Kopp top that list. If I forgot someone, forgive me ... I'll do a shout out in the next book.

A special powerful thanks to my amazing Editor, Barbara Fandrich who helps my books be all that they can be.

Foreword

The story of the *Missing Book of Possibilities and Other Lost Gods* takes liberties in all directions. There are Greek and Roman gods that bear the names of both histories. I simply chose the name I liked the best, be it Roman or Greek. They are the correct powers for the name assigned, however.

I have lots of chapters so you never have to keep reading when it's time to quit.

I have used every name I could think of for Satan and I hope you can follow those. You might get confused with the ones that sound good, like "Morning Star" but I think in context all will be fine.

Some folks will be offended by my casual use of Jesus. I understand and I sympathize. If you do read this book, you should easily see I love Jesus, and see the image I hold in my heart of him. We should have at least that in common. My Jesus had a kind and forgiving heart and I believe a sense of humor. He loved his God, his friends, and his wine. I think he would have really liked my book.

Gary Belschne

Chapter 1
– It Begins

The missing Book of Possibilities (And Other Lost Gods)

It was an exceptionally lovely little creek, on an exceptionally lovely little dirt road, in a world somewhere between the beginning and the end. The sky was as blue as, well, Paul Newman's eyes. The creek was bubbling and splashing over its very own rocks and sand, with long, green, grass gently waving in the soft breeze. A casual observer might have missed a quick, bright flash in the crystal clear water. Before a normal person might think of a possible cause, a second flash followed. Next, two upside down splashes shot from the creek. Out of the water flew two little creatures. The exceptionally lovely scene transformed into something entirely different, as the two creatures revealed themselves to be two tiny, winged fairies that laughed and tumbled in the air above the creek. On a closer examination, they proved to be very lovely, naked, prepubescent females, with long, silver wings that crackled and snapped like dragonflies. They left in the air a faint dust that smelled slightly of ginger.

"Me first," screamed the first of the two. "No me," exclaimed the second. "It's my turn and always has been. You follow me, 'cause I found you." "But I wasn't playing THEN," the first retorted, "and now I am!" "But, we are ALWAYS playing," retorted number two. This seemed to be a strong argument, as the first little creature hovered in midair, and held her little chin in her hand. Then, seeming to come to some conclusion, she replied, "Right, you are! Fly for your life, 'cause I am right after you!"

They resumed their joyous little chase in and out of the water, with more giggles and squeals than any normal space of time should contain. Suddenly, one of the creatures stopped dead in midair, with the second crashing right into her behind. They spun through the air but righted in midair. "What, what, WHAT?" demanded the crasher, rubbing her little nose. "I about broke my sniffer!" "So sorry, little sister, but there is something in the mist and it's coming our way if I am not wrong." The little fairies positioned themselves behind a small rock on the bank of the river and peeked down the road.

The road was dirt, as described above, and slightly winding. It wove itself through the woodland where the creek resided. The trees bent over the road and created an arc, just as they should. As far as a normal fairy could see down this road, it ended in a cloud on the ground, which you or I might call a *fog*. Just inside of this cloud, one could barely make out the form of a person who seemed to be moving in the direction of the creek. Naturally, as whoever it was came closer to the creek, they went further from the cloud and so it became clear as the day itself. The person was in white robes, with long black hair and a beard. Having a beard, it was decidedly a man. As more details were revealed, it could be seen that this man was wearing sandals and a most lovely halo. Even in this far-away land, it was obvious even to the most simple of us that the man emerging from the cloud was the Lamb of God, the Alpha and Omega, the Good

Shepherd, the Messiah, Immanuel, Jehovah, the King of the Jews, the Light of the World, the Prince of Peace himself. Yes, it was none other than Jesus Christ...

.... and he had no idea where he was.

Chapter 2
– A Confused King

Jesus held his hand to his face to protect his eyes from the sunshine. He shook his head and tried to clear his thoughts. He turned 180 degrees to look from the direction he came. He seemed to stare into the fog. There was nothing to see but fog. He looked at his right palm, then his left, then rubbed them both together. There was no evidence of damage from the spikes that had been driven through them. He looked down his robe and confirmed his side was also unharmed. He could see his feet but knew before he looked that they would be as solid as the days before his troubles. He had a vague notion that those troubles were now in the distant past, but where he had been, and what he had been doing, were beyond his current recall. He could clearly see the edge of a forest close by, but, realizing he had no plan, he sat down where he was, just outside the fog in the middle of a lovely little dirt road, somewhere between the beginning and the end.

Jesus was not tall with light or blonde hair or blue eyes as some would have liked, but rather, he was average stature with dark hair and eyes and a large decidedly *Jewish* nose. I am not suggesting he was not attractive. He emanated a gentle strength, and was surrounded by a force that could only, honestly, be described as *love*. He was by any measure, beautiful.

Jesus sat for a period of time, which as this was obviously not Topeka, I will not judge. Somehow, he came to the conclusion that, since he was not physically damaged and seemed to have excellent energy, he might as well stand back up and wander down the road.

Looking left and right, he could see close-cropped fields that we would all recognize as grass. It was beautifully cut, with no sign of weeds or drought. It edged the forest perfectly, like a billionaire's summer home.

It didn't take him long to reach the forest and walk through the arch of trees to the edge of a bubbling stream. Still, having no idea where he was, or what he would do, he sat down on the bank of the river and listened to the gentle song of the waters. As he was about to wash away to perhaps some other place, he heard what seemed like a very quiet giggle, then giggles, coming from the far side of a white rock. This rock was about the size and shape of a Roman soldier's helmet and sat on the edge of the clear creek. Jesus watched the rock and soon a very tiny little head with wild yellow hair appeared, then, just as quickly, disappeared to even louder and more abundant giggles.

Having just arrived in a place and time that he knew nothing of and being about as disoriented as a person or deity could be, seeing a tiny little head didn't shock him as it might have in Jerusalem. The laughter continued and soon the little head popped up again, this time sticking its tiny little tongue out at the Son of God and quickly ducking again. A soft smile crossed Jesus's lips and he slowly rose to his feet. "Hello, little one," he tried. Suddenly, two little heads popped up from the rock that looked a lot like a helmet of Roman creation by the banks of a lovely little creek, in a place between the beginning and the end. One squished its face and crossed its eyes, the other put its thumbs in its ears and blew what you and I might call *raspberries* at the Light of the World. Jesus lumbered through the creek to the edge where the rock resided and peered over the edge. He saw two little fairies each holding its little hands over the other's mouth, trying with little success to stifle a continuous cascade of giggles. They were so consumed with unconstrained joy that they did not quickly notice the giant watching them from above. It was only the obstruction of the sun that distracted the little ones from their self-absorption. They slowly lifted their little chins skyward and peered into the loving eyes of the Messiah.

Slowly they stopped their giggling and removed their hands from each other's mouth. They stared into Jesus's eyes, and he into theirs. It was like each side was drinking in an unspeakably wonderful moment, and each side was reluctant for the experience to end.

Finally, Jesus softly said, "What in the world are you?" The two little fairies looked at each other, as if to decide what indeed they were.

"Well," said one tiny one, "the technical word might be "Fairies," but that's just technically. I personally think that is too simple an answer. What do you think?" She looked at her counterpart.

"Oh, I totally agree…but, then again, information is not one of our best features. I think being *us* is what we do best. Don't you agree?" The other nodded aggressively. "*Thinking* is a total waste of time. Having to know things crowds the melon and confuses the fun! But one thing I know about you," she flew up to Jesus's nose and put two little hands on each side of his nostrils, "OOOHHHH...you are COMPLETE." She hugged his giant nose, and kissed him gently on its tip.

The other fairy also flew up to Jesus's face and hovered inches from his left eye. She stared in it, then flew to his ear. "I love you," she whispered.

"I love you too," replied Jesus. "I am *Jesus*. What are your names, that I might address you properly?"

They looked at each other, as if unsure about how to reply. "I guess I am *me*, and she is *her*." The other fairy shook her head with passion. "OH NO, YOU DON'T!" I am ME, and YOU are HER!" A predicable argument broke out, with finger waggling, and head shaking, and serious hands on the hips. It seemed as if the part of the information they considered useless was their names. Jesus stepped in.

"OK, OK, ladies. Just for my benefit, as information has always been a necessary burden to me, I will call you *Sing* and *Song* because ... well ... I love music and I love you too! The little ones looked at each other and then at Jesus. They both frowned. "UUUGGGHHH!" declared the newly christened Sing. "It covers me like long oily wool on a hot summer day! I don't know if I can still even fly!"

Song chimed in, "It's like when I dive in the mud and have to plod around like a troll!" She stomped around like a robot with chains around her feet.

"OK, OK," said Jesus, "Just for me, just for now, ... then you can cast off those burdensome names."

They looked at each other, then smiled. Sing said, "OK, <u>Jesus</u> ... Look at you, '*Song*.'" She began to laugh and laugh, rolling on the ground.

8

Song retorted, "Back at you, 'Sing,'" with equally amused laughs, to boot.

They continued their merriment, then began flying around howling each other's new names, with multiple splashes in and out of the river. Jesus too could not contain himself and laughed like the first supper. He jumped into the creek and splashed around like a trout. Finally, they settled down a bit. The fairies lit on the helmet rock and Jesus sat down on the bank of the river. For a time, they all drifted in the peace and quiet, within the constant gurgle of the little river.

"Maybe you can help me," began the King of the Jews. "You see, I have just sort of appeared here and do not know where I am, or why I am here. Is this Heaven?"

"I don't think so. It's a kind of place that got kind of lost, I think," said Sing. "At least that's what everyone says, but we would be the last to ask. Honestly, I don't think we care much." Song nodded in agreement.

"Really, you need to ask Hermes. He's the God of Travelers."

"But also the God of Thieves," added Song, "so watch your pockets!"

Jesus rose to his feet. After his experience with the little fairies, it was not impossible for him to accept that a mythological god was his best bet for clarity.

"It has been a real treat to meet you both, but I feel a need to find answers to some questions, so I thank you for your friendship and will try to find our old friend Hermes or Mercury, or whatever he is called in this world."

"So you know him?" stated Song.

9

"I know his story," replied Jesus.

"Well," said Sing, "we think your questions will lead to information and only cause clutter in your melon, but if you feel the need, go in peace, but please come back to see us. Hopefully, before that information eats you alive!"

They flew up and kissed him on either side of his face, then flew off down the river, splashing and laughing, as this was what they were created for.

Jesus watched with a smile, then he turned to face down the road. Only one direction was not back to the fog and everyone knows that fog is no place for answers. He began his walk, not too fast and not too slow. He knew without thinking that there could be a very long way to go.

Chapter 3
- First Meeting

*A*s Jesus walked the road, he carried much more confusion than he was used to. In Jerusalem, he was received at a very young age as the promised Messiah and treated as such by his inner circle. His intellectual prowess and his natural curiosity, combined with continuous religious training, made debate with religious leaders with fixed ideas almost too easy. His very religious roots, combined with the firm belief of his mother and the adults around her, allowed him to grow into the role of the Lamb and prepared him to accept his future, as terrible as that might be. Even as a young child, if he doubted his identity he did not show it, except possibly in private to his God.

But, now he was confused. This place was nothing like he expected. It was not the *Throne of God* and it certainly was not *Hell*. There were Greek fairies here, for heaven's sake, and he was, at this moment, supposedly looking for the Greek God Hermes. I must be dreaming, he thought, but at the same time he knew that was not the case. This was not a dream. It also was not what he'd believed, with his entire soul for his entire life, the future would be. To describe the Lord as *confused*, would be a colossal understatement. His only course was to continue down the road and search for answers, whatever they might be.

The road was as pleasant as it had been at the beginning. It was encompassed in soft breezes and blue skies. It retained the gentle leafy trees, which created a tunnel that

12

was not dark and wet, but welcoming and a brilliant green. It was difficult, if not impossible, for Jesus to be unhappy as he wandered on. There were creatures in the woods, but they kept their distance. They were not the creatures of old earth, but they had retained some of those characteristics. There were rabbits with hair of gold and birds that looked more like tiny flying dragons. He saw a stag that looked at him with intelligent eyes and softly whispered, "My Lord." But all kept their distance. It was not out of fear, he judged, but out of a sense of respect and awe. He understood without asking that these simple creatures had no answers for him, so he continued on and allowed them their distance.

It seems that the proper amount of walking is required to get from place to place in this world and when Jesus walked that *EXACT* amount, he turned a corner in the road and came upon a clearing that held a garish wooden wagon with items for sale hanging from every available space. It had wooden wheels, with three of the four intact and one crushed flat. It was half-swallowed by the ground, and appeared to have been there for a millennium. It had a sign across the entire length of the top, painted a brilliant but tattered red, which screamed, "Mercury's House of Oddities – All Items for Sale or Trade." Hanging by one hook, quite crookedly, was another smaller sign that simply stated, "The God Is In."

Jesus walked up to the wagon and addressed it with the customary, "Anybody home?" A large head appeared, bearing a decidedly filthy headband with dirty white wings that flapped ... barely. He had a scruffy beard and long hair, both blond and both judged messy. He was eating something we cannot describe and had his mouth full to the brim.

"Ummmmm.....thorry...must ma minute..." he choked, coughed, then swallowed a huge ungodly bite. "What can I do for you, Pilgrim?" he finally managed to say as he stood up in the wagon. As he stood, legions of crumbs scurried down his ample belly and crashed to the floor. Other items that had collected on his person also found their way to the uppermost layer of junk residing on the floor of the decrepit wagon.

"Well," replied Jesus, "I would guess by the sign that you are Mercury, although you hardly look like the images I have seen in both writings and stone."

"None other!" chimed the God. He looked down at his bulbous belly and said, "Yeah, I guess I have kind of let myself go. There are no messages here to speak of and I have given up on delivery, but I do have some excellent items I can be talked out of, if the coins required are met."

"I am not in the market for the ... um ... *fine items* you refer to; however, I do need information that I have been led to believe you possess."

Mercury looked a bit disappointed, but perked up. "Well, I do have some excellent maps of the gods, for travelers such as yourself. They are hand drawn on birch bark, by *yours truly*, with an eye for detail. On the back are simple histories of the gods with warnings where required. Some folks around here can be darn right dangerous."

Mercury stopped his chatter and really looked at his guest for the first time. "Say, I know who you are. You're

Jesus of Nazareth! You're the guy who put us all in this miserable excuse for a world.

"Oh, my God," he continued, as he climbed over a mountain of junk and exited the rickety wagon, "you are something!" He walked over to Jesus and put his hands on either side of his face. He looked deeply into the Lord's eyes and sighed. "Now I understand. We didn't have a chance. You are .... complete."

"So I have been told," replied Jesus.

"We are just Gods of man," continued Mercury. "We have had strengths and weaknesses each of our own to help humans understand and justify their own situations. Our stupidity and suffering allowed man to forgive their own lacking and to put themselves alongside the Gods, even when their lives were pathetic and hopeless. Our courage and valor also inspired them, at times, to achieve more than they might have. But we failed to tend our flocks and they wandered away. You, however, are different. You are .... what is *possible*. It is easy to see why we were sent here ... where those, with few who believe in them belong, but you ... it is sad to consider that you too have fallen from the simple minds of man."

Mercury looked at himself and tisked. He brushed off some crumbs and tried to straighten his sandals. He tried to put the wings back on either side of his ankles. They were hopelessly tangled, so he soon gave up and looked back at the Savior.

"I myself expected we would be seeing you. When you are twisted in the minds of men into something you never were, it is the same as being rejected or forgotten. You cease to exist. With you, it was only a matter of time. They are merely humans and being complete is only perfect, after all, and surely destined to slip through the holes in the simple minds of man."

Jesus sat on a large rock on the edge of the clearing. "It seems I have much to learn. You will be amazed at how little I know of what you speak. Will you spend some time with me and answer truly the questions in my heart?"

Mercury sat on the grass. "I am limited in my knowledge to realms within my powers. I can explain your impact on travelers and on commerce and thieves ... often, much the same. Of these things I know. For the rest, you will be better served with others who I am certain will be honored to help you. For now, you just relax, Pilgrim, and I will attempt to fill you the best I can. Lord knows, I have had time to think about you and what has become."

Suddenly there was a lovely loaf of white bread, a soft fillet of white fish, and two large goblets of red wine in between the Gods. Jesus smiled. Mercury laughed and said, "Cute. Well brace yourself, Jesus my new friend, you are in for quite a ride."

Chapter 4
– A Dark Arrival

Somewhere on the exact other side of this place, between never and forever, we find a swamp that is as repulsive as a homeless man's butt crack. The muck and slime possessed a stench that lived somewhere between rank sulfur and human excrement. Clouds from the putrescence rose from the stagnant waters that were inhabited by the predictable tufts of land and weeds, snakes, and insects. Two incredibly beautiful women also sat in the mud to their waists, quite naked from what could be seen. They both were full-bodied, with no fat, and had long black hair and olive skin. Their breasts were full, with nipples the size of silver dollars and the color of polished copper.

"I am sick of this," simply stated Eris. "I can't continue forever like this. What is a God with no humans to torture?"

Her role as the Goddess of Discord had been greatly reduced in a world without man.

"You are always bitching, you piece of sludge," spat Apate. "You think you are the only one who is without purpose? I almost wish our existence could end like the squishy pieces of meat called humans did. How could this not be worse?"

Like Eris, Apate, the Goddess of Treachery, found little to do in a land without man. Fooling with the other inhabitants of this place more often than not ended up with more loss than gain. Lots of no-win situations.

"I do love the mud," cooed Eris. If it weren't for sex, I would go mad with boredom."

"I love the stink, too," moaned Apate. "It smells like the most vile acts and perversion."

Apate's head lifted. "What was that?" She looked deeper in the swamp, to where there was no view through the swamp gases.

Eris sat up with a frustrated look, but she too looked in the direction of a decidedly notable splashing sound, the sound of someone or something walking through the waste.

At first, they could more feel the presence emerging than see it. It was a wave of nausea and foreboding that both thrilled and terrified the two women. They watched intently as a figure slowly appeared out of the mist. Slowly the vision cleared with the presence of the most beautiful creature either Goddess had ever witnessed. He was easily five meters tall, with the powerful face of a God. He possessed long black hair, massive arms and chest, with a perfect waist. His thighs were powerful, but not unbalanced. He was balanced in every way and beautiful beyond description. He was covered in jewels and gold. The most dominant overall effect was not the beauty, however, but the waves of evil that emanated from the creature.

The women, in spite of being Goddesses, trembled in his presence. They crawled to their bellies and fell silent.

The truth told that this being was none other than Beelzebub, Lucifer, the Beast, the Antichrist, Abaddon, Belial, Satan, the Father of Lies, the Angel of Light, the Son of Perdition.

It was the Devil himself,

.......and like the gentle Jesus before him, he had no idea where he was.

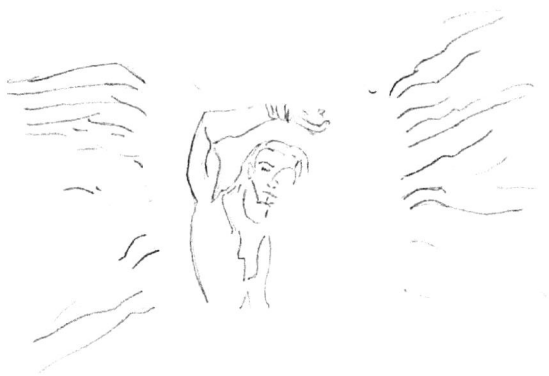

Chapter 5
– Satan

"*W*here the HELL am I?" spat the Beast. "What game does it NOW play? I am sick of this INDIGNATY! I am sick of this MADNESS! I am going to find that pathetic, so called 'God of Creation' and pound him between my palms into dust."

He slammed his fists down into the mud, which threw debris in all directions, and created a mighty thunderclap. He held his fists to his face and emitted an ear-shattering   scream. "YEEEEEEEEEEEEEAHHHHHWAAAAAAAA.....DAMN YOU!!!!!!!"

Suddenly he stopped, sensing the presence of other beings. He swung his head in a circle, piercing the swamp. His eyes settled on the two Goddesses.

The women struggled with a feeling they had never experienced. They felt fear ... a feeling reserved for lesser creations.

Satan looked upon the two beautiful Goddesses and smiled. He laid his head upon his shoulder and rolled his eyes. Drool dripped from his trembling lips. He slowly raised his head, and his smile changed into a look of physical, sexual hunger. He launched himself at Eris and rammed her head deep into the mud. Apate screamed and struggled from her perch. She only managed a step before the Wicked One grabbed her by the back of the neck. He held her off the ground in one hand like a toy. Eris had dug herself from the mud and she screamed in terror. Satan clawed her back until

20

it was ragged and covered in blood. He howled as a beast, and the swamp echoed with the sounds of unspeakable horror. The screams of a man or a woman in savage death are the ultimate images of despair, but pale when compared to the sounds of a Goddess who has never experienced the terror of panic. Now multiply times two ... The swamps suffered for time immeasurable under the weight of it.

All things end in time and this torture too fell away. Silence returned to the swamp. No creature dared to make a sound. The stillness was complete. The scene had changed around the Wicked One. The muddy water was a deep blood red and body parts were strewn across the scene like flotsam after a hurricane. The massive Dark Angel stood in the center of the waste. He remained in the swamp with his head drooping, eyes closed, with breath that came and went like a massive bellows. Saliva dripped from his quivering lips and his muscles trembled. Slowly, his breath calmed and a gentle smile graced his angelic face. He lifted Apate's head, which he still held in his hand, and tenderly kissed the lifeless lips. He gently set it on a tuff of crushed grass and turned away.

"Now to more important things," he muttered and lifted clear of the mud with extended golden wings. He was once again clean and perfect in his majesty. Before surprise, he was gone.

The swamp was quiet for a time.

Then, the waters of the swamp began to churn. The blood and bone with a life of its own made its way to each other to rejoin as one. Soon two Goddesses stood whole again in the swamp and stared at each other in silence.

Finally Eris spoke.

"Things seem to have changed in our little world."

"True, my sister, and perhaps not for the better. This one is not from our legends. I fear this is the Fallen Angel from Christian myth."

"So that is fear. That is how humans feel," said Eris. "I almost feel sorry for them."

"Don't waste your feelings ... it seems this thing is upon us ... for better or worse. This could truly be the end times." The two sat back down in the swamp and considered.

Somewhere quite far away, but still within the confines of the massive swamp, another dark creature took note. Its entire thought process consisted of only one word ..."Finally."

Chapter 6
– The Search Begins with Pan

*7*he soft *whoosh* of the golden wings made surprisingly little sound. The fallen prince scanned the ground below him and sniffed the air, attempting to locate the God of All. His anger was at maximum. His desire to finally destroy his nemesis and assume his rightful place as God of All, enveloped his entire consciousness. He had come to believe this was his destiny. All of the hateful things, the temptation and attempted destruction of human kind, were for that purpose and that alone. In the mind of the Son of Perdition, there could be no other solution and he was ready.

The grounds below him were changing from dark and dying to spots of green. There were signs of occupation with a simple hut here and there and a cart path or trail winding through the terrain. He was a bit disappointed at his earlier lust and violence. It was not that he regretted anything, except for the fact that he had learned nothing. He might have held off a moment longer. But they were so .... *available*. He was now confident that there were more fools in this place and he would get the information he sought. He could sense clearly that the one he hunted was here, in this place. He could not hide. There would be an end to this.

Satan did not wish to speak to just anyone, however. He wanted information, and that would not be available to *peasants*. He was searching for someone of stature.

After a time, again in its proper time, Satan saw a creature of interest. It sat on a hill with a staff in its hands.

23

Satan was standing before the creature in an instant, his evil emanating from him like brilliant color, his golden wings spread full and erect in his majesty. He towered over the creature and stared. It was half-man, half-goat and the spitting image of the creature ignorant humans had created to represent the Devil himself. He knew at once this was a creature that never existed. This was Pan, the Greek God of Shepherds, and he was fast asleep.

The puny creature's disrespect annoyed Satan. It should feel him. It should tremble in awe at his presence, but no, it slept! He debated with himself if he should just crush its head and be done. He restrained himself with a promise that when he had the information he needed, he would do what he was created to do. He would make it suffer.

He lifted his foot and placed it on the forehead of the little God. He pushed the sleeping creature over to the ground, where it simply curled up, let out a soft fart, smiled, and began to snore.

"Wake up, you filthy piece of dung," screamed the Antichrist. He pounded his hand on the ground, creating a massive thunderclap.

"Whooooowanawanawanawana,"stammered Pan, as he simultaneously rubbed his eyes and scratched his balls. "What a noise!" He stuck one figure in each ear, opened his mouth, and began stammering, "Mamamamamampapapapapapoooooo ooommmmmmmlalalalalalala...." It seemed he was having a hard time hearing after the thunderclap.

"I have questions of you," stated Satan.

24

"Huh? Huh? What, What, WHAT?" yelled little Pan. "Who are you? What'd you say? I can't hear you. Musta got struck by lightning again ... damned Zeus!"

Satan rolled his eyes, and debated again about simply crushing this one and moving on. "Hear me." he commanded.

"Oh, OK, OK, they popped, they popped, got you clear as day, now. Wow, you're a big fella aren't you? Oh, wait a minute, wait a minute, I know who you are. You're that Satan fella, right? Sure, you are. Nasty bastard by all accounts too, aren't you? You and sweet Jesus put us in this place, well not exactly, physically, but, well, you know, I suppose." The little Greek God sat quietly and stared at the God of Evil. "Wow, if I am not mistaken, you are, well, COMPLETE, in a totally nasty way."

"ENOUGH," hissed the Devil. "I do not have the time or patience for you. You will tell me what I wish to know and be done."

"OK, OK, Mister Devil, sir ... but I am a God too you know and you should show some respect for that after all."

"SILENCE," spat the Devil. He stared down at the little satyr. "You are insignificant and pathetic and far beneath me. I am the Anointed Cherub and the Angel of Light and will rule the universe. You will answer my questions and be done."

Pan waggled his finger at the giant demon, "Look here, Mister Devil, sir, all I was saying was—"

The Devil put his nose against the tiny Pan's nose, and quietly said, "I ... will ... speak ... now."

Pan was quiet, but looked a bit put-out that his point was not taken.

"Where am I?" asked Satan.

"Well, as I am not having fun right now and I do like to have fun, I am not going to tell you the story in a fun way. I am just going to keep it simple. I will answer your questions, but quick and easy so you can be on your way and I can be on mine—"

"WHERE AM I?" screamed the Devil.

"You are in a land where Gods all go when they have no one on earth that REALLY believes in them. There, I said it ... simple and quick."

"This is not possible," muttered the Devil; I am the Prince of Darkness. All mankind fears me. This is not possible."

"Well, there are other ways folks show up here too," said Pan. "If folks twist your memory, so you no longer resemble yourself, you end up here. Actually, I thought you would have been here a long time ago, and that Jesus fella too. I mean, they made you look like me and all I like to do is play my flute, watch sheep, get drunk, screw, have fun and such. I can't imagine a creature less like you." He looked the Devil up and down and sneered.

Satan noticed the slight, but reminded himself he was way above this pathetic creature and his disrespect was meaningless. He would suffer when the information was complete.

"Tell me more," he demanded.

"Actually, humans have made a fool of you, if you think of it. They named a ham after you ... Yeah, PIG BUTT,

'Deviled Ham.' What a JOKE! They say, when a baby is cute, 'He's a cute little devil.' They actually had a comedian who dressed up like a woman and cried, 'The DEVIL made me do it' and EVERYBODY laughed and laughed! Yeah, not much like the gorgeous, nasty, hunk of God standing before me. They have this holiday, called Halloween, where millions of little children dress up like another image of you, all red with a tail and stupid little horns and go from house to house, asking for candy. It goes on and on. There is this tiny, sucking, vacuum cleaner..."

"ENOUGH," spat the Devil. "I am convinced, and it is of little matter. I need to know where the God of All Things is. I will deal with him and this parlor trick will be made right. Even the stupidity of man is of little consequence to me. It is the one God that I will crush and be done."

"Wow, aren't you full of yourself," puffed Pan. "If you are looking for Zeus, he will be on his throne. If you think you can whip him, you will have your hands full, even a nasty brute like you."

"Your Zeus is nothing to me. I seek the God of All."

"Zeus is the God of All here, and if you need the boss, that's the guy." Pan was getting squirmy, and it was obvious he had had enough of the Most Wicked of the Wicked.

"Very well, where do I find him?" replied Satan. "At the very least, he will know more than a pissant like you."

"Around here, it takes as long as it must and the direction is of no consequence. Just begin your search, and when the perfect amount of time necessary has been spent, you will be there ... and YOU are the pissant," snorted Pan.

He turned and began to stamp away. Satan jumped on him, lifted him in the air and shoved him into his mouth. He gulped him whole and let out a huge belch.

Finally done with him, Satan thought to himself. He walked to the top of the hill and considered his options. The rumble in his stomach was small at first but totally unheard of for the God of the Night. It grew more and more severe and moments later he emitted a giant burst from his ass. The tiny Pan squirted out complete and unharmed. He was covered in a nasty slime, but shook his head, stared at Satan, wiped his face, and asked, "Can you do that again? That was ... AWESOME."

Satan sadly shook his head. On giant spectacular wings of pure gold, he slowly lifted off the ground and was instantly gone.

Chapter 7
– More Gods, Mercury and Mars

Jesus and Mercury had been speaking for some time. The fish was gone and several glasses of fine red wine had been consumed and miraculously replaced.

Jesus began, "Thank you, my new friend, for having patience with my confusion. I can see there are others I need to find, to complete my understanding of the times on earth since my departure. I am most amazed by the twisting of reason to ideas and beliefs beyond the imagination of my purpose. I was to be the bridge from Judaism to direct communion with God. I was supposed to be the Chosen One of the Jews. While Gentiles have a place at the table with my Father, my message to them was not direct ... and now, I am their 'GOD' and ignored by my own people. While perhaps this was Yahweh's purpose, it was beyond my imagination. I am not convinced, and as I am in this place it would seem humans have lost sight of me. Now, I too have lost sight of *me*.

"The magnitude of the world is one thing that amazes me the most. The church that claims to come from the heart of my apostle Peter, worth many billions of dollars, and full of terms I do not understand—but the ultimate truth, I see very clearly. Much good done, but from what you have said, equal evil also done. Is this not the ultimate condition of man? I am sorry that the church has fallen so often to the temptation of riches. I could see this clearly when I was on earth. One might say that my greatest displayed anger was in the temple, with the moneychangers. When money is involved, sin is always close beside. The idolatry amazes me! The concept of a hierarchy of saints, the papal infallibility, this is not what I believed. This is not the message I brought. That this church was the creation, somehow, of my simple and beautiful Peter, is also difficult to believe. We spoke often, he knew my heart. This could not be. The concept that I am God ... not just the message of holding God in me, but the actual, one God is also ... difficult. Often, I cried out for God's mercy. Often, I prayed to and offered praise to my God. That I am somehow God is a burden I am afraid I cannot bear. Although perhaps I am God, if all humans are God as we are all his creation and an extension of him.

"And is it so with you, as well, my friend Mercury, or am I in a dream between reality and fantasy? Why would my mind create such a fantasy? This truly is beyond my imagination."

"I have no answers for you, my friend," said Mercury. "I feel for your confusion. It is difficult enough to accept our prison of non-belief, without trying to imagine the complexities of your situation. As I said to begin with, I am limited. For true answers you will have to speak with others."

"Where would you have me go, then?" asked Jesus.

"Oh, just around the corner, I guess. This place is not like earth. It seems to decide where you need to go. Continue down the road, with purpose, and you will get where you wish. If you have no specific direction, it seems to know what is needed, and it is there you are led. The questions you have and what is in store for you, I cannot tell, so my advice is to just continue down the road.

"Be wary, my friend," cautioned Mercury. "I feel another has come to this world, and I fear he brings a great evil."

"I have felt it too," replied Jesus. "He is not a stranger to me, and I should have expected his arrival."

Jesus stood up and dusted his robes. Mercury also stood, and took Jesus's hand. They hugged each other, and Jesus turned and walked down the road. Mercury watched the Lord disappear around the turn in the road, and wondered how a small, gentle Jesus could carry such a large load. He shook his head, then climbed back into his wagon. This is a message worth delivering, he thought. Now where are my clean wings?

Jesus had much to think about as he walked this road, in this place. As he walked, he marveled at the handiwork of God. It was so much more than he knew. If a place like this could be filled with the Gods of the Greeks and Romans, it was true that, indeed, all things are possible. He always believed that all things were part of God's perfect plan, and now he began to weave this world, too, into that plan. He felt without doubt that the Prince of Darkness was also here. He knew, with a mixture of fear and resignation, that this would end in confrontation, as it always was to be.

He began to hear noises that evolved into massive grunts and groans, combined with clangs and crashes. Words became clear.

"Die, scoundrel, die! Take this and that, parry, bend, strike, repeat."

The next bend in the road revealed a massive warrior with plated armor of polished metal, in a brutal fight with an invisible foe. His helmet was polished bronze, with a brush of horsehair down its middle. He wore a short-skirted armor of polished steel. His shins were protected by ornate metal, as were the tops of his feet. He had massive arms, with knots of muscle. His neck was like that of a furious bull, corded and knotted. His thighs were as powerful as a stallion. Jesus watched with amazement as this level of warrior was eons beyond that of mortal man. The warrior jumped with dexterity and ducked with amazing quickness, all the while challenging and cursing *the no one* he was engaged with.

"Now, now, NOW!" he screamed, as he lunged with his massive sword again and again. Suddenly he sprang backward, spun in midair, and ended with his blade neatly set upon the soft throat of the Savior. He had Jesus by his hair, with his head tilted upward.

"Easy, easy," he whispered softly to himself. "A moment, Ares ... breathe, that's it." Slowly, he released Jesus and stepped back, breathing like a racehorse.

"It's you," he said. "I did not think you would come to me. What could you possibly want from an old battle horse such as I?"

Jesus stepped back, trembling, with wide eyes. He had not known such fear since the cross. "I, I don't know," he stammered. "I was just walking down the road, I, I, I—"

"Oh, calm down, Jesus. I mean you no harm. When I am the warrior, I am difficult to stop. When I train, in my mind, I envision a great enemy, and it took me a second to see you. You, of course, have nothing to fear from me."

"And, of course, you would be Mars," said Jesus, as he slowly commanded his heart to quit trying to escape his chest.

"Ares, Mars, be you Greek or Roman what difference would it be to me? I repeat, what would you have to do with me? You are the God of Peace, and I am the God of War; what greater divide?"

"I do not know why I am here," said the gentle Jesus, "but I am told that if we found each other in this world, it is for a reason. You are not my opposite, as you battle for reason, including justice and honor. Hate, treachery, deception are the enemies I know, and the one who commands such."

"You do not know me, Jew. I am not the God of Justice, I am the God of War. I am the Perfect Warrior, and as such I do not judge the war, I fight, and I fight perfectly. A soldier does not ask if it is good and proper to kill the enemy. He kills the enemy. It is for kings and politicians to choose the conflict. If there was choice and reason in every blow there would be dead soldiers only. In the time it would take to ponder such things, I could slay a battalion—or be slain. No, don't accuse me of making judgments. These things are not for me, or for those who follow me."

"But you must, at some time, choose your king," replied Jesus. "And here, your honor and reason come to play."

Mars looked into an unseen distance. "Yes, you speak the truth. Some warriors do choose their kings. They travel the world to fight the great fights, for the great truths.

Most are not so fortunate. They must fight for even an evil king, with evil intent."

"How can this be so? Could they not fight and die, rather than support such a king? Would this not be the choice of a perfect warrior?" The Christ had not considered war often because of his conviction that love and peace were the greatest weapons, and death was only the bridge to God and reward.

"So, if your wife and thirteen-year-old daughter were to be sex slaves for the army of the wicked king if you did not fight, this would make no difference to you? That your mother and father were to be tortured matters not?"

Jesus shook his head. "There is a road to salvation through every life. The suffering of the flesh is not as difficult as the tortures of the soul. I hear what you say, but I will say it is better to suffer or die in justice, love, and honor than to exist in this world in the service of the damned."

"Again, I say to you, I am not the God of Justice. When I am involved, these heavy matters have been decided. It is only significant to me that the war is waged well, the sword is thrust properly, the bow is strung, the arrow slipped, the ax wielded, and that the warrior performs well in the act of war. Morals, truth ... my God, TRUTH? Have you never dealt with humans? Their truths are so complicated, even they can't say which side they are really on. Each has its wicked and each has its righteous. How in the world can a simple soldier judge?"

Jesus smiled sadly at the huge God of War. "You speak truly, but I know your heart. In each case you defend, you would do the best you could, and this is the righteous thing. Evil confronts us every day, in all ways. It is the decisions we make that define our souls. A proper warrior has his truths and will die rather than betray them. He would not leave a buddy on the field; he would not be a traitor or slay the defenseless. A soldier, perhaps more than most, understands these things and knows that ultimately, to win the war, a list of undeniables must be obeyed, or all will surely be lost."

Mars slowly nodded his head. "I might argue the details but not the spirit of what you say. There have been times...and perhaps the most important still to come ... when warriors must decide. I feel a great evil alongside your great good. If you need my sword when that time comes...I am in your service."

Jesus smiled and touched the warrior's arm. A moment of joy rushed through them both as they knew each other and were momentarily one. Mars sat on the ground with his sword between his legs as Jesus turned and walked down the still lovely little road.

Chapter 8
– Satan and Nodutus

Satan's fury was beyond description. Not at the foolish little goat man that had showed him so little respect, but rather at the God of All who had somehow transported him to this strange place. He tried to think of the world he had left and the success he had enjoyed in destroying attempts at peace and love spread by agents of the One God...a God he would, without doubt, destroy and replace. He thought also of the pathetic little Jew who was supposed to wage an epic battle and throw him down. The idea was so absurd, it was beyond consideration. He only revived these images to reinforce the weakness and folly of the efforts displayed by his enemies. The Wicked One actually laughed as he reviewed his cat and mouse game with the little Jew. He had twisted everything the "King of the Jews" had said and done, and had easily confused pathetic humans. He thought of peace, which he had overshadowed by war. The very image of the "Christian soldier," of pistol-packing Christians, made him smile with pleasure. The simple message of the Christ itself, he had twisted to an unrecognizable religion with factions and intolerance. He had used the ambitions of caesars and kings to rewrite the message to reinforce idolatry and greed. Forgiveness was replaced with judgment. That the simple truths of Jesus remained in their "Christian" Torah annoyed the Wicked One, but there was enough deception wrapped around those simple truths to cloud even the most diligent pilgrim...and Satan had little trouble amplifying that confusion.

"That's better," he said to himself. He laughed out loud and reprimanded himself for letting the enemy anger him and thus distract him from his purpose. He had succeeded in every effort with man, and would take that apparent power with him as a crown when he destroyed the present God of All.

His ego sufficiently restored, he focused his energy on seeking his ultimate enemy. He could feel that the Christ was in this world, but he was comfortable that he was beneath contempt. He was of no consequence, simply a pathetic little Jew.

He soared above this new world and surveyed the land. There were more creatures, but nothing worthy of his notice. There were more questions than answers regarding this world, but Satan considered them insignificant when placed next to his ultimate quest. After a time, he could not but realize he was getting no closer to his enemy. While not going in circles, he was just flying from nowhere to nowhere. His frustration and anger returned. He settled to the ground and smashed his fists on the ground.

"You cannot hide from me," he screamed. "You are pathetic and weak! Show yourself," he demanded, with words that shook the earth.

"OK, OK, for Zeus's sake, don't yell! I am not really hiding, I was just already on my knees peeking from behind the rock." An awkward looking young God, of sorts, stepped out and stood before the massive God of Everything Evil. "It's nothing personal, you see, but you are a big one and seemed to be kind of angry, though I am not sure what I might have done."

Satan looked with disdain at the unexpected entity before him. The person was about the size of a human male, with a tan toga of a material not easily determined. He had a ring of wheat stalks woven around his attractive blond head, which he wore like a crown.

"Who or what in hell are you?"

"Well, I am Nodutus, actually...and a God of this land, the last land and probably the next, I guess."

"You are a GOD? This is beyond belief. Are you evil or other?" He sniffed the God up and down. "If you are evil, it is not apparent."

"Well," began Nodutus, "I am not evil by nature or purpose, so I guess I would be *other*."

"I have but one question of you, then we will be done ... Where is the One God? How do I get to him in this twisted world?"

"I do not know of a 'One God', but it might be possible. If he is here his memory is so twisted by humans, he has ceased to exist. Just like you and me."

"Do not dare to speak for me, you maggot. My patience is thin, and your very existence is in peril."

"Oh, I doubt that! And although you are big and bad, you certainly are not the boss of me!"

Satan slapped his hands together around the small God's head. Blood and brains squished between the Dark Lord's fingers and covered the ground.

Satan briefly reprimanded himself again, for having terminated an entity before finding answers for his questions. He gazed at the fallen body surrounded by body mush.

Suddenly, the gore began to come alive. It started flowing in ripples toward the body in the dirt. It quickly filled in gaps and holes, and in mere moments, returned the small God to whole.

"Whew," he spat, "was that necessary? Big God, oh yeah, Big God! .... Like to see you do that to Zeus, or even Mars! ... Then, we'd see whose brains got smooshed!" He picked himself up as Satan stared at something he had never witnessed. Not in all eternity.

"What powers do you hold, small one? What manner of God are you?"

Nodutus's anger was slowly replaced by a visible uncomfortableness. "Well, I am a God, after all ... yes, indeed, a genuine God, just like everyone here. A God is a God after all."

Satan grabbed him by the front of his toga and pulled his face close to his. "What God ARE you?"

The smaller God sighed. While he could not be killed by the God of All Evil, he still would rather not have his head squashed again. "I am the God of ... tying knots in stalks of wheat." He puffed out his chest but also visibly shrank in stature. "If it is necessary that you know."

The Devil stared down at the smaller God. The incredible disrespect he felt at having to communicate with this lesser being, drove the Prince of Darkness to a most violent fury.

Suddenly, he smacked his hands on the ground and screamed, "COME BEFORE ME, YOU PATHETIC GOD OF ALL! SHOW YOUSELF, YOU COWARD! STAND BEFORE ME, I COMMAND YOU!" He paced in circles, screaming and jumping up and down. "I WILL NOT TOLORATE THIS FOR A MINUTE MORE!!!" He raised his wings in a mighty arc, lifted his arms in fists to the sky, and screamed into the air, "NOWWWWWWWWWWWWWW!!!!!!!"

The mighty Dark Angel stood with his fists raised and his chest heaving. Gradually, he dropped his arms and dropped his head with eyes closed.

"Nothing, huh?" said Nodutus after a respectful time. "I know how you feel ... no respect. Sure, I am just the God of Tying Knots in the Stalks of Wheat, but I am still a God after all. I have BEGGED Zeus to give me something else. I mean, I have tons of time. I could do all kinds of cool stuff, but he just looks at me and laughs. Oh sure, poor little Nodutus ... no respect. Man he can be an ASS! I feel your pain, dude."

The Devil sat with a crash on the ground of this strange world between the beginning and the end. He wrapped his wings around himself and was motionless.

The little Greek God walked over and sat next to the Lord of Darkness. He sat in silence and solidarity, sadly shaking his head at the hopelessness ... Oh Zeus, the hopelessness. Every once in a while he sneaked a look at Satan, to see if he appreciated the bonding.

After what felt like an eternity to Nodutus, the Wicked One slowly unwrapped his wings and sat staring at the little God next to him.

"How do I find him?" he whispered. "How do I find him?"

Nodutus wrinkled his brow, now feeling a sense of camaraderie with Lucifer. "It's not that easy," he began. "In this place, you cannot walk ... or fly from place to place. It is more that time and purposes conspire with intent, to complete goals." When the perfect time has come, you will be there. If I were you I would continue with purpose, but do not expect time and space to be as they were where you came from.

"Say," said the little Greek God, having had a thought, "I do believe you will find Zeus, and maybe when you do, you could help me out. I mean, he might listen to you. Would you consider asking him if he would give me another thing to be God of? I have lots of ability, and stand willing to do whatever else I can ... I mean how many knots can a God tie in stalks of wheat?"

He looked into the eyes of evil and instantly understood this was not going to happen. The Devil jumped on him and ripped him into pieces, throwing some to the wind, eating some, and mashing others in his powerful fists. He jumped into the air, spread his mighty golden wings and flew into the sky, leaving what was left of the little Greek God strewed across the land ... except for a thin ribbon of Nodutus streaming from his ass.

Chapter 9
– Dionysus

Jesus's mind was full of questions. He wondered what God the Father's purpose was in creating this space and time. He felt the wickedness of Lucifer and was becoming convinced that both of them being in this place was no coincidence. He walked on, playing out possible scenarios regarding their inevitable confrontation. None was pleasant, and he wondered how love alone could possibly destroy a being like Satan who had such violence and wickedness at his disposal. Jesus felt familiar feelings of fear and doubt.

As he continued down the road, he rightly reasoned that such thoughts and concerns were of no value now. He could sense that both the distance and time until such a meeting were a ways off. He understood that his Father God had a perfect plan, and Jesus, as always, would accept whatever his role was to be.

As he crested over a gentle rise, he saw another resident of this reality. He recognized him from the writings and the drawings of the Greeks and Romans. The God was sitting on a stone bench on a small rise in the road. Leafy boughs arched over his head creating a cozy sort of open-faced tent. He was wrapped in the fur of the fox, with a ring of grape leaves wrapped around his head. This was obviously a man, but with an androgynous appeal. Without a doubt it was Dionysus, the God of Wine, and Jesus was truly glad to see him.

"Well, look who's here," said the affable deity, "and if I am any judge of character and circumstance, you have been long on the road and are ready for a fine taste of wine."

Jesus smiled and nodded. "You are not only the God of the finest liquid that our God has created, but also a mind reader. I wander and worry, and worry and wander ... in this way, this world is so much like the last. A drop of wine would be the perfect medicine for a mind so afflicted. It seems you are alone today, so perhaps not inclined to your female followers, the maenads, and the wilding they bring."

The two shook hands in a way that was really more of a hug.

"No, no, sweet Jesus, it is only me, with a fine bottle of wine and a friendly shoulder to cry on. I have heard the news of your travels, and your questions, and would love to help where I can, while we take vicious advantage of this innocent bottle of wine."

Jesus sat near the bench on the shoulder of the road where the grass was soft and trim. "It seems my friend Mercury has found my situation to finally be a message worth delivering."

"Yes, indeed," replied Dionysus. "He has new spring in his step. I swear he has lost thirty pounds if he's lost an ounce. The wings on his feet don't huff and puff so when they lift his carcass, and my maenads have begun to notice him more... though, when it comes to a good bawdy round of sex, they were never very discriminating. It is miraculous what a bit of the grape can do to enhance the attributes of a potential lover. But, I wander. Relax, my friend, and let me look at you."

The true Party God looked Jesus up and down. "Yes, yes," he said. "You are something else. Not much to look at, as far as the purely physical, but your aura is ... well ... AMAZING, and the total effect is delicious!"

Jesus squirmed a bit where he sat, not quite sure if the stare was purely platonic. "Calm down, Romeo," said the Lamb of God. "I am comfortably sure that that bottle of wine would not be enough to bend me to your appetites. But, let's focus on the wine and the many common things we do share."

Dionysus poured two goblets of a rich red wine, and the two gently eyed each other.

"Well said, my new friend," said Dionysus. "I can easily see that your purpose is beyond ours and this place. It is no wonder we were cast upon this rock. We are truly not of your stature in a cosmic sense. I do thank you for enjoying wine and in doing so, saving it from zealous followers of the religion your simple life spawned. They made every other pleasure of man wicked and in doing so, more often than not, made many simple people sinners and victims of persecution, torture, and death. My followers suffered greatly, but I do not blame you. Forgiveness seemed to be high on your list of teachings and very high on the list of things your followers chose to ignore."

Jesus thought for a moment, then began, "I do not know all of what has transpired since the cross, but in this, I thought I was so very clear. Judgment is for the Father. It is not for us. Let the one who has sinned the least cast the first stone, I said. I said that people should look first at themselves before they condemn others. I said that the ones who judge on earth will be harshly judged in Heaven. How clear did I have to be? My message was of love and tolerance. Tell me honestly, what went wrong?"

"Humans are pack animals. They need someone ahead to lead and command. They need someone behind for them to lead and command, and way too many seem comfortable in following without any thoughts of their own. How would this be without judgment, without well-defined right and wrong? Tell me what to do, so I can tell someone else what to do, and when they find someone weak and outside of the pack, they are justified in judging them. In your simple deeds they created a complex system of sins and duties. Simply put, anything that brought humans physical pleasure is a sin, and what they consider *surrender and sacrifice* was a positive. As you might imagine, I would disagree."

"It is not as I preached. I came to free the people from the Old Testament. Free them from the harsh law, from the *eye for an eye*. Free from the stoning and the sacrifices. I was the Messiah that bore the sins of man. I took on the collective karma. It was never meant to be easy, but I tried to make it simple. Love could conquer all things. The Ten Commandments showed a simple path, a path upon which I was to be the light."

"I think part of the problem was that you did not really address physical love," stated Dionysus. "You were without a companion, and left the details of those relationships to the wandering, simple minds of man. I might ask why that was so."

"My life on earth was short and focused. I was a rabbi with a specific task, to fulfill the prophecy of the Messiah. From my earliest days, I was cast in this role and focused all of my attention to its successful end. There was a Mary in my circle that I cared for, and perhaps in time ..." Jesus stared into the distance, and both Gods fell into their own thoughts.

"Well," began Dionysus, "In this you left a mess. Sex is, without a doubt, the most confusing, misunderstood, commanding experience in life. All physical relations involving physical love begin with raging lust and desire, and it gets more confusing from there. Even after a lifetime, humans will easily rate *interpersonal relationships* as the top of their list of mysteries. But, of this I am not an authority. There is one, whom I assume you will meet, who is perfect in these ... shall we say ... *affairs*. I, myself, am a master of casual, recreational sex and general drunken debauchery.... and proud of it!" He lifted his glass to the Son of Man and drank a long draught.

"Even in these things, there is love," began Jesus, with a thoughtful look. "If there is mutual respect and tenderness in the physical, and peaceful playfulness in the spirit of the wine, I do not see the sin. I can confess to a couple of evenings with the apostles where an evening began with a glass of wine and spiritual debate, and ended with jokes, slurred speech, and hearty singing of songs. A morning or two with a pounding head, I would admit to, also."

"A 'couple of evenings'?" asked Dionysus with a smile.

"Well," replied Jesus with a little grin, "perhaps a few.

It does remain a dangerous game, however. Love is easily turned to lust. The God-given drive to reproduce can make men do wicked things. The need for love instilled in women and men can make them confuse love and power and put them in harm's way. Misinterpreted scripture can mislead humans to replace love with hate in this regard."

"Tell me truly," began Dionysus. "Do you condemn love other than *man and woman* love...the love of a man for a man, or a woman for a woman? Do you judge like your followers do?"

Jesus thought for a moment.

"What I tried to say was that sin is universal, yet is also personal. I tried in many ways to say that man was not to judge. Judge not, lest ye shall be judged. He who is without sin, cast the first stone. Why do you see the speck that is in your brother's eye, but do not notice the log that is in your own eye? How can one, especially one without love, truly understand the content of another's heart? I tried to show that judgment of others is only vanity. It is, if closely observed, sinful in nature. Let the caesars of the world bring judges to support the laws of men. It is not for those that truly seek the kingdom of God. If those who wave a religious flag and crusade against those they condemn were to reflect on the content of their heart, many would recognize hate, and hate is the sword of Satan, the worst sin of all."

Jesus continued, "I would say a man or woman knows their own heart. If there is cruelty or disregard for their partners, or lust without love and respect, then there is sin. But, this could be man and woman sex, as well... and most often is. If rather there is love and commitment, if there is respect but above all love, then I would not judge. A man or woman knows their own heart. Sin is evil, and evil is as obvious as the sky. I would say, do not sin. The world can be a difficult place, and it is easy to see that everyone needs someone to hold onto. I would not condemn anyone to suffer a lonely heart."

"Humans are clever creatures indeed," commented Dionysus. "They have created devices to prevent conception. How do you regard this?"

Jesus thought for a moment. "With more than seven billion people on earth, it is no wonder they recognized a need to refrain from having children. The number is beyond belief. I would imagine my Father's hand was in these creations. He would not long allow the starvation and disease that would surely follow such masses."

"It has helped, but not put an end to such suffering. I have another thing to tell you that is hard to fathom. People have begun to regularly, intentionally, end a mother's pregnancy. It has become almost accepted for many people. The more extreme of your followers fight this procedure, at all costs, and there is much hatred on both sides of this issue."

"This was done in my time as well, and in this my heart breaks. How can this be so? It is beyond reason that a mother could consider an option like this."

"So it would seem. However, do not judge all so quickly. They have also found ways to monitor a baby from conception to delivery. They can see every finger and hear every heartbeat. They are now able to determine the health and wellbeing of the little one as it is growing. Sometimes, as you know, things do not go well."

"Yes, this is true," said Jesus. "The loss of a baby is a difficult lesson, perhaps the worst, but, death is a part of life's lessons."

Dionysus continued, "True, my Lord, but man has also learned how to prolong these young lives, and this sometimes leads to very long and painful suffering. A quick return to the arms of the Lord is not so bad, but a prolonged, tortured life was not, I believe, intended either."

"So, if I understand you," responded Jesus, "some loving mothers choose to save their babies from such man-made suffering, by termination. In this sense, while this would be a painful decision, it is not so horrible as I first imagined. Again, if the motivation is love, the same pain is felt and the same lessons are learned as an early death for the young one. It is in a sense an early death, and would you not rather return to the arms of the Lord than suffer in a life not intended? Surely, God would never allow innocents to suffer. Even an animal will not suckle a damaged offspring. These decisions would not be something I would consider lightly, and as in all things, the heart and soul of the mothers and fathers must judge and also must bear the burden of their decisions. Woe be it to those who would callously harm an innocent. Woe be it, also, to those that judge harshly, for they will surely be judged. The ancient Torah was a harsh master also, and so it was that I was to replace it with the New Covenant."

Dionysus said, "Self-righteous humans have both Torahs, as you call them, and freely choose from each to serve

51

their wicked intent. The two books, the *Old Testament* and the *New Testament* make up the "Christian" Torah.

Jesus lifted his empty glass to the God of Wine and simply said, "It's empty."

"Well," said his new friend, "let's fix that." He poured Jesus another glass of fine red wine.

They both leaned back in the grass.

Jesus began again, "I do not know much of this 'New Testament,' can you explain some of it to me?"

"I can," replied Dionysus, "but again, I am not the smartest God on this rock ... I do love my wine, but part of its allure is that it takes the edge off of intelligence and provides a peaceful oblivion."

"Well, I am also feeling a lowering of my brilliant mind, so perhaps we can discuss the simple storyline." Jesus smiled and clinked glasses with the handsome Greek.

"OK, my friend, I will tell you what I know ... as best as I can under my usual circumstances."

"Can I assume my Torah was written by one of my apostles?"

"Well, sure," began Dionysus, "you could assume that ... but you would be wrong. It was written in small part by a couple of them ... maybe ... but mostly by others. The times and persons are quite unclear. Some were of or near your time, most were tens, perhaps hundreds, of years later. Then, perhaps as much as four hundred years after your death, the writings with a total of twenty-seven books were agreed upon, and it has existed with minor changes since then."

"Have you read my Torah?" asked Jesus.

"Of course," replied Dionysus. "With eternity on our hands, and being that you basically demolished our religion, it has been required reading for all of the ancient Gods. Required only by ourselves of course, but required nonetheless. It is ... *colorful* to say the least. I like the books where you and your deeds are primary, but the rest can be interesting too. Revelation is a hoot!"

"Do you have a copy?" asked Jesus.

"We are Gods, O Complete One, you have but to ask." Dionysus held out his hand and instantly a scroll appeared. "I could do a modern book, but thought you might enjoy a model from your time."

"Thank you, Dionysus. This is a comfortable site and the wine is excellent. If you don't mind, I will rustle up some bread and cheese and devour that and the Torah as well. I am indebted to you, my friend."

"Nonsense, relax and just shout out if you have a question or a need. I will be at your service."

With that, Dionysus was gone, and Jesus was left to find out what the world had made of him within the words of his very own Torah. He bit off a piece of bread and took a sip of fine red wine. This should be interesting, he thought, as he unwrapped and began to read the scroll.

The Gospel According to St Matthew

1) The book of the generation of Jesus Christ, the son of David, the son of Abraham......

Chapter 10
– Satan's Swamp

It seemed Lucifer's bowels had been cleared of the remains of the simple little Greek God. He made a mental note not to eat any more of them, as there was actually some discomfort in their discharge, and it was just damned ignoble. He considered everything that was happening as just the God of All fucking with him. This only fed his hatred, as if it could possibly grow any larger.

As he soared in the blue sky, the sun reflected off his extremely beautiful golden wings. When he flapped his wings, it was with no perceivable effort and with a rhythmic motion that supported the notion that this creature was an essential part of the whole. His hair was jet black, with eyes like onyx. His face was smooth and perfect, with features strong and bold. His muscles were defined with a perfect symmetry to the whole. He was woven into the fabric of creation as fundamentally as the earth and sky. If one was close enough to wonder, they would question how this unbelievable creature with a beauty that was difficult to even behold, was so consumed with evil. He'd been thrown from Heaven for challenging the Creator. What a loss for him. What a loss for Heaven. How could he devolve spiritually to encompass all that was evil? How could he become the receptacle for all of the wicked things in creation, this creature of unspeakable beauty? Though he would forbid the thought of it, there was a very definite, defined sense of sadness that resided at his core.

It did not take any effort for him to fly, and he could fly as long as time itself, but he knew without thinking it was for no purpose. He was getting nowhere. He decided to stop the game and land until the God of All was ready to meet him. He was now playing God's game and could not win. When he did come to his face, and he would, it would be an equal game and there he would prevail.

He came to a great swamp and landed in its middle, far from anywhere any of these so-called Gods would desire to be. He settled in the mud and wrapped his wings around him and rested. Even in his confidence, he knew, to defeat the God of All would take everything he was capable of. Though he never seemed to tire, in that final struggle, when the most giant wills of all clashed, to win his rightful place and become the true God of All, he would need to be focused, he would need his strength.

Chapter 11
– Jesus Reads His Torah

$\mathcal{R}$evelations 22:20: He that testifieth these things saith, "Surely I come quickly." Amen. Even so, come, Lord Jesus. (21) The grace of our Lord Jesus Christ be with you all. Amen.

And so, Jesus finished his Torah with the end of the book of Revelations. His head was spinning from the things he had read. His general reaction was confusion and something close to sadness. When he combined the stories told to him by Mercury, Mars, and Dionysus regarding the evolution of the church and the Torah he had just read, he was convinced his message had been, either intentionally or unintentionally, misunderstood. His people, the Jewish Nation, ignored his message. The Catholic Gentiles replaced their world of Gods with Jesus and a massive hierarchy that, in truth, resembled the Greek or Roman Gods with what seemed to be a lot less humor. The angel Gabriel would replace Mercury for messages, St. Michael or St. George would hold up warriors for Mars, and St. Vincent is the reigning Saint of Wine, being a less joyful Dionysus, and on and on. The Pope would replace the Oracle, and Priests were Priests. Jesus could come to no other conclusion than that he had ... failed.

Jesus considered himself the Messiah. He believed he was to deliver the Jews from bondage. It was thought, in his time, that this meant he would conquer the Romans and restore the Jews to the control of Jerusalem. It was thought that he would win back the land that God had given to them.

Jesus, being complete and, through intense prayer and study, came to believe differently. He believed that he had come to deliver the Jews from a larger bondage. He came to deliver them from the harshness of the Old Testament.

Jesus believed that forgiveness and love were primary in the eyes of the one and only God. He was convinced that an eye for an eye, and the difficult mentality of the ancient Jewish tradition, should come to an end, and that God loved his people and had compassion for them. He wanted them to be happy on earth, as well. His message was that sacrifices and suffering for one's religion had to give way to love and charity. Forgiveness was primary, and it was not a single sin that would define a person but, at death, the whole life lived. A life of sin with a true repentance and an understanding of God's love at death would be judged more kindly than a life of religious austerity and obedience with a hateful heart. Jesus did not know that he was truly made "complete" by God, and so had a crystal-clear understanding of these truths. He was often baffled by human confusion. He thought he had made things simple and that he set the word in motion to grow and prosper. Now it would appear he had thrown a curveball. It was no wonder he found himself in this place. There was a Jesus in charge on earth that *this* Jesus did not recognize.

The gentle Savior stood up and dusted off his robes. He thought about saying goodbye to Dionysus, but felt there was nothing really more to be said. He left the scroll in the place where he had sat and continued down the road. He was decidedly down in the dumps.

It didn't take long for the holy carpenter to run into another resident of this world. It was a naked young man with wings. He was very beautiful, with a romantic aura. Any relatively educated reader would recognize him as Eros, or in Roman-speak, Cupid.

He saw the Jewish God first, head down, shuffling his feet in the dirt in the road, obviously not a happy traveler.

"Hey, Jesus, I thought your days of suffering were over," spoke the young God of Love. "You look like you need a hug."

"Why is it that folks seem to be trying to get into my robes in this place?" asked Jesus. There was no humor in his comment.

"Calm down, man. It's just my aura and of course this incredibly hot body of mine." Cupid positioned himself like a twenty-first-century gay model. "Don't hate me 'cause I'm beautiful," he said with humor.

"Well, put your diaper on, if you don't mind, and I won't feel like I have to watch my ... back."

"Sure thing, O Complete One." In an instant he was covered with a linen loin cloth. "How come the Light of the World is shining so dim?"

"I have come to realize I have failed in my purpose on earth."

"Well, join the club, Messiah. Everyone here has failed to make their case to humans, that they are still relevant. Of course making a case to a human, and having it stick, has been shown to be about impossible. They are like curious birds who bounce from one shiny thing to another. They can't even love for a lifetime. I like a good affair as much as the next guy, but true love is supposed to last. Perhaps they do miss my arrows. When I shot at someone, it STUCK!"

Jesus found a large log just off the road and sat down. His dejection was palpable, and for the Hope of the World to seem, so hopeless, was depressing indeed.

"Jesus," began Cupid, "you have to pick yourself up here. You did everything you could. You did a lot. You said and did the right things. You said that the most important thing was love. Don't judge yourself by what humans do. They are, at their best ... confusing."

"They have indeed confused me. It will take me some time to process this. You are right that humans are difficult. I was one. There is one who twists their minds and is committed to confusion. Even now, he haunts me in this very world. It is a full measure of my burden."

"You need to stay strong, Jesus. Whatever happens, you are still the Hope of the World. Never doubt the power of love. Your heart is pure, and humans still love you. Through the twisted memory, you still shine through." Cupid sat on the log next to Jesus. "I know what you need. There is someone special you need to meet."

As if on cue, the very beautiful Aphrodite appeared. She sat next to Jesus on this small road, on the opposite side of Cupid.

So, in this land, somewhere between here and there, and now and then, on the side of a lovely little dirt road, sitting on a log on the grass, was the Roman God, Cupid, on one side, the bare-breasted, breathtakingly beautiful Roman

Goddess, Aphrodite, on the other, and the very confused King of the Jews, Jesus Christ, in the middle.

Aphrodite leaned over, looked Jesus deep in his eyes and kissed him full on the lips.

Chapter 12
– Satan's History

𝕸eanwhile, back at the swamp....

The Beast sat perfectly still, with his wings wrapped around him like a cone of gold. The outline of feathers etched in the golden surface was delicately displayed to make the image, again, breathtaking. But deep in this swamp, there were few to appreciate it. Just how many is a question unanswered, but for sure there was one, and it carefully watched the Son of Perdition with caution and purpose.

The giant serpent was twenty meters long, with scales of pure silver and eyes as red as rubies. It appeared as ancient as the Wicked One himself, and possessed a presence that was outside of time and space, but was also an undeniable part of the whole.

The creature floated upon the surface of the swamp with only its head up and alert. Its head was the shape of a spearhead and the size of a warrior's shield. Its eyes were raised and focused, with its pupils black and fixed. Its red, forked tongue shot in and out, as if searching the air for ... something. With the exception of its tongue, it was motionless. It contemplated the new arrival with interest. If a snake could smile, it smiled.

Satan fumed within his golden pyramid. He tried to rest, he tried to calm himself. He realized that there was no purpose in wasting the energy, the hate, when he would need all of it, soon. Very soon, he assured himself. He thought of that time, eons ago, when he fought his first battle with the God of All. He had marshaled his army. He led a great force against the might of God's army, archangel against archangel. The clash of the mighty was like nothing since the beginning of time. The very universe trembled, and the fabric of reality stretched to the edge of destruction.

Satan pictured himself as he was in Heaven. He was the Light Bearer, the Morning Star. He, Lucifer, was the highest of the Seraphim, the very Chief of the Angels.

Then, the God of All made man. He considered those weak pathetic clumps of clay his masterwork, his Crown of Creation. So let him fawn over these puny, stumbling creatures, thought Lucifer. Let him be distracted, for in time they would prove to be useless and weak, and the God of All would lose interest and turn back to his own. This did not happen, but rather, God proclaimed that humans were greater even than the angels in Heaven, and demanded that all bow down to these ... *creatures*. Yes even me, he thought, Lucifer, the master of God's hosts, was to ... bow down.

To Lucifer, this thinking was madness. It was blatantly apparent that man was not near the creature that the hosts of Heaven were. Behold our glory and majesty, and consider the simple image of man. The comparison was ridiculous. To Satan it was now obvious that the God of All was not without fault. It was obvious to him that it was possible for him to error, and if this was so, he was certain to have other weaknesses, weaknesses that Lucifer was sure *he* did not possess. Surely he, Lucifer, was as powerful as this flawed God of All. Before man, he would have not considered such thinking, but this creation of man, he was now convinced, was the beginning of God's undoing.

Satan nestled into the mud and considered what had gone wrong. He was still convinced that his premise was correct. Man was nowhere near the equal of the Hosts of Heaven. God made a mistake, was flawed, and in being flawed was vulnerable. After eons of brooding over his failure, he was also convinced he knew where he went wrong. He had attempted to amass a great army of like thinking angels, to battle the legions of those loyal to the God of All. He had been successful, but at the end was still outnumbered. He wasted energy battling God's army, when he should have been battling God himself ... one on one.

The Wicked One recounted the days before the great battle. God's foolishness in his pride for man seemed so obvious to Lucifer, he gathered his multitudes and build a throne equal to the God of All's in Heaven. He instructed his followers to ignore the command of God to fall on their knees at the foot of man. He was the most mighty of the mighty, and countless were willing to hear his command. There was one, however, Abdiel, who disagreed. He believed that even Lucifer was no match for the might of God. He argued with Lucifer and returned to the side of God. He was forgiven in Heaven and praised for his rejection of sin. He was a traitor, thought Satan, and would be dealt with harshly, after his return to rule Heaven. This is when God put together an army to attack Lucifer's throne. It was to be led by Gabriel and Michael, the angel who had taken Lucifer's place.

The army approached the halls of Lucifer's throne. As Lucifer knew all things in Heaven, there was no surprise and he had prepared his followers to battle. The massive hosts of Heaven lined on two sides, and faced each other. These brothers beyond time were now separated by sin. Separated by a sin against a creation so outwardly pathetic, but still a creation of the God of All, who put it above all else. And now, creatures of unimaginable majesty faced each other and knew for the first time, confrontation. They were about to create something new. They were about to create war. Perhaps this was a more appropriate result of the birth of man.

Satan recalled how he first faced the traitor, Abdiel. He called him to task for his treachery. Then, the mighty Lucifer was named a fool, by this one who knew not loyalty. It was then the first blow in Heaven was struck, as Lucifer grabbed the lesser angel by the throat. Instantly, the battle was engaged. Creatures that had only known peace and love were instantly immersed in hate and violence ... all over the creature God called "man."

Seven days the battle had raged. The forces and momentum surged back and forth. The battle was even, as the power of the angels themselves was even. The force of the battle shook all of the heavens and threatened the very existence of creation. Then, Michael came forth with a massive sword, such as was never seen in Heaven. He wielded this mighty weapon and struck Lucifer himself. It was a vicious and devastating blow. It nearly rent Lucifer in half, and he was carried by those that followed him to the rear of the battle and safety. Satan felt the blow as he sat in his wings. He felt it as if it was happening at that moment. He hated Michael for its delivery and considered how this changed so many things in time. He remembered how he lay on Heaven's floor, in a pain he had never experienced. Those loyal to him fought heroically and held the forces of God at bay. He was an archangel, however, and not subject to the cycle of life and death. His body quickly mended as the battle ceased for a time.

Lucifer recognized that Michael had struck him not through a greater power, but through a greater weapon. He devised in his mind a much more massive weapon and ordered those that followed him to build a giant arsenal. The instruments created were huge cannons, such as were never imagined then and now. They were loaded with mysteries known only to the Evil One and devastated all they touched. They fired with the dawn of the new day, and all hell and fury rained down on the army of God.

For a time it looked as if the soldiers of Lucifer would prevail. They had created great machines, to make up for their lack of numbers, and pounded the gates of Heaven. Lucifer could feel the fear and concern from the essence of his brothers with whom he now fought: Anael, Zadkhiel, Jophiel, Chauel, Uriel, and even the mighty Gabriel, Raphael and Archangel Michael himself, the one who was now elevated to Chief of the Angels. They, at that moment, knew fear and doubt.

Michael commanded that his army lift the very mountains of Heaven, and bury Satan and his cannons with them. This was done and Heaven was silent, as the wicked army scrambled from beneath the rubble.

With the wicked weakened, the God of All descended in a great chariot and pushed the disoriented army, along with Satan, in retreat. The God of All had cleverly created a hole in the very floor of Heaven, and Lucifer and his army, confused in retreat, fell from the Gates of Heaven to Hell. They were, in mass, cast from Heaven, 133 million strong, defeated. Glorious angels became demons, evil spirits and devils. Satan remembered his words to his followers, that it was better to rule in Hell than to have to suffer the foolishness of God in Heaven. He assured them there would come another time and another battle, which would bring them all to the glory they richly deserved.

Lucifer had failed, but now dedicated his time to ridiculing humans. He made them look ridiculous. He tormented them and twisted good intentions to evil ends. He was certain the rest of the hosts of Heaven could not help, but would eventually come to the same conclusion he had. The God of All had created a flawed creature. The "Crown of his Creation" was a failure, and certainly, they would also rise up and throw out this God of All. Lucifer would rise again and take his rightful place.

Man, however, proved to be a difficult and confusing creature. For every evil man, there were many who tried to do good deeds. Then came the Messiah, the little Jewish carpenter that preached love and forgiveness. His message on earth was food for the souls of righteous humans, and the small list of followers began to grow. It was easy, in that time, for Satan to have him crucified. He clouded the minds of men with ease. The Jewish population was generating dozens of "messiahs" so having them throw one to the Romans was child's play. Little did they know, he was God's true, "complete" human creation. Even Christ himself walked willingly onto the hills of Golgotha, supposedly fulfilling the legends of his people. It was almost too easy. But the words the Christ had spoken carried beyond the crucifixicn, and kept countless hearts from Satan's control. While annoying, this was a small matter for the Evil One, who had ample sinners to feed his raging appetite, and of the true believers, their souls were the *most delicious* when they fell. Oh yes, these humans were so flawed. But, so was the army in Heaven, and the remaining angels were not flocking to his side. It appeared that the little Jew gave them hope.

No, thought Lucifer, the time for armies in Heaven is over. There is nothing left except the final confrontation. Man was a mistake, and because that is so, God is flawed and I can prevail.

I *can* prevail, he thought.

The serpent watched and considered the presence in the swamp. It knew who and what the Evil One was, and knew he would come. Time was not of value in this place, it had learned, and it was content to hover and to softly breathe, its forked tongue darting in and out.

Slowly it began to move. It slithered across the swamp in the direction of Abaddon. With fifty yards left to cover, it silently lowered itself below the surface.

The great swamp was quiet and waited.

Chapter 13
– A Gathering of Gods

"*Y*ep, no doubt about it, he's a big one and mean as spit. I also have to point out, he is as glorious as glorious can be, and that out-gloriouses Zeus by a mile, and, I might add, I have come to know the Beast, inside and out!"

Pan strutted around the small gathering, quite proud to be the one in the know.

"I can't imagine a little Jewish carpenter taking this character on even if he is "complete.""

"Yes," continued Mars, "It would seem our gentle friend is a bit out of his weight class. It's hard to imagine the little fellow fighting at all. He seems to be just about the 'love thing.' If I had a millennium, I doubt I could teach him to thrust or parry or even to duck! I can't envision a less likely champion."

Mercury continued, "I am not even sure our hero is even a God, in the sense that we are. If this Satan rips him up, do you think his body could find itself again?"

Dionysus spoke, "I do not pretend to know the power of this King of the Jews, but let's not forget his existence overthrew Zeus himself, and threw the Gods from Mt Olympus. While it is doubtful he could punch or kick, he is not without weapons."

"Perhaps," replied Mercury. "Still, I am convinced this man was not created for violence. It's not in him. Humans elevated him to a God on earth and it was they who turned their backs on us, and so we were overthrown. Jesus had *champions* on earth and he needs *champions* here."

"Agreed!" shouted Mars, "and every fiber of my being longs for battle. I have missed my wars and am ready to serve. This little King is worthy and his enemy is also worthy. This is the final battle I have longed for. I, for one, have had enough of this land of nothing, that holds us captive. If champions he needs then champions we will be!"

Little Nodutus spoke up. "It is the God of All he seeks. Do we know where this God might be?"

"Do we even know *who* this God might be?" asked Mars.

The gathering looked at each other and it was obvious they had heard the legends, but uncertainty was the only thing certain.

Mars thought a moment, then said, "We need to speak with Zeus. If we are to be victorious, I am sure we will need him. I am sure he would want to be there. He might even know this God of All."

The little group nodded their agreement as if one.

"Very well," continued Mars, "I will bring this message to New Olympus and see what I can learn. While I am certain Zeus will join us, I believe we should begin to gather our heroes. Divide our Gods amongst yourselves and put together a great 'Collation of the willing.'" I can feel the Wicked One and sense there is little time to waste."

Little Nodutus spoke up again. "Say, Mars, if you are going to speak with Zeus, do you think you might ask him to consider giving me some other powers? I am thankful to be a God and all, but being the God who makes knots in wheat is kind of weak. If I had a better thing, perhaps I could fight a better fight, don't you agree? This seems like a good time to ask anyway."

The great God of War looked at the little God. "You cannot know, my friend. This King of the Jews was brought down on earth by a simple kiss. It is not always muscle that is the key. How your talents play into all of this is yet to be seen. I will try to speak with him, but as you well know, he is not easily swayed."

Mars waved his mighty sword in a circle and was gone. The remaining Gods set out, each to find the number amongst them willing to take up the mantle of the King of the Jews.

Chapter 14
– Jesus and Aphrodite

*A*phrodite slowly pulled back from the lips of Jesus.

"Oh my," she softly spoke, "that was wonderful. Should I be surprised? I would wager few have shared such a kiss with the Light of the World. It is easy to see that you are love itself, and complete in its purpose."

They looked into each other's eyes and saw the depth of perfect love. They saw the power and the suffering, such unnecessary suffering. They saw the missed opportunities.

Aphrodite, the Goddess of Love, began again. "There is so much I would tell you. So much I would ask you. The love I feel for you is ... without limit."

Jesus smiled softly. "I have never met one such as you. I did not know you truly existed. You make my heart race. I find myself .... again confused."

"Well," said Cupid, "I think I'll take off for now. I would love to take credit for this, but I have not lifted an arrow." The beautiful man-God sighed a deep sigh, smiled softly, and was gone.

"In my time and to my purpose, I did not share a woman's love. To bring a woman on the journey I was destined to travel would have been ... *cruel*. There was one, however, that made me wish things were different."

"Ah, yes, the other Mary." Aphrodite smiled. "I watched. Perhaps you were right. What you were asked to do was hard enough. Yet she would have been a worthy partner... and willing."

"I know. I saw the look. No, that's not quite right, we shared the looks. But, it was not to be. The reasons are many."

"I understand, but I also wonder. How can you truly understand the ways of man without experiencing the love of a woman? Your scriptures say that you were made flesh to suffer the pain of man. You were made complete, but I would ask, was not your experience....incomplete?"

"Ah, yes ... my scriptures. I fear that a great number of those represent my failure. I was somehow not clear enough, somehow not a good enough teacher. I lost my people, and my Torah wanders like the people of Moses."

"As to being incomplete, I would agree. If the Messiah's role was to be God made flesh, then I would be incomplete. If it was to deliver the Jews and to be the bridge to the God of All, then this part of my experience was ... not necessary."

They sat on the log for a time in silence. He gently reached out and held the beautiful Goddess's hand. They existed briefly in the bliss of each other's company.

They sat again for a time, then the Goddess spoke.

"I sense in you, oh Lord, a ... lonely heart. You are in this place and suffer with confusion over the acts of mankind. This weighs heavily on you. And behind it all, we all can feel the presence of a creature that legend says comes for you. Please know that this place is a place where we have been sent, because others do not believe, but it is also a place where every bend in the road is for answers.

"I love you, Jesus, and I have an answer for you." The lovely Goddess lifted his hand and placed it on her naked

72

breast. "There is one more thing for you to complete, and by your words, I know you would not let either of us, tonight, suffer a lonely heart."

The wind was softly blowing, just enough to make the trees whisper. The birds softly sang a gentle love song. The sun rested comfortably on the horizon in a suite of colors, red to gold.

Aphrodite took the gentle carpenter by the hand and led him down the road to a place where we can be sure two hearts joined. Two hearts that were perfect in love and respect ... and who among us would judge?

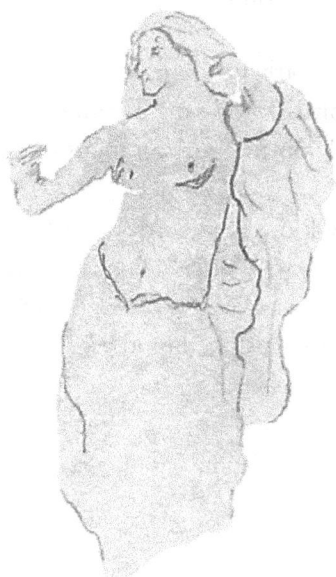

Chapter 15
– Satan Meets the Snake

*7*he surface of the swamp barely rippled when the serpent lowered itself beneath its waters. It moved quickly down through the water, into the mud, and below. It moved steadily toward the unsuspecting Lucifer.

Beneath the cone of gold created by his magnificent wings the Accuser finally rested and simmered in a cloud of hate and malevolence.

It seemed he had just finally settled, when he began to feel a slight shifting in the mud beneath him. He felt the presence, recognized the spirit, and saw the snake's face within his very cone, all at the same moment. Satan threw his wings apart and stepped back from the ominous creature.

"You fool! Do you play games with me?" Satan glared at the smiling serpent (if serpents could smile).

Satan continued, "It has been *ages before time* since I have felt your presence. What wonder that I find you here, in this place where fools reside, and time and space fold into each other."

"Yessss, my Lord. While you are new to this world, I have been here since early in the life of humanity. I knew you would come to this place, as all who exist in the memories of man must." The snake coiled in front of Satan, and lifted his head equal to him and looked deeply into his eyes.

"You plan a plan. I can feel it, but perhaps you might listen to the advice of an old friend?"

"Your advice would only serve yourself, as any can witness," said the Dark Prince. "There is nothing you can know, that I do not know. Nothing you can possess, that I do not already possess. You are merely a whisperer of lies and deceit. What possibly could you have that would make the slightest ruffle in my needs?"

"What you say is true. Do not hate me for how I was made. It is even said, that it was *you* that created me, and was a part of me. If this is so, would you not listen to the advice of your own self? I have been here sssssoo long. Perhaps I have some .... experience?"

Satan looked deep into the shifting ruby eyes of the Deceiver. They were constantly shifting, with pupils that were one moment full and dilated, then focused pinpoints. They pulsated back and forth and seemed to draw the Devil in, to assure, to convince, to control.

"ENOUGH," shouted the Father of Lies. He grabbed the snake by the throat and squeezed him, until his neck was the width of a pencil. The snake writhed and squirmed, and wrapped its body around the arm of the Devil. His face was no longer smiling and he could barely hiss, "My Lord, I only meant to asssure you, I have knowledge of value. Pleasssse, my Lord, let me go."

"You fool! Who do you think you are speaking to? You would play your simple tricks on me? I did create you. You are not a *God* like the other puny Gods in this world, and I am quite certain that YOU I could easily destroy."

The Beast threw the serpent into the mud and stood over it, waiting for a challenge, any challenge. He was tired of everything and the violence in him grew beyond hate. He did not believe this creature could help him and would have enjoyed ending its pitiful existence .... painfully.

"Master," hissed the snake, "forgive me. I have been too long in this swamp, and time has dimmed my memories of your glory, of your majesty. Forgive my failing. Please, let me serve you. Please, let me worship you." It slowly recoiled itself and raised its head, to once again look into the Dark Lord's eyes. It wanted to make clear that it was ... begging.

"Very well, then," began Satan, "speak and quickly, as my patience is at its end."

"Yes, my master, yesss. Please, sit down and rest, calm yourself that you may hear my words and perhaps, consider....other *options?*"

Lucifer once again settled in the swamp, and the serpent coiled itself, just out of its master's reach. While it did not know if it could actually die, it did know it could feel pain, and the throttling it had experienced still throbbed in its neck.

"As you have become aware, this is not the *earth* where we find ourselves. It is a place where Gods who have been *forgotten* or whose image has been distorted to the point of being unrecognizable, find themselves. So it is with us. Naturally, a place is necessary, as forgotten memories do exist, and have to reside somewhere, and truth certainly exists outside of the limited and flawed capabilities of man. So to that end we find ourselves here."

"You speak drivel!" spat the Wicked One. "What does it mean to me *what* this place is. I have one concern, and one only, and that is to find the God of All, and put an end to him. When I rule in Heaven, creatures in this place, and the earth with its pathetic humans, will squirm in perpetual suffering. They will suffer as I have under the thumb of this God of All."

"But, master, the challenge is to come face to face with Yahweh, and there is no reason for him to allow you through that door, which is controlled by necessity and his whim. As you realize, this is *his* game we play. He made the rules, and so it is these rules we must play. When you create necessity, you hold the key."

"Tell me more. If this is true, that when I have a desire to do something, the path will be clear, then why have I not fulfilled my desire to face him? Why do I find myself with idiots and fools? What you say makes no sense."

"Consider, O Lord of Unspeakableness, you have not been trying to see any others, or accomplish any other goal, or answer any other question, except to come face to face with Jehovah himself. This is the one path that is not made clear by this rule. It is his game and he has created another rule. Things will happen 'when the time is right.' This is controlled by many things, and most are free of his control. You know him, and he loves to have all earn their progression. A waste of time, but then, when time is infinite there is no such thing as *waste*. So, through this door we may enter. It is necessary to set up a path through action that will require him to let us in. Then the time will be right."

Lucifer smiled. "You do have value, serpent. It is a fortunate meeting. Do you have a suggestion for me regarding ways to open this door?"

"Remember, in this world all things happen when the time is right. Our meeting is no accident. It shows that we do have room to move here, in spite of the will of the Almighty."

"I am encouraged," said the Dark Lord. "I feel that you have more, that you have a plan. Continue, so that I may consider it."

"You are aware that the Complete One, Jesus, is also in this world?"

"I am."

"He is the key. He has been misunderstood on earth to the point of being unrecognizable, and has appeared here. He wanders amongst these lesser Gods and searches for his history. Since he has just arrived he has not had time to review the doings of man since his crucifixion—nice job by the way—and is just beginning to realize how you have twisted his story. He is confused and unhappy...again, nice job!"

Lucifer could not help but look proud. "Yes, I have twisted his truth. I am glad he is discouraged.

I have sown many seeds of evil and hate, but I fear he will find out that this too is not all I had hoped for. Man is a slippery creature and twists reason to their purpose. His kernel of goodness exists still."

"This does not matter," continued the snake. "Humans are of no consequence here. For some reason, and it might be that his only true form was human, he does not know that Jehovah is here. He cannot feel him. For some reason the Almighty hides from this one. Jesus knows that this place is for *forgotten Gods* and that is how he considers himself. He does feel you, however. Your aura is overpowering. He considers himself to be a sacrificial Lamb of God. He has read, in his *man-created Torah*, that he is destined to conquer you and destroy sin. What his beliefs are, I cannot tell, but this certainly is part of his new reality."

"A joke, of course," spat Satan. "He is a flea, and beneath consideration. It is on a plane with God believing man is the crown of his creation, and if it is written, it is another example of the flaws of the God of All. This is another reason why I will be able to crush him. Only the blind would not see his weakness."

The serpent continued. "Now we can see that, because this notion of an epic battle has been planted in the mind of the Complete One, he will feel compelled to battle you. I agree, this for him is *madness*. The poison you have planted within the human soul has created a legend of ultimate war, to free them from sin and suffering...so human. They desire sin, but want someone else to clean it up for them. So, this poor carpenter is the lamb they have led to slaughter, and would lead to slaughter again. Now, perhaps, even he believes this. This is where we shall place our wedge and force the hand of God. This is where the universe shall turn and you, Lucifer, will ascend to the throne of God."

Lucifer stood in the swamp and spread his mighty wings. The thrill of what the serpent envisioned was more than he could hold within him. He lifted off the ground and seemed to be ready to fly away.

"My Lord, my Lord," hissed the serpent, "there is more, there is more, there is MUCH more!"

The Devil refocused on the snake, the teller of lies, the Deceiver, and settled back to earth.

"Is it not simple?" he asked. "I have only to want to see this Jesus, and it will be fulfilled. I will hold his head in my hand and threaten to crush it, if I am not brought to the throne and the one I seek."

"Thissss, I do not believe," continued the snake. It takes a combination of desire to see and the time being right for this to be accomplished. I believe the time is not right. There is more we should do.

"The simple Gods of this place have gained a certain attachment to the King of the Jews. Even as we speak, they are gathering a force to help him battle you. They also see that he would be easily crushed."

"I can destroy them all, with a thought," boasted the Lord of All Evil.

"Careful," hissed the snake. "Remember, they will not die. They are immortal. Please do not doubt me, I believe you can crush them all, but also they will keep coming back...and there are some with considerable weapons. Never underestimate your enemies."

"This gets more and more complicated. If the God of All was not such a COWARD, he would face me! YOU HEAR THAT, YAHWEH? COWARD!"

The Devil stamped about the swamp and howled ... "AAAAAAHHHHHHHHHHYYYYYEEEE EEEEAAAAAAAAAAAA!!!!!"

"Patience, my Prince," continued the snake. "You are not without allies. There are many within these legends that are wicked and would joy in a turnover in Heaven. They will follow us, and because of the nature of this world, we can get to them."

Satan calmed himself and breathed, "But, I do not want a war. I had a war with an army that was eons beyond what could be mustered here, and we failed. There is no purpose to it."

"You are, of course, right, oh bombastic one. However, we do not fight this fight. The Gods of *this* place fight. They fight until there is a clear path between you and the carpenter. When you meet and hold him in your hands, it will force the God of All to intervene. Then, and only then, the time will be right. This world will open the door to the throne you seek."

Satan smiled a wicked smile at the serpent. "Who do we find first, my lieutenant?"

The snake seemed pleased at the promotion. "Let us find the God of Hell himself, the mighty Hades, and build our army from there."

"Excellent," spoke Satan. "Wrap yourself around me, and we will begin."

The snake coiled himself around the mighty archangel and they lifted off the ground. Its head was coiled to the rear, and a careful observer could recognize a wicked sneer. The serpent would do all it could to assist the mighty Lucifer in finding the God of All. It would cheer him on, and carry his coat, as the Beast strode out to challenge Jehovah. Did it believe Satan could overthrow God? It did not. The odds were he would be crushed in an instant. Only a monster with an ego like Lucifer's could believe otherwise.

The snake was happy to lead him to his demise. Of course, then it would gain its rightful place as the God of All Evil, and come to reign in Hell.

Yes, it thought ... I have waited a long time.

Chapter 16
– Mars Meets with Zeus

Mars knew that the best way to rally the Gods would be to enlist Zeus himself. The big man would not only bring the most powerful force to the fight, but would also ensure the allegiance of the masses. Who would stand against the God of the Gods? He realized there would be some who would love to challenge the existing power structure, and some would relish the idea of an evil-dominated world, but to defy Zeus was to risk his wrath. Historically, this had proved to be an unwise position. Mars understood that Lucifer, or Phosphorus, as the Greeks called him, was a step above the *normal* misbehaver. This was the top of the evil ladder, and a worthy adversary to Zeus himself. Yes, it would be wise to make sure Zeus understood what was happening, and to be sure he was prepared to lead the charge.

The path to the new Olympus was easy in this new place, straight ahead from anywhere, with the simple purpose of getting there. For general travel, the time was always right, and in the time it takes to make the decision to go, Mars was standing before the throne.

The throne of Zeus was not exactly what one would expect. In this world there was no actual Mt. Olympus, so the new Olympus was just a field of grass. This was upsetting to Zeus, so he commanded some of the Gods to haul dirt to the field, and build his new Mt. Olympus. Well, this went fine for the first couple of wagonloads of rock, but the Gods were not used to physical labor, and historically they had humans to build their temples. Suffice it to say, the construction soon

84

lost steam, and the new Mt. Olympus was simply a sort of *gravel bump* in the field.

The throne itself was made of wood, and was kind of rickety for the same reasons. There were no humans to dig and donate the gold that should have covered the royal recliner, and the Gods tasked with the woodworking were really only Gods designed to inspire humans to do woodworking. They actually had no real talent of their own.

So, there sat Zeus. He was no less striking with his fine physique, his long hair and beard. He still possessed his mighty eagle and scepter. Lightning bolts cracked over his head. The scene was only slightly diminished by the mound of gravel and rickety throne.

"Hail, mighty Zeus, God of the Gods and ruler of .... well, *this* place, I guess," offered the God of War. "I come with news of major import, and seek your support and council."

The mighty leader slowly turned his head from side to side. He lifted his scepter over his head and flexed his mighty muscles. His pectoral muscles twitched from left to right, and brought to mind the more talented headliners at strip clubs. His posturing seemed to be an attempt to establish the pecking order, and to somehow awe the God of War with his magnificence. What with the place they were in, the lump of gravel, and the rickety throne, Mars was not overly impressed. He rolled his eyes and put his hands on his hips.

"Are you finished?" he asked.

"Yeah, well you could at least show me some respect, and pretend to be *somewhat* impressed," mumbled the Top God.

"You know I am your servant, Mighty Zeus, but for now, we have urgent matters that overshadow matters of form."

"I am aware, my friend. There has been a series of events that dramatically change the nature of our little hideaway. It would seem this world has a larger part to play in the evolving universe."

"Exactly, my Lord, this is why I am here. Are you aware of the nature of our visitors?"

"Of course I am," retorted the big God. "There is the little Jewish carpenter, the one who threw us out of our homes and cast us into this place. The one who replaced us in the hearts of man, and there is the God of All Evil. Oh yes, and there is the Complete One's legend, in his Torah, which tells of an epic battle to rid the world of evil, and bring in a new world of peace, with rivers of honey and streets of gold. Yes, I know the story, and now it would seem this battle is to take place here in the land of the lost. Could it be any more appropriate? The humans would be duly impressed if it happened on earth, but of course they would completely forget about it or turn it into a comic book within a generation. There is nothing new about this. How many epic battles have there been? The first mighty battle to overthrow the Titans, the great wars of the Greeks and Romans, the holy wars, the wars to end all wars. All were duly fought with heroes and valor, and all were duly forgotten. Man has the loyalty of a fish, and the memory of a flea."

"So true, top dog, but now we have a battle that has little or nothing to do with earth or humans. It seems it is perhaps a truly cosmic struggle that might actually, dramatically, alter the future."

Mars looked at Zeus, and Zeus at Mars. In one voice they said, "Or not!" They both laughed, then regained their serious faces.

Mars continued, "This time, things are different. We are in this place where it seems different things are possible, and we are involved in a struggle that is completely outside of our time and space. This is different."

"True," said Zeus, "it is easy to feel the power in this one. It would seem the little Jew would have a tough time with the Evil One."

"No doubt, my king; this is why I have come to enlist you in the struggle. With your power and leadership, we will be able to combat this demon and allow the forces of good to triumph."

"Without a doubt," replied the God of the Gods, "with my power we would surely win the day. Too bad I won't be able to help."

"What?" Mars stared at the greater God with disbelief. "It is crucial, you must help or the Complete One will be smashed. I fear if Lucifer is able to gather the willing evil Gods, we will be overpowered. Even I cannot stop such an attack. One word from you and they would not dare do battle with the Dark Lord. You must reconsider."

Mars looked at Zeus with passion. He knew this was the deciding moment between victory and defeat. He knew that without help they would lose to the powerful God of All

Evil. There was little doubt. He had been certain Zeus would lead the Gods, and his refusal shocked the God of War.

"I am sorry, my friend, but in this I am neutral. Well, almost neutral. Naturally, I prefer love and peace to hate and chaos, but I do not care for this carpenter, either. He came with his love and suffering, and undid our entire existence. He might have shown us some respect, but....*nooooo!* Well, let him fight his fight, and then they will be finished and go elsewhere. I strongly suggest you let this Jesus fight the Beast. Let them fulfill their scripture. There is no place in this for us."

The God of the Gods waved his hand, and Mars found himself back at the gathering place, his hands still outstretched, pleading.

Chapter 17
– Lucifer Meets Hades

Satan had just about had enough. He was playing by the rules and still was flying to nowhere. The serpent had had enough as well. He was not a flying creature and had been sick almost from the moment of liftoff. There were remains of rabbits and deer with a few mice and moles thrown in, all over the back of Lucifer's magnificent armor. The snake's eyes were glassed over, and his giant head slapped in semi-consciousness on the back of the demon as he flew. His tongue was hanging out, and if one could hear above the sound of the whipping wind, one might hear the snake softly sobbing.

"Enough," said Satan and wrapped his wings around him. They plummeted toward the ground, gaining speed, faster and faster until they were a blur. The snake had come around enough to scream, "maaaaaaaaaaaaaaaaaaaaaaaaaaaaaaaaaaamaaaaaaaaaaaaaaaaaaaae!"

The instant before they hit the ground, they disappeared with a soft "pop." They suddenly found themselves at their destination. Satan whirled around, prepared for anything, with the giant snake's head swinging like a bolo. He squared himself before the only entities in what they now recognized as a rather small, dirt and gravel, walled cave. While it seemed hard to believe, they now stood in the new throne of the God of the Underworld, the brother of Zeus, the mighty Hades.

Hades himself was large, as a God should be, but perhaps a bit too fat, with long black hair and beard, and massive breasts. He sat on a throne of roots, chewing on what looked like a potato. As odd a picture as this famous God created, it was made even more so, by a creature that was propped up by his side.

It appeared to be a giant carp.

Hades spoke as the serpent slithered down from the Dark Lord's back.

"Welcome, welcome, welcome," said the God of Death. "I just knew you would come. Fishbone, bring our guests some fine wine and meal, nothing but the best, yes, yes, yes!"

He looked at the face of the carp, which opened and closed its sucker mouth with a "smack, smack, smack."

"Oh, very well, Fishbone, I will get it myself." He waved his arm and instantly Lucifer held a goblet of wine and what looked like a potato. The same sat before the still swooning snake. He smelled the wine and immediately heaved up the remnants of a turtle.

"Oh my," spoke the God. "It would seem you are having some traveling issues. FISHBONE...get our guests some towels and toilet water, so that they might freshen."

The carp opened and closed its puckered mouth with a "smack, smack, smack."

"Very well, Fishbone, I will get them myself." The Lord of the Underworld again waved his arm, and two towels with two buckets of water, each with what looked like daisies floating on the surface, appeared in front of the travelers on the floor of the small gravel cave.

"More madness," Satan spoke to the snake as the serpent gargled some water and spat.

"Oh my, my, my, such a mess! FISHBONE, clean up that snake spit IMMEDIATELY!" The fish's eyes merely bugged out, and he replied with his standard "smack, smack, smack."

"Very well, Fishbone, I will tend to it." He waved his arms and all was clean.

The Master of all Hate and Evil stared at the pair before him in disbelief. He moved forward and spread his wings. He leaned over the underworld master and hissed, "Focus, you fool. The wheels of time have come full circle and I have come to crush the God of All. You will help me, and for your reward you will serve me in Heaven."

The God of Myths looked up at Satan and whispered, "Will there be a spot for Fishbone, too?"

Satan looked at the carp in amazement. "Can it do anything?" he asked with a sneer.

Hades looked at the giant carp. "Well, I do not really know."

Satan raised his mighty fists and was about to smash the unlikely pair when the serpent, who had regained his sensibilities, slithered quickly between them.

"Easy, easy, eassssy, allow me, my God, pleassse allow me."

Lucifer spun around and stared at the snake. He slowly controlled his breathing and stepped back into the gravel cave.

The snake slithered up the path to the pile of roots that made up the throne, and lifted his head to stare into the lesser God's eyes. His eyes widened and his pupils dilated and contracted to a soft gentle rhythm. His head moved slowly back and forth, and soon the God of the Underworld was moving his head as well. Just when the snake was sure he completely controlled Hades, the mythic God spoke softly.

"Hey, Fishbone .... Look, his face looks just like a palm frond, with big buggy eyes."

It was obvious Hades was not impressed so the snake stopped his motion.

"Hades, O great God of the Underworld," the serpent had obviously decided to change his tactic, "we come to enlist you in a great army. It will end the God of All forever, and lift you to the highest levels of Heaven. No more will you need to live in the dirt hole with no one to speak with, save a .... Fishbone. Rally the evil willing of your Gods, and we will lead a great army. Too long have you wasted away in this place. Your body is soft and your mind is without challenge. Come with us and regain the majesty you knew on earth. There is a place for Hades in the highest of the highs, where a God of your stature belongs. There will be great riches and beautiful queens, treasure beyond even your imagination. Send out the word, rally your own, and we will march to glory."

The God of the Underground seemed to grow in stature. He seemed to focus and a great cloud seemed to lift from him.

"Yes, yes, by the Gods, it is time. I have lost all senses in this hole. After the dark majesty of my underworld, I come to this place, and it was all I could do to dig .... *this*! You are right, serpent. With Lucifer to lead, and with the might of our Gods of darkness, I can once again reign supreme, with power...with wisdom...with the brilliant light of Heaven. I, Hades, will replace Zeus himself and lead all of the Gods ...."

Satan and the serpent slyly smiled. Now they were getting somewhere.

Hades continued, "With my loyal FISHBONE at my side!"

They all turned to look at the carp, which merely pursed its puckered lips and responded, "Smack, smack, smack."

Chapter 18
– Gods of Love, the Morning After

*A*phrodite's home was a lovely, large, entirely white tent with a carpet worthy of the Gods...it was entirely white and was mostly covered with large white pillows. All objects within seemed to glow with an internal energy. The effect was a heavenly feeling of living in the clouds.

The Goddess was up, and appeared to be brewing what smelled like very strong coffee. She was wearing the Lord's linen shirt on her top and on the bottom only the soft color pink of her perfectly shaped ass. The shirt was naturally loose, so an occasional beautiful brown nipple came peeking out to check and see if her guest had awakened.

The smell of strong coffee finally did its job, and the Son of Man raised himself on one elbow, from the beyond soft comfort of the pillow bed.

"Good morning, handsome," chimed the Goddess of Love as she did a perfect belly flop on the bed and rolled on top of the carpenter's son. She looked him deep in the eyes and continued, "I hope you're hungry, because I am making quail eggs and dates, and I am an excellent cook, if I do say so myself." She kissed him full on the lips.

Jesus smiled at the sweet Goddess and replied, "The coffee smells wonderful, as do you, sweetness."

"Well, if you would rather, we could enjoy something else that is sweet, and from all of the practice we had last night, something you have become rather good at."

Jesus rolled over on top of the Goddess. "As tempting as that sounds, oh temptress, I have been overcome by the smell of your coffee. I also wonder how a man can wake up in the morning and be ....so .... exhausted! Seriously, I love you very much and am ever a part of you. There is a new understanding in me and a feeling of fulfillment. This morning I find the sky a bit bluer, the sun a bit more golden, and the air as crisp as the first morn. My Father God again is perfect and is loving beyond measure with this amazing gift to man."

Jesus rose from the pillows and helped the Goddess to her feet. He was perfectly naked, but walked over to his pile of clothes and put on his linen wrap. This left him with his chest bare but his modesty intact.

Jesus poured himself a very small cup of exceedingly strong coffee and sat down at a low table on the floor. The Goddess bustled around a corner of the tent that was apparently used for cooking.

"You know I could wave my hands and create perfect food, don't you? It is also a fact that we really don't need to eat here at all. But in both of those things ... where is the fun? I love the smells of the preparation and I love the fact that this is a gift from me to you. Food can be so .... romantic, don't you think?"

The beautiful, forever young Goddess looked lovingly at the handsome Hope of the World. She briefly considered the unimaginable suffering he had been through and the impending confrontation she could feel was coming. Suddenly, she burst into tears and fell his arms.

"You are just too, too much. Too much love, too much suffering, too much giving, too much sacrifice. There is no end in it for you."

She hugged him tightly, as if in her arms he could be spared from not just what was to come, but the past as well. Even a Goddess was hopelessly lacking in an effort of this kind. There was nothing left to do but to love him in the here and now. To love him really good. She smoothed his hair as he held her and looked deeply into his eyes. Tears were streaming down both of their faces.

"Just stay with me," she said softly. "I cannot take away your pain or fight your fight, but I can hide you, perhaps forever. We can be together and exist in perfect love. You can take me as your wife. We can have *little Jesuses*...another major part missing from your completeness."

"If it were only me," said the gentle Messiah, "I would stay until the earth refused to spin. I would stay until the sun burned into a cinder. There would be no force in Heaven or on earth that could take your hand from mine. But, it is not only me. It is written that I have a purpose left to fulfill. I cannot walk away from this. It would take away the things in me that make you love me. It is my love for others. It is my strength. It is my life and my message. I know you know this, and I know you understand."

"Is it not against your love to fight, even a creature as abhorrent as the Evil One? If you do this, do you not follow your foolish humans as an onward Christian soldier, a Crusader? You would follow this path and reinforce the notion of battle as a solution for man? Can a physical confrontation really be a path to enlightenment? This is folly. Your love would be better served staying here with me."

"In so many ways you are right, gentle Aphrodite. I am not a fighter. The only time I was physical was in throwing the moneychangers out of my church. I did not attack them, however. I attacked the money and turned their tables. Money is a *great Satan* when it comes to my message, and judging from what I have heard, it has played a major role in the perversion of my word, but that is a different story. For my part with the Wicked One, I am not convinced it will really be me fighting. My Father would not put me in the role of a Gladiator. I am not built for that. I can only completely believe in the purpose of my Father, and in the unstoppable power of love. Those are the weapons I will rely on."

"I fear you will be crushed."

"So be it, if that is the desire of my Father. Not my will, but his will."

The beautiful Goddess forced a smile and released herself from the hold of the Savior. She squeezed his hand and walk across the tent to the food she was preparing.

Jesus took a deep breath and smiled at the wonderful smells in the tent. He smiled at the wonders of the evening before, and of the gentle hand that led him to such feelings, to such joy. He smiled at the love that this woman Goddess carried. He smiled at her lovely pink ass that rode just below the shirttails of his linen garment.

For the moment, the questions he had were silent, and the fear of the future was nonexistent. There would be time enough for that on a different day.

Chapter 19
– The Army of Good Evolving

ars had had his question answered by the mighty Zeus, and it was not to his liking. It would appear the best warrior in the *good guy* column had no appetite for battling the Christian God. While the logic behind the decision was sound, Mars truly did not see it coming. It was true the followers of Jesus were brutal in their complete dismantling of the Greek and Roman mythology. They stole their solstice holidays and claimed them for their own. They twisted their traditional celebrations and called them something Christian. This was so clever as the beloved parties could continue, just with a different purpose, and honestly for humans it was always about the party ... not the *purpose.*

In keeping with this sinister twisting, the Christians also demonized some Gods who were, for the most part, harmless. The worst was taking the gentle Pan and making his image that of the Great Deceiver .... who looked absolutely nothing like him. The evolving puritan tone of the ever-suffering Christians, led them to be particularly appalled by the constant partying and sexual appetite of the little goat God. Their spiritual self-flagellations required they put an end to all unnecessary pleasure, and little Pan was an easy target. They turned his playful image into the image of the Most Wicked of All. Honestly, an absurd transition.

So there they were. Mars sat on the ground in this field, in the middle of the beginning and the end, at the gathering place. His sword was on his lap and his dick was in the dirt. There seemed to be no possible way the remaining Gods willing to fight for the Christian God would be enough to turn back the Evil One and those who would follow him.

Mars made a fateful decision. While it seemed to be true that they could not win this battle, that did not change the fact that they had to fight. There was right and wrong in the world, and to fight for the right was the duty of any great warrior. Mars understood more of the acts of war than any other God in this place. He alone would understand the hopelessness of their cause. This fight was not just any fight. If the legends of the King of the Jews were correct, this would be the battle at the end of the world, Armageddon. This would be a battle that Mars, for one, would never walk away from. He stood up from the ground and dusted off his armor. He stood erect and spread his feet apart with his sword planted firmly in the ground between. He lifted up his noble head and smiled a slight smile. He did not know if Satan could end his life. He was outside of his own legends. He did know, however, that a hopeless battle in the defense of love and justice was more than a worthy way to end one's days, and if this was to be the end, he would end fighting the most fearsome enemy of all. His smile broadened as other Gods appeared in the gathering place. What more could he ask for?

Mercury was the first to appear, with Diana, the Goddess of Hunting. They walked across a small stretch of green grass to face the God of War.

"Well," asked Mercury, "where is the big God? I have spoken to all who would support the side of The Jewish King and have found several willing. As Zeus commands, many more will follow."

"In that, we have a slight problem," replied Mars. "It would seem the mighty Zeus is still upset with the carpenter. I don't know, I guess being thrown down from Olympus and made to rule from a mound of dirt has put his nose a bit out of joint. It makes things more complicated, but changes nothing. This will be an epic battle between good and evil, and if he does not want to play, then the loss is his."

"This is grave news, Mars," responded Mercury. "I do not believe we have a champion who can match the Most Wicked, not even you, my friend."

"What you say is true. However, this does not guarantee defeat. This battle plan has changed. We cannot win man to man. We must fight smarter. Where we would have charged and conquered, now we must dodge and duck. We must work on a plan that will trick the trickster, and somehow even the odds. I am glad to see you, Diana. There is no bow in the universe to match yours. We need every advantage we can muster."

The Goddess of Hunting smiled and nodded. There was no fear in her, though she, too, understood the gravity of the situation. The Gods had never fought outside of their own legends. They were treading on new ground, and very much in peril.

Others began to arrive and were soon deeply discussing their situation and debating strategy. Their company included:

Mars, the God of War

Mercury, Messenger of the Gods

Diana, Goddess of the Hunt

Fortuna, the Goddess of Fortune

Janus, the God of Doors, and Beginnings and Endings

Minerva, the Goddess of Wisdom, Science, and War

Felicitas, the Goddess of Good Luck and Success

Hercules, the God of Strength

Honos, the God of Military Honors and Chivalry

Mithras, the God most worshiped by the Roman soldiers

Pietas, the Goddess of Duty

Bacchus, the God of Wine

Nodutus, the God who made knots in stalks of wheat

Mercury assured the company that there were others who had business to conclude, but they would come to the meeting place as time allowed. Everything in this place was, as all knew, in time.

The big question, now was, who and how many the Evil One could muster, and how they matched up. Mars knew all the Gods of Heaven and was pleased at those who were before him.

Mercury spoke, "I understand that Satan has enlisted Hades himself from the underworld. He will surely rally the wicked, and help gather dark forces. He also knows their strengths and weaknesses, and will be an able general."

Bacchus spoke, "And what of Fishbone?"

The gathering looked at each other, then broke into laughter.

Mercury responded, "Do not underestimate Hades. While living in a sand hole has taken its toll on him, he is still the brother of Zeus himself, and one of the three. He is, perhaps, the most mighty of those of us who would join this battle."

The three, of course, were the Gods of the Gods, the brothers who defeated the Titans and ruled Heaven and earth. They were Hades, God of the Underworld and the Dead; Neptune, God of the Waters; and Zeus, Ruler of the Gods.

"Speaking of the three," began Diana, "has anyone approached Neptune? He might be willing to fight, and would be a great asset."

Mercury replied, "I did not find him. He has not, in fact, been seen much since we first came to this place. Since there is no great water to be found, it is not obvious where he might be. However, the time might have come to approach him. When the time is right in this place, the *where* will be right in front of us. I will set out immediately."

In a wink, the God was gone. The remaining troop began to gather in groups and discuss the possible strategies that might keep the little Christian God from falling under the crushing wheels of the Great Pretender.

Chapter 20
– Back on Earth

*B*ack on Earth:

Charlie was probably the first to feel the difference. He was dumpster diving, as usual, and found a pie plate. Not just any pie plate, but a magic one. More on that later The point is, he was the first person on earth to know that things had changed.

Charlie Pilgrim was the Pastor of The Church Under the Viaduct for Displaced Believers.

In this church, all were welcome.

At this church, when they passed the plate, it was not for collection, but rather, a plate full of bread that Charlie himself had dumpster-dived for behind the Brilliant Bread industrial bakery. The loaves were left over from the retail store the bakery maintained in front of the massive complex. It was really pretty good bread, with very little mold, and Charlie's flock was usually hungry.

Charlie had walked a winding path to the church he now preached at, the church he'd also created. He had once been a minister at a giant mega-church called The Only Real Church of Jesus in downtown Los Angeles. He'd not been the head minister, but was what was termed an "up and comer." He was adept at rallying the masses with screams of "Praise the Lord!" and "Amen!" He threw in countless exclamations of "Can I get a witness?!" and "Halleluiah!" He was famous within the leadership for preaching the sermon that reaped the largest collection in church history. For his efforts, he got a new Cadillac.

After a time, Charlie began to question the motivation behind the church and also question his own motivations. One day he was just gone. He left his shiny Cadillac; his no-rent-necessary, five-thousand-square-foot home on the beach at Malibu, and his trophy wife, Annette.

He just left.

The church leaders sadly explained he had had a nervous breakdown and asked the congregation to pray for him, and show their support with generous donations. The lovely Annette moved in with the senior pastor, Abraham Sincere Godly. He had always shown a fondness for the extremely buxom follower, and now showed kindness in taking the abandoned bride to his bosom. His holy connections expedited the couple's quick divorce. The Reverend Godly's third wife was not thrilled, and reportedly took up residence with a local musician who played drums for a band called Stillbirth.

Charlie took to the street to find what he had been looking for in the beginning, religion. He prayed for guidance and for clarity. It was not just the church he had found himself in that confused him, but the religion itself. Naturally, over time, the hypocrisy of his mega-church stuck in his throat. He was in fact a very good man and that was inevitable. He was also confused when Bible scholars and true believers saw nothing but truth in text that Charlie found full of inconsistencies and a storyline that seemed to drift further and further from the early words of the gentle Jesus. They saw answers where Charlie saw only questions. He felt in his heart a great love for his Savior, but a growing discomfort with his religion.

So with prayer, fasting (he didn't have any money anyway, so that was easy), and meditation, he set out to create his own.

It turned out to be a simple religion and one that he was surprised had not been created before. He took only the words and deeds of Jesus himself from the Bible, and that was that. The rest was non-existent in Charlie's church, and did not seem to be missed.

Once he had his religion completed, Charlie set out to find a church. He began preaching on the streets to the folks who were in the most need. He tried to imitate his Savior and asked his followers to give up their worldly goods and to follow him. It turned out that the great majority of his evolving flock had no worldly goods, so were more than willing to give them up.

To support a building in LA would have cost big time money, and Charlie could see this would lead right back to the mega-church and the reality he had just left, so he chose not to bring members to his church, but to bring his church to his members. The perfect spot ended up to be under a viaduct on the I-5 freeway that crossed a small waste-water canal near Downey, in south-central LA County. It was a massive concrete overpass that had acres of useable, protected ground under it, especially in the dry season. This was also where Charlie set up his home. His objective was to find salvation in the wilderness, in the center of one of the most massive congregations of humanity that was ever collected in the history of the earth. With his tidy sleeping pad on the ground, under the protection of concrete, this place, in all ways, was perfect.

There was already a sizable population residing under the bridge, so Charlie had a ready-made congregation. Not all were excited about a preacher in residence. There had been several who had tried to fill this role before, and had been found out to be thieves and charlatans. They were given the boot. Charlie, on the other hand, was honest and sincere, and before long, his simple message began to resonate. His church began to grow and grow, until it leveled out at about thirty faithful, with maybe a dozen or so more coming for the bread.

Of all of the popes, bishops, ministers, priests, gurus, and holy men in the world, Charlie was the one to find "the holy pie plate" .... A discarded old pie plate he found when dumpster diving for bread. He just thought it would be useful for something ... to someone. It wasn't even dented. Then, when he was cleaning it, a voice called out to him. "Yeah, oh, Charlie the Chosen. Verily, you have been selected, as Moses before you, to lead God's flock to the New Covenant."

It said much more, but you get the idea.

The visions that he saw in the plate showed him a world beyond, and the message was clear ... something *big* was going on. Satan was gone, and the light that had been the hope of Jesus on the earth was ... turned out. It would seem they had both landed in this *other world* beyond the plate.

Charlie could feel it, also. Somehow, in his simple honesty, he had been chosen to see through to the World of Lost Gods. He could see the story unfolding, of Jesus and of the Gods of the Greeks and Romans. He could see the epic struggle beginning, and he understood that he was indeed watching the unfolding of Armageddon. He had encouraged others in his flock to watch the story in the plate with him, and it became apparent that only Charlie Pilgrim was able see the story unfolding. As all prophets before him, folks began to think he was crazy. Though the members of his congregation were used to crazy people of all descriptions, Charlie was certain he was not one. As the minister of his flock, he was going from respect to ridicule. He knew he had been chosen, and took the responsibility seriously. He made his way to the top of the bridge to pray for guidance.

Charlie folded his hands and opened his heart, and waited for more words with direction from the plate. No words were uttered. He stood at the edge of the viaduct looking down at a traffic-packed I-5, and felt an uneasy compulsion to alert the world.

Chapter 21
– Neptune

Mercury flew into the air with the objective of finding Neptune and convincing him to join the struggle against the evolving satanic forces. He knew there was no great ocean in this place and had no idea where the God of the Sea might be living. He had made himself scarce for a very long time.

He was surprised when he found himself on the edge of a desert. Not a giant Sahara desert, but a chunk of sand about two or three kilometers across. In the center there appeared to be a clump of palm trees, perhaps an oasis. Mercury made his way in that direction.

As he came close to the center, he began to hear a loud voice, apparently in the middle of telling a story.

"Yes, by Zeus, the wind was blowing ... A hundred knots if it was one. The ship was listing side to side, and even the dolphins below were getting a might seasick. The air was as thick as your mother's brown gravy, and the captain could nae see the rocks to her bow."

Mercury came through the palms and saw the giant God of the Sea sitting in the middle of a small pond on a single rock. He was surrounded by a circle of camels that seemed to be listening with rapt attention.

"It would seem that all was lost," he continued. "Then, the captain cried out, 'Oh, mighty Neptune, we be lost. Save us and we will commit our miserable lives to your service.' Now, I don't really need any filthy swabs serving me, as you can imagine. I had every mermaid and Sea Queen at my disposal. But, I have a mighty heart to match my mighty deeds, and it was mightily moved ..."

Suddenly, the pontificator noticed the godly messenger and gave a hearty shout, "Hey Ho ... if it ain't my old friend, Mercury. Come here to me, island boy, and join me in some kippers and brie. We might even have a tot of rum as well."

The giant Sea God winked and motioned the messenger to a clear patch of sand by his side.

Mercury gently flew over the ring of camels and landed next to Poseidon. He wrapped his massive arms around the smaller messenger and nearly crushed his hat wings as he bear-hugged him.

"So, what in this world are you doing in my little kingdom, my friend? No wait, I can tell you! There is mischief a-brewing, and it's blowing a foul wind, which will hit like a mighty typhoon. It will rattle the spars and make the halyards scream. I can feel it like I can feel my own long sword, if ye know what I mean. I can see the Evil One in my mind's eye. It's not a place I care to look."

"What you say is true, Neptune. There is a battle coming. On one side a gentle carpenter, and on the other, the most foul Lucifer. It is a mismatch and we fear the Evil One will triumph. We believe it is our destiny to take up the sword for the side of righteousness and help defend the good against this danger. I have come to enlist your trident in this struggle."

"I see," said the Sea God, as he stroked his massive beard with the tips of his trident. "I would not choose the Evil One to rule the universe. He is truly one nasty bastard. I can see a future of darkness and fire. As you easily know, fire is the enemy of water. I do not relish the thought of ruling a world of steam. That being said, this Jesus of Nazareth is also a problem for me ... and for you as well. He has taken our believers and cast us into this *world of the forgotten*. He is no friend of mine."

"I understand this, mighty Neptune. I am not happy to be here either. It is a place that is devoid of believers, and has made us all lesser. I am not sure that this Christian God is aware of this or if this was indeed his intention. If you have watched his life, as I am sure we all have, you have seen that he was truly interested in saving his people, the Jews. He did not give much thought to the beliefs of the Romans. I would guess he did not intend to be made into a God to replace all Gods. I would wager that this was the doing of the humans. It was the invention of our followers. In a sense, our demise is our own fault. We got too involved with the petty goings on in Olympus, and gave little thought to the screwed-up lives of humans. Jesus did care about his people, which translated to all people. He has a simple message of hope and of love, which we had too long ignored. I truly think the fault is ours that we have landed in this place. Look at the other Gods of Earth. The Buddha God still exists, the Hindu, the Muslim, and many more still reside on earth equal to the Complete One. We fell away, and it would appear by the presence in this place of the Jew King, in time, the others will also fade away. The humans will turn their backs on them as well. While it does stick in my craw, I see this and do not judge the carpenter harshly."

"Aye," said the salty one, "what you say is true. I have always judged intentions as to be a driving force. If a mariner is caught unaware in a mighty blow, I am more apt to guide his hand. If it is that a mariner challenges the sea, and in his vanity believes he can master it, I do take pleasure in bringing him to his humble knees and smashing his ships to smithereens. It is difficult to swallow all of this, however. Zeus on his sand hill, Hades in his sand hole, and me in the middle of my sand sea... with no one but camels to entertain, it has been a true humbling. What I would give to have my sea back. To ride the waves and dive the deeps, great Zeus, I miss it so."

"I share your grief, my brother," replied Mercury. "There is nothing I wouldn't give to be back on Mt. Olympus. I am reminded that time is long and the future is hard, even for a seer to see. What I feel strongly now is to fight this fight. It is not just for the King of the Jews, but it is also for what is right, what is truth, what is love. It is against all hate and treachery. It is a worthy fight in itself, and what happens to us after this may or may not be altered, but we have been called. We find ourselves here, at this time, at this place. Perhaps this battle is not from our mythology, but it will exist in time and space, and will create a story all its own. The more I think of it, the more proud I become to be a part of it. I will not sit on the side as this epic struggle begins."

"Well said, my friend. You are right, and right again. Count me in! I will join my brothers and sisters in this. Actually, I do not think these camels understood a single thing I said. They are dumber than fish! Let's go to the gathering place and prepare for this battle's proper time."

They were gone in a wink and left the camels to fend for themselves.

Chapter 22
– Army of Evil

*T*he three leaders of the rebellion stood in a ragged opening in the woods, before a gathering of willing evildoers.

Hades, true to his word, had been able to recruit a very impressive gathering. It included:

Vulcan, the God of Fire

Discordia, the Goddess of Discord

Invidia, the Goddess of Envy and Jealousy

Libitina, the Goddess of Death, Corpses, and Funerals

Nemesis, the Goddess of Revenge

Tempestes, the Goddess of Storms

Trivia, the Goddess of Magic

Somnus, the God of Sleep

Portunes, the God of Keys

And, Cloacina, the Goddess of Sewers... who stank.

There were, reportedly, others who would join the fray, after taking care of immediate business.

Some in the gathering were obvious in their evilness, and others simply had disagreements with someone on the other side and wanted to settle personal scores. They all felt they were on the winning side, and looked forward to rewards that included major promotions in Heaven.

Lucifer arose before the gathering and spread his mighty wings. He began to *glow*, taking on an aura of power that he had not, to this point, displayed.

"Friends, if I may call you such, I am pleased with the gathering before me, and the efforts made by the mighty Hades."

Hades smiled and puffed himself up a bit. It had been a long time since he had had much respect, and he enjoyed the attention. The group was noticeably lacking his pal, Fishbone. The serpent had convinced him they needed him to stay and watch the throne of Hades, in case there was an assault on that regal hole in the sand. Hermes, in his foggy mind, was secretly glad that he did not have to carry the very large carp around. He was determined that the loyal Fishbone should never know it was a ruse, and also should reap equal rewards in the new Heaven.

"It may not be apparent to all," continued Lucifer, "that this is the last battle in creation, and the first dawning of a new day. The present God of All will fall, and I shall take my rightful place and reign in Heaven. Your pathetic lives to this point will be replaced with a power and majesty you cannot even fathom."

It was easy to see that this Wicked Angel was beyond anything that was seen on Olympus. His ultimate power was now evident, and the energy that flowed through him was of a magnitude no one present could have imagined. This reinforced their belief that they would ultimately be victorious.

"A great battle," preached Satan, "is defined by not only the mission but by the power and majesty of the enemy. In this, we are not lacking. Your Gods have assembled a mighty army to try and guard the key to our success, the little Jewish King. This Jesus is as a flea to me. When I crush his

114

throat in my mighty grasp, the will of the God of All will be broken, and he will be forced to face me. In this meeting with Jehovah, I will not fail. I have found him to be imperfect, and thus flawed. I have no such imperfections, so it is obvious that I am superior. It will be the power of Satan that triumphs, and the power of my perfection that will rule creation. I do not wish to fight any but the most holy. I will not spend personal resources with your inferior Gods. You will fight to open a path to the pathetic little Prophet, and I will do the rest. Go now, and plan how this will be accomplished. I too shall prepare."

Lucifer wrapped his mighty wings around himself, and once again became a cone of wings, golden and ominous, that emitted an aura of evil that was beyond the experience of any in the company.

They stepped back, forming a ring around their leader. They stared in awe, and each envisioned their own coming glory at the side of this magnificent beast.

For his part, the serpent slithered into the bushes. He, too, would have nothing to do with the all too human-like Gods. He had other purposes ... and they were all his own.

Chapter 23
– Charlie Meets Buzz

Charlie honestly wanted nothing to do with this. His heart's desire was to follow the example of the Lord, and live a simple and righteous life. This did not include suffering on the cross, and he understood that to bring a message to modern Christians telling of an army of Roman Gods fighting at Jesus's side, was as insane as anything he might do. At the very least, he was bound to be labeled a heretic or simply mad.

But how to explain the plate? If Charlie did not believe the plate, then the only other logical explanation was that he was indeed mad. He was either chosen or mad. At this point, Charlie himself was not sure.

The compulsion to tell the world, however, was as strong as Cuban coffee, and Charlie had no real say in the matter. He was driven like Budweiser draft horses, like Wall Street CEOs, like mothers of baby beauty queens, like ... oh well, you get the idea. His church no longer believed in him. Actually, they thought he was nuts, so his leaving was of little loss to them. He packed a small pack with what little he still owned, including the holy pie plate, and headed down the highway.

Charlie's plan was a simple one. He would go and speak with the leaders of the world's churches and see if any of them could see the plate's message too. He was smart enough to know that his explanation alone would just get him ridicule. Someone else had to see the plate and support its message. Now, Charlie did not know any of the world's great religious leaders, but he did know someone who did ... the leader of his old church, Pastor Abraham Sincere Godly. He set off to pay his old boss a visit.

The trip was not an easy one, as Charlie did not even have enough money for the bus, and the Reverend Godly lived in a villa by the sea in Malibu. He walked down I-5 to the nearest exit ramp, and then headed cross-country, occasionally sticking out his thumb, hoping for a ride.

Charlie had walked for most of the day when an absolutely perfect, 1964 orange and white VW Microbus with twenty-three windows and a sliding roof, pulled up to his thumb. A long-haired man, perhaps in his fifties, stuck his head out the window and said, "Hop in, dude!" Charlie climbed in the little classic, and the driver continued, "You look like you could use a bit of a break today, and more specifically, a ride. Where are you headed, my man, and while you are at it, why don't you share your life's story with me over a tasty bit of the bud." He passed a smoking bowl of herbs to Charlie, who did not have time to object.

"Well, I don't really smoke this stuff," said Charlie. "I seem to have a hard enough time with reality."

"All the more reason to tok up, citizen, all the more reason! By the way, my name is Mathew Long Haden, but most folks just call me 'Buzz.' Guess it's 'cause I'm *buzzed* most of the time ... get it?" Buzz looked at Charlie for confirmation that the reason for his nickname was clear. Charlie smiled and nodded his head. "Yeah, I get it."

"And, what be your name, my most recent companion?"

"I guess I be *Charlie*," said Charlie, still holding the smoking pipe.

"Tok up and pass, brother," smiled Buzz, "don't waste the holy herb."

Charlie looked at the pipe, shrugged his shoulders and took a puff. Immediately, his lungs exploded and he coughed until he was sure he was going to puke.

"*Righteous* ......!!!!" exclaimed Buzz as they headed down the road in the sweet little bus toward Malibu.

Now, Charlie had never smoked the evil weed, and this was *particularly good* evil weed. Buzz was famous for it. Our hero soon found himself in a fuzzy pretzel world, with brilliant colors and cartoon characters. Buzz was a perfect cartoon character. Charlie found so many normal things to be quite abnormal, and had a difficult time holding his laughter to a minimum. He also found a slightly drug-induced heart connection with his new friend, Buzz. That's when he took out the plate.

"I have to share this with you, Buzz," confessed Charlie. "It's a holy pie plate, and I can see another world in it."

He held it up for Buzz to see.

"Can you see anything in this plate?" Charlie questioned hopefully.

"Ohhhhh," said Buzz, quite willing to believe anything, "far out, dude!"

He strained across the seat to look into the plate that once held pie. He wrinkled up his nose and raised his eyebrows up and down. "I got nothing, dude, zippo, nada. Is it turned on?"

"Don't need to turn it on, Buzz, it's a holy plate, and the good Lord has given me images to see."

"Cool," said Buzz with wide eyes. "Tell me what it says, Charlie ... please?"

"Very well, my aged hippy, I will begin at the beginning and end when there is no more to tell. Before I start, however ... perhaps another puff?"

The two adventurers cruised down the road to Malibu, in a little orange microbus that seemed to hum a happy tune as it swayed back and forth to rhythms reserved for only such magical vehicles.

Chapter 24
– Buzz Joins the Fray

𝐵uzz pulled the little bus into a cul-de-sac that terminated at the driveway of the palatial abode of one Abraham Sincere Godly. The property was naturally gated, and guarded by two very serious-looking guards dressed in uniforms. They each had automatic weapons over their shoulders. They eyed the two characters in the perfect little bus that was still idling suspiciously, just down the road.

Buzz didn't seem to mind the small army, if he noticed them at all. "I am telling you, Charlie, this is the most amazing thing I have ever heard. This is a BIG DEAL! We are talking about the big one. The first peace-loving hippy, sweet Jesus himself, against the biggest bummer in the whole universe, that scum bag Devil guy. And the Roman dudes are REAL! That is so amazingly cool!"

"I got to tell you this, Charlie. You look at me now, that's it, right in my eyes. You are now my brother, and I am your brother, and it is now WE that are going to do this righteous thing. My heart is in this, Charlie, you got to say 'yes.' I know I can't see the message in the pie plate, but I can hear the message in your soul. If you dump me, I will follow you, if you run, I will run, if you say 'no,' I will say 'yes.' I am your new-age Christian soldier, Charlie, and I will not be denied!"

Buzz looked at Charlie with pleading, honest eyes, and Charlie was persuaded. "I am proud to have you with me, Buzz. We will walk this walk together, and tell the world that creation hangs in the balance."

They shook hands with a Buzz-created shake that had about seven steps and ended with their pinkies hooked.

"Besides," said Buzz, as he put away the bowl, "I got about 300 million dollars from winning the lottery a while back, so I am sure THAT'S gonna help."

Charlie stared at his new brother. "You have what?"

"Oh yeah, I'm *loaded*." Buzz stopped as he considered the double meaning. He looked at Charlie and laughed. "And I have lots of money too!"

Charlie shook his head. "The Lord has his hands in this, Buzz. Without a doubt, you have been chosen. I believe in a path like the Lords where money has no meaning, but it is much easier to do without when you have much more than you need! We are up against evil just like the righteous army in the land of forgotten Gods is. They are just as nasty here, in their own twisted way, and we will need all the help we can get."

"Agreed, Kemo-sahbee ... suppose we pay a visit to your old boss-man and put this peace train in motion!"

Charlie looked dubiously at the two nasty looking guards that were looking back. "No place to go, but forward ..."

Buzz and Charlie got out of the bus and walked over to the guard shack. The guards look at them like they were potato bugs and sneered, "Yes, is there something we can do for you?"

"Yes," said Charlie, "would you tell Reverend Godly that Charlie Pilgrim is here and would like to have a word with him?"

"And what would your business be with the preacher?" said one of the nasty guards.

"That would be between the reverend and myself. Now please pass along my request."

The two guards looked as if they would rather shoot the two and be done with it, but one of them reluctantly picked up the phone and rang the mansion.

While Charlie had left the giant Only Real Church of Jesus, he had never had a real falling out with the Reverend Godly or his flock. Charlie had just become quietly disgusted, and had packed his things and left. Reverend Godly and the rest of the minions actually thought Charlie was crazy and had a breakdown. Who in their right mind would walk away from the treasures and potential power that Charlie had in his hands. Many felt that he was the anointed one and would surely follow the Reverend Godly when he decided to retire from his burdens and harvest his rewards. That would seem to be still some time away as the reverend was still bearing his burdens in his mansion in Malibu.

Charlie and his unlikely wingman were granted access.

The not-so-humble pastor led the unlikely duo into a parlor that looked out at the ocean and the mile-long private beach the parsonage controlled. He was a large man with a dominating aura. He had long silver hair, and everything he said and did seemed to be part of a polished act.

"Yea, the prodigal son hath returned! Charlie Pilgrim, as I live and breathe ... and you have brought one of your new friends into my home." He looked Buzz up and down and ignored his offered handshake.

"Can I fix you a drink?"

"Boy, howdy!" said Buzz. "I'd love a margarita with crushed ice, no salt, and a lime ... please."

The most reverend ignored Buzz and repeated to Charlie, "Can I fix YOU a drink?"

"Sure," said Charlie, "I'll take two margaritas with crushed ice, no salt, and two limes ... please."

"Very well," responded the preacher, who pushed a button on the wall and ordered the Mexican refreshers. "Sit down, please, and tell me what this little visit is about."

Buzz and Charlie sat on an overstuffed white leather couch that looked like the hide might be made of white tiger or the like. It was way too soft and luxurious to be simple cowhide.

"I have an issue, Abraham, and I could use your help. I need introductions to the most holy Christian men in the world, and I know that you can do this for me."

The pompous preacher stared at the two. "You must be kidding. Why in the world would I do such a thing?"

Charlie pulled the plate from his backpack and showed it to the preacher.

"Can you see anything?" he asked.

Pastor Godly looked at the plate. "Oh, course I can. It's a goddamn pie plate!"

"Whooooa, preacher dude," said an offended Buzz, "that's no way for a preacher to talk!"

"Fuck you," sneered the leader of one of the largest churches in LA County.

"Hang on, Abraham. Listen to what's going on here." Charlie told some of the story to Godly. He didn't tell specifics, just said he was getting messages from God in the plate, and had to tell the world.

"Oh yeah," spat the preacher, "prove it."

Charlie didn't know what to say. He was about to confess that he could not, when he noticed something had changed. The story on the plate continued, but there was a word banner at the bottom, like you see on football broadcasts. The one currently scrolling said, "Ask about Mabel Moneysworth."

Charlie read it twice to make sure what he was reading were instructions for his current situation. It was.

"Reverend, I have been instructed to ask you about Mabel Moneysworth."

The most Reverend Godly turned most noticeably white. "What the FUCK, Pilgrim! You play a dangerous game, boy."

Charlie stopped him. "Wait, there's more." The plate displayed, "404763218."

Charlie said, "404763218."

Again, the preacher blanched. "How could you know this?"

"It's the plate, preacher. These things mean nothing to me, and quite honestly, will mean nothing to me in the future, if you could kindly help us out with a couple of introductions."

The preacher rubbed his chin and looked back and forth at his two unlikely visitors.

"Well ... I ... guess ... I ... could make a call or two."

Charlie smiled and replied, "That would be most kind, preacher ... most kind, indeed."

The two margaritas arrived, and Buzz and Charlie sipped on them with delight.

"I'll bet that's mighty good tequila, ain't it, Preacher?" spat the gentle Buzz.

"Yeah," grumbled the Most Reverend Godly, "damn good!"

Chapter 25
– Apollo

Jesus held Aphrodite gently in his arms. She rested her head on his shoulder as they stood in the road near her tent. Their time together had been brief, but powerful. What would you expect from two Gods of Love?

Jesus lifted her chin and looked into her tear-filled eyes. "Thank you," he said. "You have given me a wonderful gift, and I will treasure it always."

Aphrodite cried softly. "Will I see you again?"

"I have no idea. I still have so many questions, and a future that is not clear. When I was on earth, I was so certain. In many ways, I was so wrong. Now, I am facing the ultimate enemy and I do not even know what is real and what is not. I am hungry for more information. I will need to clarify my mind before I am faced with the ultimate confrontation."

"Jesus, your heart was never wrong. You should not define your success or failure by the deeds of man. Judged by your own deeds, you are without fault, perfect in your nature and complete in your creation. Find out your information, but hold it at arm's length. To hold guilt over the foibles of man is to suffer from the mental poisoning of the Evil One. Do not be fooled."

"Very well, my love...I will try and be objective in my self-appraisal. I think perhaps your judgment is twisted by my incredible good looks and winning personality." He smiled and separated from the beautiful Goddess. "I do need to continue my search. My heart feels that wheels are spinning, and time is growing short."

"If you want information, seek out Apollo. He is the God of the Sun, but also of music and poetry. He is the God of Healing and taught medicine to man. He is also the God of Truth, who cannot speak a lie. He has an inquisitive heart and a talent for unraveling some of the mysteries of man."

"I would ask you where I would find him, but in this place I would guess we will find each other. Farewell, sweet Goddess. I am certain we will meet again, somewhere in love."

With that, the *hope* of the last world and it would seem of this one, walked down the little dirt road and faded into the future.

As was the way in this strange place, it was only a bend or two in the road and Jesus stood face to face with Apollo. The Roman God was sitting on the grass softly playing a lute. The music was gentle and soothing, and Jesus sat next to him without a word. The music seemed to lift and fall, and to create images of life as a melodic wheel that spun in circles in time. No words were necessary, and the magic of the music itself soothed the Jewish King's soul. It put him at ease and created a bond between the two spirits.

The music ended, as all things do, and the two sat smiling at each other.

Apollo broke the spell. "Greetings, O Complete One. What a ruckus you have created in this world and the last. Isn't it amazing what chaos simple love and truth can bring about? Even now, my brother and sister Gods gather to form an army to defend a simple Jew from the ravages of the most

Evil One. And he too gathers the wicked of my kind, to bring about your end, and move the universe toward his evil intent. Wherever you walk, the very walls of creation shudder. Yet, you are so simple, so kind, so loving, so ... *right* in all things. You are truly the greatest mystery of all."

"I seem to be a mystery to myself as well. I have been learning of my past since I have been here. I can recall little of the time between the cross and appearing here. I seem to remember a feeling of spinning and peace, an affirmation of love and what I would term a sense of healing. Time was not defined. It could have been eternity, or merely a moment. I have since learned it was roughly two thousand years. I am ... amazed. The events on earth, and the evolution of my deeds and purpose are of concern to me. The thread of logic seems to have been broken into many pieces and each piece seems to have created its own threads, which were in their turn broken, creating more thread, and so on. Truth has been surrounded by a web of confusion, misunderstanding, superstition, and idolatry. Created, it would seem, to satisfy thousands of ulterior motives. It is no wonder I find myself here in a world of forgotten, or completely misunderstood, Gods. I have read my Torah, which is now called the New Testament, and happily, some of my words and deeds still exist. I thank God for that. This is at the beginning of the Torah, and from there, it seems to depart to places I do not fully understand. Now I am in a place and time where it would seem I am about to do battle with the Archangel Lucifer. This seems to fulfill scripture in the Torah that I was not a part of. Is the truth the truth I lived, or the truth of these scriptures? What else do I need to know if I am to fight this fight? I cannot imagine my Father in Heaven would want me to be a warrior. I am no soldier. My only weapons are love and peace. Could this possibly defeat a monster like the Evil One, who has no respect or regard for either? "

Apollo looked at the Christian God with sympathy. "You are asking questions that are beyond my simple understanding. However, if you understand the basic nature of man, it is easier to unravel the more complex issue of individual acts of those on earth. You were born complete and perfect, into a world that was and is neither. Your followers and the ones you loved battled mightily to try and copy the image that you created, but they were not blessed with the understanding you were born with. As temptation and the unimaginable complexity of life closed in on them, they did the best they could and made decisions based on acts of your short and simple life and words, the closer to your time, the more pure the message. As with all things, time corrupts. Within your own people, the Jews, your message was discredited by the power structure of the day. They had much to lose, and fought viciously. Most Jews followed them then, and more returned to them as your word became the religion of the Gentiles. When there is great danger in the world, it is natural to find your way home. The Jews faced many dangers and found few to trust outside of their own. In time, your deeds were discredited and you fell away like rust in time. Also, the promise of the Messiah to lead the Jews to their New Jerusalem was not quickly realized. Two thousand years is a long time to wait."

"For the ones who follow you, you have literally become God himself. You have become what they call the trinity, or the three-in-one. This is a central part of their dogma. You have become God the Father, God the Son, and God the Holy Spirit."

"Interesting, and I guess, literally true. God the Father is in me, and I, Jesus the man, surrendered to him completely. In that sense, all that is in me is of God. This would be the Father. I am, of course, the Son, as the seed gives all men the ability to become the sons of God, and the manifestation of the completeness of God's law is the Spirit. In that sense, I am literally, the *three in one*. However, to say that I am the Completeness of the God of All things is difficult. If you surrender to the void, do you become the *all* of the void or a *portion* of the void? If you are eaten by a tiger, your flesh becomes the flesh of the tiger, but are you the entire tiger? Do you displace the tiger that existed before he ate you? Not so ... the one .... the Almighty was before time, and will be there when there is nothing else, when words and history, religion and events have no meaning."

"Now I must battle Satan, whom God created. How could a creation be greater than the Creator? If I were the God of All, this would seem to be an easy victory. Somehow, I feel that is not the case."

"It is not surprising that things have taken this turn," continued Apollo. "It is man's nature to create comfort and simplicity. That is why we prospered for so many centuries. We offered simple explanations, and an answer for any question. We had priests that told our stories and made up ones if our stories were not adequate. We ourselves are at fault for not working harder for humans, and to reward us they turned their back when a better, more compassionate

131

solution arrived. That, of course, was *you*. We let our priests define us, and this led to a distortion of our intent. The same is with you. Your priests, after time, began to define you. Their natural pride turned priests to saints and, although they would not agree, they turned saints to Gods. Their saints could answer prayer and perform miracles. They even have a living saint in their pope, who is reported to have a direct line to God, and has been deemed "infallible." Like a caesar, a living God on earth. This is in spite of verified acts of sin and unbelievable cruelty some of these popes committed. With humans, their religions must grow or they seem to wither and die. Your simple truth was merely a seed for the soil of their fertile minds. They even turned the most hideous implement of torture, the cross, into a thing to worship. I would have to say that their nature allows these things, but the Wicked One's hand is also always in play."

"The cross was certainly not my fondest memory. Would they worship a sword or a spear if that had taken my life? Would they kneel to an ax or an arrow? I do not know enough to judge, but I have heard enough to know the vision I had for man has not been manifest. It was my wish to give them peace in their hearts, through simple acts of kindness. I wanted them to know there was a forgiving God who loved them, and would not be harsh to judge. I wanted them to know the unending grace of the God of All. I wanted them to see through the hollow promise of earth's treasure, and to clearly see the path to the riches of the spirit on earth and beyond."

Apollo began to play his lute again. Its melody wafted through the air like a sweet perfume. Jesus sat and hung his head.

"Cheer up, Jesus, my friend. It is all so much more complicated. As you, above all, know, there are mysteries yet to unfold. Love and goodness, and the God of All nct only have a part to play, but play the only part. You did what one who was born *complete* would do. You are a faithful servant. There is no place for shame in you."

"As you say... but in truth, I long to be with my Father. I am tired in spirit and feel lost in this world."

"You have another great role to play I am afraid, and it is not an easy one. But, have faith that you would not have been created lacking. It doesn't seem to be the way things work."

Apollo began again to play his lute as a dejected Son of God again walked down the little dirt road, somewhere between here and there.

Chapter 26
– Travels on Earth

*P*reacher Godly was not particularly pleased with his traitorous protégée. He was also not one to bow easily to blackmail. Sure, Charlie had somehow found out about Mabel Moneysworth, the church's most generous benefactor. It was true she had been dead for eight years, and also true that the church had not found it necessary to inform anyone of that fact. It was furthermore true that they had continued to draw generously from her accounts while they quietly gave her a most pious, quiet burial in her lavish back yard garden, but the reverend felt no remorse and felt justified that he was doing the Lord's business while stealing the widow's money for the good of his church.

Charlie had not been in the inner circle that made such difficult decisions, and had no way that the preacher could think of to find out. That he did find out was not, however, impossible and the reverend made a mental note to do some internal investigation to find a possible leak.

The number, however, was a different situation. 404763218 was the number of a little retirement account the church had generously set up for the Reverend Godly, in a small bank located in a place simply described as "offshore." Of course, for privacy concerns the reverend and the church's CFO were the only ones who knew of the account's existence. That the Reverend Godly was also the church's CFO made this even simpler, and made the fact that Charlie had known the number all the more concerning.

The good preacher did not believe in miracles of any kind, and in the magic pie plate, specifically. Charlie was a threat to him and to the church itself, and must be dealt with. Abraham Godly was not above retribution, but found that Charlie's request lent itself to a cleaner solution....at least for the good reverend. He would give him the introduction that he had requested. Close friend Horace Grande, a visible religious leader of the largest evangelical church in the world, a man well known in the world and a man well known to Pastor Godly, was a man who would squash Charlie and his hippy friend like a bug. He wouldn't bat an eye or shed a tear. He, like Reverend Godly, understood the complexities of religion, and the burden involved in creating, evolving, and maintaining churches that not only delivered the Savior's message, but also created massive political cultures, a living church that was more than willing to defend itself against all threats. One that was willing to use the mighty "fist of God" to crush thinking that might negatively impact the accepted beliefs subscribed to by the divinely led leadership, and if insignificant humans got crushed in the process, so be it. The fight for the spirit is an ongoing war and collateral damage was, and has always been, a part of war.

Oh yes, smiled Abraham Godly, Charlie and his buddy might expose him to Reverend Grande, but he would be forewarned, and Charlie and his buddy, Buzz, would quickly be delivered to the arms of Satan himself who would be waiting for all those that would challenge the foundations of the church.

"Man, that was AWESOME!" exclaimed Buzz. "I have no idea who that lady was and what that number meant, but it sure brought old Abe around!"

"To be honest, Buzz, I don't know what all that meant either. It just showed up in the plate. I just read what the plate said."

"Yeah, dude, that is one righteous plate. We are on a mighty mission, my brother. I can't believe we have a pass to see the Preacher Grande. Man, that is like seeing the *Beatles* of religion in America. I have watched him on TV, dude, and he is like a one-man, fine-tuned, rock and roll show. I watched him on peyote once, and I swear, as the music and preaching grew and grew, the dude grew angel wings! My friends said it was the peyote, but I know for a fact that that stuff opens doors ... you know what I mean? This guy is something else, and if anyone can see something in that plate, he should be the dude."

"Yeah, he is big time alright. I probably agree with your friends regarding the peyote ... not that I would know, but remember, Satan has wings too, and the message in the plate is not all that kind to the status quo in religious circles. The good Reverend Grande might not take kindly to what it's saying. Also, I think Reverend Godly caved in pretty easily. He has a lot to lose as well, and I, or the plate, did ... well ... kind of blackmail him in a way. We will see, I guess, and it's not like we have a choice. The plate is in the driver's seat and you and me are just along for the ride."

"Right you are, good-time Charlie. Now, let's get to basics. How do you want to get to Columbus, Ohio, to see this uber preacher man?"

"Well," said Charlie, "it would be a heck of a long ride, even in a sweet little microbus. I think we need to consider options. I probably should have hit up Pastor Godly for use of the church's private jet. Seems like, at that moment, he would have given us anything we asked for. I guess I'm not much of a planner, Buzz. You have any ideas?"

Buzz wrinkled up his brow and appeared to be deep in thought. "I think that first we need a hit on the holy pipe. As far as inspiration goes, it usually helps me out."

"Help yourself, Buzz, but for me, I am going to ride the straight and narrow highway until this mission gets accomplished. I need all the brain power I can muster."

"Suit yourself, *my cap-ee-tan*, As for me, it seems to boost my horsepower, but as for the high-on-life thing .... I can dig it!" Buzz took a mighty pull on the little pipe as he directed the little bus down the road.

"OK .... OK .... My mind is coming into focus. We need to get to Columbus to talk to this Grande dude. It's a long way from California to Columbus. It's about almost all the way across this great USA country of ours. PHEwwwwwwwww!!!" He blew out a massive cloud of illegal substance. "OK, OK .... I am getting an idea....Here it comes .... Here it comes ... can't use their church jet... Yes, yes, of course, it's so simple, what if we used my jet?"

Charlie looked at Buzz in amazement. "You have a jet?"

"Sure, dude ... it's a beauty! I bought it from the Grateful Dead. Of course this was quite a while after Jerry had died, but it still was, *the Dead's* plane, man. I haven't changed it at all .... It's CHERRY!"

137

Charlie looked at a grinning Buzz .... "Far out, dude!"

The little microbus cruised effortlessly down the Pacific Coast Highway, heading for the small airport in Lakewood, where Buzz kept his plane. Charlie took the plate out of his pack to see what was happening on the other side of reality. The plate displayed its continuing message to Charlie. It didn't show every bit of the action but showed clearly what needed to be known. Things were seemingly tilted in the favor of the Prince of Darkness. It was tough to see how he could be beaten. Even in a little pie plate, it was easy to see that this monster was a creation way and above anything that could stand against it. Charlie bowed his head and prayed a little prayer, both for his own strength, and for the strength and safety of he who would once again take on this evil force. A thought quickly blew across Charlie's mind. He sure hoped this time Jesus wouldn't end up like last time ... tortured to death.

Chapter 27
– More Gods of Good and Some Strategy

*T*he gathering of the willing were chattering like chipmunks at the gathering place. Apollo, Cupid, and Aphrodite had arrived, and Mercury had returned with Neptune in tow, but several others who said they were willing to fight had not yet arrived. Their number was still less than twenty. They had figured that Satan's army could not be much more in number, but in time both might grow, so the final numbers remained difficult to predict. Still not many considering the historic proportions of war, but remember, these were Gods so it would be one hell of a fight!

It was agreed that it really didn't matter where they met in battle. The terrain was all pretty flat and there were no existing forts or battlements that could be used for defense. It seemed the gathering place was as good a place as any, and they began to lay out a strategy dedicated to defending the little Savior and defeating the wicked archangel.

Mars really wanted to throw up. He alone knew the odds they were facing. Lucifer was in a class of his own in power, and was also not confined by such concepts as honor and discipline. He would be impossible to predict. In truth, he would be impossible to defeat, at least through powers. There would have to be a serious amount of trickery to even have a chance.

He looked over his troops.

In his mind, he separated the warriors from the tactical support. There was a third group consisting of Cupid, Bacchus, and Nodutus that he simply considered "other."

These warriors were:
Mars ...of course
Diana, with her bow
Mercury, with talents in all forms of weaponry
Bellona, the War Goddess (sister of Mars)
Hercules, the God of Strength

The tactical team was:
Fortuna, Goddess of Fortune
Janus, the God of Doors
Felicitas, the Good Luck Goddess
Honos, the God of Military Honors
Mithras, the God most worshiped by Roman soldiers
Pietus, the Goddess of Duty

Mars divided them into two groups, with the warriors considering defensive positions and offensive positions, and the tactical group primarily thinking of strategies that might level the field.

Cupid just flitted around rubbing backs and messaging scalps. Bacchus kept the little army refreshed in fine wine, which in turn kept their spirits up. Nodutus just sat in the grass and pouted.

Mars moved from group to group encouraging every player and adding an idea or two in the process. He was determined to use every power to its maximum potential. The key would be to keep the evil army off their plan and to be prepared to capitalize on any mistakes. Mars was convinced his enemy would have to make a big mistake for them to win this battle, and the right God or Goddess at the right time must be ready to strike at that very moment.

While the Christian Torah pictured Jesus leading the charge, Mars was doubtful after meeting the gentle Savior that this would be possible. He felt it prudent to marshal the Olympian Gods and if the little carpenter was to be of any help, so much the better. He could not rationally rely on this. His strategy had to include simply keeping the evil monster away from Jesus, and hoping for a miracle, a mistake that would lead to his demise. He thought that the odds were greatest that Lucifer would march through them like rotten sake through a sumo wrestler. It would be impossible to hold him back. He was determined, however, to try and form a plan that would give his little army a chance and that would give Jesus a chance as well.

From the warrior side, the options were pretty straightforward.

The archers, probably Mercury, Aphrodite, and Diana, would hold back and rain a hail of arrows on the enemy. The evil Olympians would not be killed, but massive injuries that they would have to mend would slow them down.

The warriors, Mars, Apollo, and Hercules, had no equal in all of the Olympians. They would lead a charge that would hack the enemy lines to pieces. Again, they would not die, but the more severe the damage the longer it would take them to repair. Mars would lead the charge and face the mighty Hades. Most thought this battle alone would be epic, and most agreed Mars had a chance.

Neptune was one of the three brothers that ruled the Gods, and although he was no warrior like Zeus or even Hades, as such, he was a God of the Gods. He demanded that he be the one to face the Evil One. The entire assembly was inspired by the God of the Sea and the courage he displayed.

The remaining Gods would remain between the frontal assault and the archers. They would wield the powers they had at the openings they could see. In truth, it was this group from which hope sprang. It would not be arrows or brute force that won this battle, it would be the thing that could not be predicted that might, and this was a very small might, turn the tide.

Damn Zeus, thought Mars. If he were with us, there would be hope.

The gathering of the willing discussed strategies and tactics and debated back and forth about the possible outcomes. Everyone was focusing all their energy on the task at hand, and did not notice a small rise in the leaves at the edge of the clearing. If one was to look very closely, they might notice a long, forked tongue that darted in and out of the cover, and realize that the tongue was well within hearing of every word spoken.

Chapter 28
– The Evil Army Grows

*O*n the opposite end of good and evil, the gathering of the wicked willing was having a bit of difficulty dividing tasks. It seems by their nature they had issues with cooperation and teamwork. Several more Gods and Goddesses had joined their group, which added to the chaos. Discordia and Invidia were particularly disruptive with their powers of discord and envy. The group began with reasonably civil conversation, which deteriorated to screaming and yelling and hateful threats of violence. Finally, Hades had to step in.

"All right, you idiots, that's enough! Woe to us if we cannot come up with a plan for the Evil One, and woe to those who have caused this failure." He glared at Discord and Invidia. "We will divide into two camps. There will be one group that will plan the inevitable battle between the Olympiads. The other will come up with a strategy to open a path to the little carpenter."

He then laid out the divisions:

For the battle:

Hades, as leader
Minerva, Goddess of War
Pavor, God of Alarm
Pallor, Goddess of Fear

Cacus, the three-headed, fire-breathing monster killed
by Hercules and brought back to life by Hades
Volta, the monster daemonic entity with the head of
a wolf
Nemesis, Goddess of Revenge
Tempeste, Goddess of Storms
Libitina, Goddess of Death
Discordia, Goddess of Discord
Cloacina, Goddess of Sewers … who stank

For the path:
Vulcan, God of Fire – leader
Fraus, Goddess of Deception
Caca, Goddess of Excrement
Verminus, God of Disease
Invidia, Goddess of Envy
Trivia, Goddess of Magic
Somnus, God of Sleep
Portunes, God of Keys

Hades was pleased with the Gods in place and their
distribution. They would not go into the fight expecting to
win a decisive victory. Their only objective would be to create
a path to the gentle Jesus that would allow Lucifer, the
Morning Star, to crush him, and in doing so open up the
portal to the God of All. The true battle would begin here,
and its outcome would determine the future of creation.

Hades looked at the golden winged cone in the
clearing. He could easily feel the pulsating evil that flowed in
waves off the creature. He had never experienced such power.

He was truly in awe of his brother Zeus, but this was something different. To compare his powers to Satan's would be like comparing the little hill of the New Olympus to the real mountain in the heavens of earth. There was no comparison. He knew the legends of the Jewish God and of his ultimate power, but had no firsthand knowledge of this God of All. Satan did, and seemed so confident in his ability to defeat him. The Evil One did not seem suicidal. He certainly was no fool. The more he considered the situation the more excited he became. Perhaps there would be a change in Heaven, and his position at the right hand of Lucifer would position him to rule the Olympians ... and probably much more.

He turned his attention to working with both sides of the plan to guide them to victory.

He barely thought of poor Fishbone at all anymore.

Chapter 29
– Neverita

Here I am again, thought the simple Prince of Peace, pleading for love and peace but facing violence and confrontation. His heart was breaking and his mind was filled with confusion and doubt. The evolution of his word and the state of things on earth broke his heart. It all was simply beyond his comprehension. It was plain to see that he was again headed for a confrontation that would, in all probability, end up with him, once again in some horrible way, being martyred. His love of God was in no way diminished and his questioning of God's wisdom was more as a search for understanding. He had no doubt that the God of All was perfect in his plan and that the outcome would be for ultimate good. He also had no doubt that he would once again surrender himself to be slaughtered, to fulfill the will of the God of All. It seemed to be his purpose. He truly was the sacrificial Lamb of God.

The dirt road stretched on before him in an endless series of bends and straightaways, an endless road of woods and fields with countless streams and small ponds. Jesus walked and walked and it began to dawn on him that he was not meeting another God. Was this it for him? Had all of his questions that could be answered, been answered? After what seemed like days of walking, the gentle spirit settled on the banks of a small crystal-clear river. This was a deep, slow-moving stream that did not babble and splash but murmured in a soft, deep voice.

Jesus sat on its banks and listened to its stories of time before time. It seemed not to matter where a river might be, the language was always the same and the stories firmly grounded in eternal truths. A deep peace came over the Lord and, after a time, he settled into a deep sleep.

He awoke with a start. In front of him, standing to her hips in the clear water was a beautiful woman, a Goddess no doubt, in this world of forgotten Gods.

"I did not mean to startle you," said the Goddess. "I simply had to see you for myself, the one who would send my husband to his possible, no, probable death."

She looked at the holy man closely. "Yes, you are special. This is easy to see. You also are not a man of the sword. This is obvious. How in heavens name do you cause such strife? How do you claim such sacrifice? Why would a God, one of the three, a mighty honorable God, choose to risk his very existence to follow you? Your story was not for us. It ruined our stories, and threw us out of Heaven and earth. Yet, now you claim the allegiance of the very same ones that your people treated so harshly. Your power goes way beyond the simple man I see before me, even though it is for all to see that you are complete. Again complete, for the simple mortal to recognize and mimic, to realize their ideals. It has nothing to do with us, nothing to do with my husband."

Jesus could see the anguish and fear that this beautiful woman had for her husband, although he had no idea what she was talking about. Even though he did not understand, his heart broke for her and for all women who send their men off to wars they have little use for. He felt the waves of her sorrow. He reached out and took her hand then bowed his head and wept.

This was more than the Goddess could stand. She covered her face and also wept. They wept for the injustice of war, the emptiness of hatred, its unimaginable purpose, and for its eternal inevitability. They wept over their inability to do anything to stop it.

The moments passed, and this place was again quiet except for the deep murmur of the river.

Jesus looked up and into the eyes of the beautiful Goddess. "Please," he said, "Who are you, fair Goddess? Please tell me of your husband and of the danger he has embraced in my name."

"My name is Neverita. I am the Goddess of Water and wife of Neptune, who is God of the Sea, and one of the three. Even as we speak, they prepare a great war to defend you from a monster that is also not from our legends. He is one, I fear, that is beyond even the powers of the three, including my husband and the mighty Zeus. It is believed that it is possible that this creature might even have power to touch the very essences of immortality, and might be capable of destroying the Gods themselves. This is not known to be fact but it is feared, and I also very much fear."

"This is not the fight of the Olympiads. It is my fight and mine alone. Why do they assemble in my name?"

"You do not know these Gods. Oh, it is true we squabble and fight amongst ourselves, and sometimes can be vengeful and petty, but that is simply because it is the way we were created. We did not have the luxury of being born 'complete.' Do not think that this means we were created

149

without honor. It is the core of our existence and our lasting message to man. It is believed you would not have a chance against the Dark Angel. It is said he will crush you like a camel crushes a sand flea. The sides are believed to be ... uneven. No God would stand aside and watch the side of goodness and love crushed by evil. Epic battles like this are what we were created for, the more hopeless, the more worthy, the more memorable. They are all prepared to meet their end in this perceived battle for righteousness."

"All of the Gods of Olympia are fighting the Wicked One?"

"Oh no, that is not so. They have divided equally, some for good, some for evil, as they have existed on earth. The Wicked One has promised many promises of new power and authority in his kingdom to come. Those that are prone to this message have eagerly accepted it. They forget that he is indeed the *great deceiver*."

She went on, "Oh, there is more. The mighty Zeus himself has refused to fight. He believes you have led to our downfall, and that this is *your* legend to fulfill. He will remain on his lump of sand at the new Mt. Olympus. This is a decision all fear he will come to regret. Without his power, the outcome is in question. My husband has picked up his gauntlet and will face Satan himself. Few believe he will be able to even slow down Lucifer, much less stop him."

She began to cry again.

Jesus took her in his arms and comforted her. This was something he was very good at, and in moments her heart was free of fear and full of his holy spirit. She pulled back from him and stared at him with wide eyes.

"You are indeed not without power! I am refreshed and renewed in hope and spirit. Please do not let those that love you perish. We all believe that good conquers evil, and that love conquers all. In this we only have known our wits and the sword, but I now see that you wield a completely different weapon. I have not seen the monster, but I can feel him and I have known fear. I now clearly see that perhaps all is not lost, and we may soon rejoice in a new vision for victory."

She fell down on her knees and hugged the Savior's feet. "Please, Jesus, protect my husband and those that fight for you. This war has gone beyond you and the Evil One to the very Gods of Olympus. They might perish if you cannot protect them."

Jesus said, "It is not my will, but God's will. I will pray for strength and let the future be as it was written. As you have said, my sword is love and my shield is righteousness. Isn't that what this entire existence has been about, good versus evil? It is fitting that it should be resolved here. God has put this simple truth in our hearts and it is up to us to make it manifest. Love conquers all."

Chapter 30
– Mandy

"Love, love, love ..... Love, love, love, love is all you need! Love is all you need! Love is all you need!"

Buzz and Charlie sang loud and off-key to the classic Beatles coming through the tinny speakers in the Microbus.

"Oh, man, they don't write 'em like THAT anymore! The Beatles ... what can you say, man? The Beatles ... it just kind of says it all! Love, love, love!"

Buzz sang on, but the song had already changed to something by Donovan. Buzz obviously loved the oldies station.

"The plane is just a few miles away, my brother. We'll stop for a bite at the Fly Away Café, file a flight plan, then hit the wild blue yonder!"

"You're not going to fly this thing, are you Buzz?" Charlie looked at the aging, very stoned hippy with doubt ... but not too much, considering his recent revelations regarding millions of dollars and jet planes.

"No way, Jose ... I leave that up to the Blaster Master. Not a better pilot this side of Vietnam. Three hundred combat missions with only thirty-three crash landings. Nobody could belly in a fighter jet like the Blaster!"

Charlie suddenly felt a bit queasy.

Buzz navigated the Pacific Coast Highway to Santa Monica, then jumped over to Lincoln, south to Manchester Avenue, and east to the 107 where he cruised south to Jack Northrup Field. This was where he kept his plane.

"Yeah, I could anchor my jet at LA Airport, but I ask myself ... why? I prefer a lower profile. I can say with all the certainty I can muster, that ... FOR SURE ... the Blaster *likes* a low profile. So Jack Northrup it is!"

Just outside of the airport was a row of slightly dumpy cafes that catered to the folks who flew. One of them was a tin building with the front of an old prop plane sticking out the front. Its props were somehow wired so they were constantly spinning. It was one of Buzz's favorite spots, the Fly Away Café.

"Well, Buzz, you old dog," said the stereotypical prematurely weather-worn, but once quite attractive and still really pretty darn good looking, waitress, "where you been?"

"I have been there and back, Mandy, and I'm heading out again. Meet my new bud and co-conspirator, Charlie Pilgrim. Charlie, this is Mandy."

Their eyes met, and there was a slight *twang* that almost everyone heard, and a hint of electricity in the air that made the hair on Buzz's arms stand on end.

"Wow," said Buzz staring at his arms, "that's weird."

"Hi, Mandy. I am pleased to eat you ... or beat you ... no, MEET you." Charlie reached out his hand to shake hands with the waitress. He knocked over a coffee cup, which spilled down the front of Mandy's apron.

"I'm sure I saw that in the movies, or on TV or something," said Buzz, to no one in particular.

"I am so sorry," said Charlie, as he pulled out his shirttails and began to rub Mandy's crotch.

"Oh my, Charlie ... I mean OH MY ... if you are going to keep that up, we had better go back in the kitchen."

Mandy laughed and wiped the rest of the coffee from her apron. "Sit down you two before you do any more damage."

They sat down in a red, tuck-and-roll, leatherette booth. Charlie grabbed a menu and stuck his face in it, as if that would hide the fact that it was beet red.

Mandy filled a few cups at the counter, then came over to their booth with pad and pencil in hand.

"I know what you want Buzz, but how about your friend?"

Buzz always had a grilled cheese sandwich and cream of tomato soup. It was his favorite meal of all time, and no one did it better than the Fly Away Café.

"I guess I'll have a Fly Away Burger with cheese, no mayo, and bacon. Does that come with fries?"

"Honey," said Mandy, "for someone as cute as you, I'll peel the potatoes myself."

She made a note on her pad, whirled around, and walked back to the kitchen with a bit more wiggle in her behind than normal.

"I swear to you, Buzz, I have never felt anything like that before in my life. It's like I was thirteen again, and scared to death of Toby Pollack. I have been married before, Buzz, but she turned me to butter. What's her story? She got a man? You think I have a chance?"

"Slow down, Preacher..... One step at a time! No, she is not currently dating. She does have a story, though, and though she doesn't talk about it, it must of hurt a *bunch*. Legend has it that she is like the Mandy from that Barry Manilow song. Legend says that that *someone* might have been Manilow himself. That he dumped her, and broke her heart. I've seen lots of cowboys try and hustle our Mandy, but she blows them off. Can't recollect a single serious hookup for her in the years I have known her. In fact, that's the most interest I've seen her show in a long time."

Buzz looked Charlie up and down. "Well, I guess you *are* kind of cute, but not really THAT much....go figure.'

Charlie's heart was pounding when the food arrived. They ate their food and Buzz couldn't help but notice the quick glances the two shot at each other. He shook his head and quit trying to have conversation with a distracted Charlie.

As they were leaving, Buzz brought Charlie over to where Mandy was minding the register.

"Charlie, this is Mandy. Mandy, this is Charlie. Now, I ain't one to mess around and miss an opportunity. You don't know each other but I can vouch for you both. I love you both and you are both excellent people, no lie. I know some of your story Charlie, and some of yours, Mandy, and I also heard the birds singing when you met ... and I am not even stoned...much. It's easy to see possibilities here. I am not going to let two folks your age act shy and miss something that might be cosmic. But Mandy, Charlie and I got serious business involving the Armageddon end of the world. Charlie might just be the most important man on earth right now, and I am his wingman. What I would like to propose is a date for you two, one day after all of this is done. Do either of you have any objections?"

Mandy looked confused but also, knowing Buzz, not completely shocked. She looked at Charlie and he looked at her. They both smiled, you know, one of those smiles.

"Works for me," said Mandy.

"Me too," said Charlie.

"OK, lover boy," said Buzz with a sigh, "let's fly."

They left the café, got into the VW, and headed to the airport.

Buzz pulled the little Microbus onto the tarmac and through a card activated gate that led to a neat row of large sheet-metal airplane hangars. He stopped in front of one with a neatly painted sign that read "URSU, Inc."

"Here we are, boss," said Buzz. "Let's see if Blaster is in, and we'll do what Uncle Sam says we have to do to get a bird in the air. No metal detectors or TSA here, but I do tell young lovelies they have to be strip searched..." Buzz looked sheepishly at Charlie. "You don't think I would do that, do you? It's just a sort of joke. You know Mandy is a real prize,

Charlie, but I got it figured you might be one too. Can you tuck her away while we sort out the troubles of the world?"

Charlie nodded and smiled. "What's the 'URSU' stand for?"

"Oh, that's my business corporation. It's actually 'Universal Research for Scientific Undertakings.' Me and the Blaster call it 'Us Real Stoners United.' That really makes more sense."

"What does your company do?" replied Charlie.

"Well, lots of stuff, but I like the *getting stoned* the best. It's complicated, Charlie, and full of this's and that's. Some of it may prove useful; we will see as things move along."

He slid the large sliding door aside revealing a fine looking 1982 Gulfstream III private jet. From the outside it looked like the common, everyday, quite-amazing-to-Charlie, corporate jet.

Buzz picked up a long-handled broom and began to beat on the side of the jet.

"Incoming, incoming ... Rise and shine, Blaster. We have company and a mighty mission. Let's get this baby ready to fly, *amigo*..."

The side door popped open and the stairs slowly lowered to the floor of the hangar. An incredibly ragged man, dressed completely in camo, stood at the top of the stairs. His eyes were puffed from sleep, and his hair began at his head to go straight up about four inches then took a hard right for several more. He was sporting a beard that had developed a mind of its own, so his entire face could be defined by one word ... anarchy.

"Jesus Christ, Buzz, what the fuck time is it?"

"Well, O Master Blaster, it's about six p.m. if my Mickey Mouse watch ain't lying. Time for you to rise and shine."

"Shit, that's only three a.m. in fucking Hanoi. It's the middle of the fucking night!"

"Sorry, bro, but you're going to have to consider this a night raid. We are in need of your most excellent service."

"All right, all right, but my pad is a mess. You know you might have called, Buzz."

"You don't have a phone, Blaster ..."

"Doesn't matter, you don't even make an effort, that's all I'm trying to say."

The two men on a mission climbed the stairs to the jet and instantly walked into another world.

The interior of the Jet was once decked out in typical corporate comfort, leather, wood, and the like. If what Buzz said was correct, the interior design could now be credited to the most famous of jam bands ... the Grateful Dead. The seats were covered in cloth with intricate embroidery. The groupies for the Dead were legendary seamstresses, and it showed. There were dancing skeletons, grinning skulls, and many a takeoff on the American flag woven into the fabric.

Buzz acted as the guide and pointed out different and important memorabilia that was littered around the inside of the jet.

"And now this," said Buzz, "is my most prized possession." He pointed to a box frame built into the interior side of the jet. In it was what looked like a short bone.

"Jerry-fucking-Garcia's missing middle-finger bone! I shit you not!"

Any mildly serious Dead Head knew that Jerry Garcia was missing the middle finger on his right hand. He was a master at not just guitar, but banjo, mandolin, pedal steel, and lord knows what else in spite of this obvious handicap.

"Imagine what that bastard could have done if he had five fingers!" said the Blaster, who had collapsed on a couch. "He was a GOD!" He shook his head in obvious wonder.

Charlie looked at the bone in the box and had trouble imagining its artistic value. He was sure if it was real, and it probably was, it was worth a fortune to any vulgarly rich Dead Head.

The interior of the plane was messy but not dirty. There was a beaded curtain that separated the main cabin from a smaller cabin that was, apparently, the Blaster's home. Further up front was the cockpit. There were heads front and aft. All in all, it was a genuine private jet and with its unique interior, it was really a work of art. Charlie could not help but be impressed.

Buzz and Master Blaster sat at a small table. They pulled out some charts and began to put together a flight plan that would get them to Ohio. Charlie lay down on the couch and closed his eyes. He could see in his mind's eye the sweet waitress, as clearly as the story in the plate, and he smiled, but before he could put together a decent fantasy, Charlie Pilgrim was fast asleep.

Chapter 31
– More Willing, and the Army Grows

7he gathering of the Willing, on the side of the
Savior, was growing steadily. It seems the word was out and
many wanted to be involved in this epic battle, mainly for the
sake of the glory and the excellent songs and stories that
would surely evolve, but also, for some, because of boredom.
It was rare these days to have events that actually had some
significance. Some also felt the need to protect the little
Jewish God and the good that he represented.

The new arrivals included:

Caerus, God of Luck and Opportunity *T
Chronos, God of Time *T
Elipis, the Spirit of Hope *T
Enyo, a lesser Goddess of War *W
Hypnos, God of Sleep *T
Kratos, God of Strength and Power *W
Nike, Goddess of Victory *T
Thetis, Shape-shifter and a Prophet *T
Uranus, God of the Sky *W
Zephyrus, God of the West Wind *W

(*T or *W next to their name indicates if they were
assigned to the Tactical group or the Warrior group.)

It was an impressive group and a welcome addition to
the army of the Lord. As they arrived, Mars sent them to the

appropriate group for strategy and tactics. As they debated the possible battle scenarios, it seemed as if they were probably capable of slowing down the Evil Beast, but the odds of them killing him or rendering him helpless seemed extremely improbable. Of all the powers available to them, the mind-numbing concept of a creature that controlled all that was evil left them with little hope.

The simple concept of having the archers at the back hailing down arrows on the enemy was solid, to slow them down. This was an age-old tactic and almost required. It would be the starting gun of the war. It was also understood it would not slow the enemy down for long. They were Gods, after all, and would shrug off arrows. When this first wave was done, these warriors would rush to help the battle raging at the front, God to God before them.

The next line of defense were the physical warriors, Mars, Mercury, Hercules, Minerva, Enyo, Vulcan, Kratos, Poseidon, and Zephyrus, God of the West Wind. Here would be the main wall against the aggressors. It was these mighty warriors that were required to hold off the Wicked One and those that followed him. It was believed that they too would fall. Their only mission was to hold their line long enough for the miracle that was required for victory to unfold. As of yet, they had no idea what that "miracle" might be.

It was thought that much could be done to affect the spirit of the Olympian enemies. Honos, the God of Military Honors, would implant that they had no honor, so would receive no honors. Mithras, the God of Soldiers, would let them feel that they were without a direct God in their fighting, and so were abandoned on the battlefield. Pietus, the Goddess of Duty, would implant in them that they were turning their backs on their duty to fight against evil and would ultimately fail. Elipis, the Spirit of Hope, would take all hope from them, and fill the protectors' hearts with hope. This was thought to be a strong weapon. Together with the might of the actual warriors, all these things together would undoubtedly turn the tide for any normal battle. It was understood that in this case, like the physical battle, it would not hold and definitely would not win the day. All it might possibly win was time.

The Gods that were left to create the magic that might win the day were: Fortuna, the Goddess of Fortune; Felicitus, the Goddess of Good Luck; Chronos, the God of Time; Hypnos, the God of Sleep; Janus, the God of Doors; and Thetis, the shape-shifter and prophet. From these, the victory must come, from these, the magic must evolve. The plan must be clever beyond their deeds and must deceive the greatest deceiver in creation. The task was daunting.

Since so many of the group's members had responsibilities that were, if hopeless, at least straightforward, they all joined in an effort to help create the perfect plan. Felicitus would help some, and it was easy to see that luck would play a part, but they could not afford to rely on it as a deciding factor.

It was suggested that perhaps Chronos could adjust time backward or forward to alter an outcome. Chronos explained that time is a tricky reality and is probably something that the Evil One has access to also. It was agreed that if time was to be a factor, it would be temporary and would possibly have a part to play in this battle. It would have to be for a split second, and at the perfect moment in time.

Hypnos could possibly impact the Olympians but believed he would have little influence on the Wicked One. As Satan was from another reality, no one truly knew for sure what would be the impact of any of their powers. They were building a battle plan on suppositions and could only wish for the best. Elipis, the Spirit of Hope, was working overtime.

Thetis, the shape-shifter, and Janus, the God of Doors, were left. It was thought that at some time Thetis might take on the image of the Savior to distract the evil one. It was thought this might confuse the enemy for a short time but it was also thought the Devil himself would not be misled for long. He might also change to other images, which might misdirect and help to create a sense of chaos. Confusion and chaos would be required to make the Price of Darkness make a mistake. It was agreed a mistake would be necessary for any chance of victory. One on one they were decidedly no match.

Janus could make doors between realities. He could make doors through time. He could travel from here to there with the simple opening of a door. It was decided that probably the Dark One would be quick to return, and how and where he appeared might make things even more dangerous. There was a sense that there might be a place for Janus's skills and he was temporarily set aside. He separated himself from the group, and sat quietly on the grass.

In the meantime, just a short way from the gathering, in the tall grass and leaves lay an ominous villain. His long body lay completely hidden, submerged in the vegetation with no motion except a gentle *swish* of the end of his tail. He made no sound and no one suspected his presence. His eyes drooped half closed, and his forked tongue flicked silently in and out. He could hear every word from the gathering of warriors and listened intently as strategies were evolving. His mind was comfortable and efficient. He understood the strengths and weaknesses of this army and could plainly see the many ways they would certainly fail. He would stay until the right time, as was required in this peculiar place. What he did with the information he was gathering was not evident. One thing was certain, it would be used for his benefit alone. He was the serpent. He was the Great Deceiver... it could be no other way.

Chapter 32
– Godly and Grande

Charlie and Buzz had barely cleared the palatial estate of Reverend Godley when he made the promised call to his brother in the spirit, the Good Reverend Grande.

"Horace ... Abe Godley, here. I have called to ask a small favor, which I am certain you are more than able to generously consent to."

"Jesus Christ, Abe, it's been a dog's age since I have heard from you. I thought maybe after that little affair in the Philippines you might have gotten religion and decided to steer clear of my bad influences."

"Yeah, I should, you old bastard. That was one hell of a party, and we are all lucky the police were sensible enough to accept your generous donation and set us free. But as far as your parties, I say anywhere and anytime! Let's just try and be a bit more discrete with the younger women."

"Ah, yes ... but for all of the good we do for the church, I am sure the good Lord will forgive us for filling that one small appetite. There are plans afoot for an ecumenical council meeting in Thailand. Can't hardly miss that one, wouldn't you say?"

"Sounds perfect, just send me the dates. Right now, I have a small problem and I hope you can see clear to help me out."

The most Reverend Godly explained the situation with Buzz and Charlie. He explained the holy pie plate and Charlie's story of a coming battle between good and evil. He told him of the place where lost Gods go and the existence of the ancient Gods of the Greeks and Romans.

The Reverend Grande naturally thought that the whole story was insane. He was a man that did not believe in miracles and suspected strongly that there never were such things. He understood man's need to believe in a greater power and was more than willing to feed that need ... with whatever story that sold the most copies for the highest price. In America, the land of capitalism and God-fearing Christians, it was his brand of Christianity he sold.

"There is more," Pastor Godly continued. "When I scoffed at his madness, he brought up a couple of issues that he had no way of knowing. He claimed he saw them in the pie plate. Ridiculous, I know, but somehow he has found out some things that would make my life, shall we say, uncomfortable. He and his friend seem to be what might be called 'street people.' I imagine that very few would miss them if they were gone. While it is a difficult decision I know, I am afraid his information threatens the very foundation of my church. Many would be disillusioned and possibly turn away from the good Lord himself because of their disappointment. I don't believe this is a risk we should be taking."

"Cut the crap, Abe. You don't believe that shit any more than I do. What you are telling me is that you want these two terminated, wasted, wiped out. Do I hear you correctly?"

"Well, I prefer to think of it as being delivered into the arms of the Lord..."

"You just never quit, do you, Godly? OK, so if I understand you correctly, you have satisfied this Charlie's request by sending him to me. You have sent him here because you don't want to soil your own hands. You are a piece of work, Godly. I ought to deliver *you* into the good Lord's hands, you prick!"

"Calm down, Horace. When he came here, I had no idea what was coming. I had no time to prepare. Would you have had me stab him in my living room? For Christ's sake, man, I did the only thing I could. I passed him to a man I knew I could trust. I passed him to a friend, a brother in the cloth, a person who knows how to handle such ... situations. You know damn well if the situation was reversed I would have *your* back."

"OK, Abraham Godly, but by God, you owe me big time and believe me, you will get the check for this one and it will be a price you will be required to pay."

While Abe Godly's church was big, and he was a very powerful man, he knew that he was small by Horace Grande standards. He was the big leagues.

"Of course, Horace, I am in your debt and you know you can call me, regardless of any debt I might owe you."

"Very well, Abe. But, I am not happy about this. I was planning a short trip to Jamaica. I will postpone my venture into hedonism, and wait for your little ... problem. They won't even get in the door and some of my associates will gather them up and throw them off some bridge somewhere. 'Into the arms of the Lord'... as you would say."

Chapter 33
– Jesus Takes a Lonely Walk

Jesus, once again, stood and dusted off his robes. He bid farewell to Neverita, the wife of Neptune and wandered down the little road. As time went on, he became more and more confused. The complicated yet detailed life and responsibilities of a Messiah he understood, and he had little problem with that role. There was no history for the place he was in now. There were no scriptures or prophesies for him to follow. On earth, he had been raised to follow the righteous path to martyrdom. It was a bitter path, which he followed faithfully. But through it all he had the Torah, which he read and understood. It provided a road map from which he was able to find his spiritual guidance and determine the path preordained by King David, Moses, Abraham, the other prophets, and the great God and Father Jehovah. Now he had nothing. He simply had a dirt road that apparently led to everywhere and nowhere, oriented toward time and necessity, rather than cities and homes. He had only the love in his heart and the determination to do the will of the God of All to hold onto. These would be his weapons and his sanctuary. To these things he would hang on until grim death or whatever was in store for him in this insane world. In this he was determined.

He was not certain if walking even mattered on this road. He suspected that if he just sat down, time and necessity would conspire, and the road would come to him. Jesus was too wound up at this moment to just sit. He would walk and pray and let events unfold as they seemed certain to do.

The dirt road continued as any decent little dirt road might. It wound through small woods and fields, it passed by streams and ponds with creatures familiar and strange, it continued up little hills and dropped back down again. The gentle Savior walked down the center of the road kicking up small clouds of dust with his sandals. His mind drifted from his life and death in Jerusalem, to the convoluted religion his simple life had inspired, and then to his recent existence and the Gods and Goddesses he had met. He wondered about the impending war and how it would impact the present realities. Somewhere in time and space, an army gathered to fight on his behalf. Somewhere else, another army gathered to fight for a cause altogether different, in support of a creature they could hardly comprehend. If they could, they would in all probability reconsider their positions. It certainly was not the first time that deception found willing believers, and the greatest Deceiver of All molded wills to his command. In its aftermath it was certain that his followers would be dismayed by broken promises and crushed expectations. Many would argue that their lust for greed and advantage had led them to the results they would come to find and that they deserved, the treachery and pain they most certainly would experience. But Jesus only felt sorrow for them and recognized their confusion. In this place there was possibly even more reason to forgive. Evil Gods were created to support evil. Was it their fault to be what they were created to be? Is a rabbit at fault for being a rabbit, or a wolf at fault for being a wolf? Jesus wondered in his heart why the God of

All created the suffering, and as for the ones that would do him harm ... as was his way ... he forgave them all.

Chapter 34
– Columbus, Ohio

Charlie woke up with a start as the Gulfstream touched down in Ohio. Both Buzz and the Blaster were averse to international airports, with their insane congestion and tendency toward prying security, so they set down at Bolton Field just southwest of the city.

"Hey, dude, that was some Olympic sleeping," said Buzz. "I couldn't tell if you were alive or dead ... except when you were whispering sweet nothings to your pillow. You were out for a full four hours."

"Man, I needed that! What time is it, anyway?"

"Straight up eleven p.m. give or take. Just enough time to get to grab something to eat and hit a hotel for more sleep. We can call the uber-pastor-dude in the morning and ramp this adventure up a notch."

The Blaster Master came out from behind the beaded curtain that led to the front of the plane. He looked as disheveled as when Charlie first saw him, but his eyes were sharp and focused.

"Safe as a baby in your momma's arms! I ride the skies like a stallion and lay her down as gentle as a baby iguana." He smiled. "Well, you didn't think I'd say as 'gentle as a LAMB,' did you?"

"No way, man," said Buzz, "far be it from you to state the obvious. Anyway, excellent job as usual, I imagine you will be staying on the compound while we save the world."

"Right you are, man ... I've saved enough of this world. I'll get this beast checked out and filled with fuel, for whatever may come."

"Roger that, *amigo* ... shake out the cobwebs, Charlie, and let's find ourselves some sustenance."

"Ready when you are, boss," said Charlie. He tucked in his shirt, laced up his shoes, and grabbed his pie-plate-protecting backpack.

The two scrambled down the stairs from the plane and headed across the tarmac.

"Watch your topknots, you two," shouted Blaster as they walked through the security fence into the parking lot.

An absolutely perfect-looking 1964 orange and white VW Microbus, with thirty-two windows and a sliding roof, waited in the parking lot.

"Man, Buzz...how many of these things do you have?" asked an astounded Charlie.

"Oh, I guess thirty-two," replied Buzz, "but I am looking for at least eighteen more. You know, one for each state."

Next to the perfect little bus was a man in a jacket that had "URSU" embroidered in small golden letters on the front.

"Good evening, Buzz, here's your chariot," the man said.

"Thanks, Evin. This is my new friend, Charlie. We are about to break some bread. Want to join us?"

"Hello, Charlie." The two men shook hands. "As good as a bowl of tomato soup and grilled cheese sounds, I have to get back to the little woman and the munchkins. Thanks, anyway!"

"Suit yourself, my friend. Give Sandy a big wet kiss from me ... and hug the wee ones. Let them know I'll be back for Rosalie's birthday."

"Will do, Buzz."

Evin jumped into a shiny new red Camaro and cruised out of the parking lot. Buzz jumped into the driver's seat of the perfect little VW and Charlie lifted himself into the passenger's seat. The interior was exactly like the little bus they had just left in California.

"Buzz, you blow my mind. You have an office in Columbus?"

"Well, not exactly. We own a company in town that makes composting toilets. It takes no water and has no discharge. We have been selling them mostly to third-world countries, and actually I use the word 'selling' loosely. I think we give more away than sell them. They are cool though. Evin works from home and manages all of our businesses in Ohio."

"All of your businesses? You have more?"

"Oh yeah, a few, but that's boring business. Let's find some grub!"

Buzz pulled out of the parking lot and headed east on Alkire Road, then north on 62 to Briggsdale. "Now," said Buzz, "the magic pipe!" He pulled his little pipe from his pants and fired it up. "Change your mind, preacher man?"

"No thanks, my brother, but you go right ahead."

"I always do, Charlie, my man. I always do!"

There was a Denny's restaurant just off the highway and Buzz swung in.

"Best tomato soup and grilled cheese in the world at Denny's, Charlie ... BAR NONE .... except of course at the Fly Away." Buzz held the door and the two filed into the restaurant. They sank into a booth and waited for the inevitable waitress.

"You know, Charlie," began Buzz, "these preacher guys don't seem at all like I imagined. In fact, that Godly was a genuine bastard."

"Yeah, that's kind of why I left. Somewhere between sweet Jesus, politics, and money, in some churches you might see an ever-widening gap. It doesn't mean the message has changed, it's just the messengers. What with the Internet, webpages, blogs and the mass mediafication of some of these big churches, the money and power are perverting things. It should not be a surprise. Even sweet Jesus knew about money and got seriously cranky at the moneychangers in the temple. Politics might be even worse. Folks just seem to have a need to try and force people to be like them. It's fine in the teaching of the church. If a person doesn't agree they don't have to join that church, but to try and make those teachings law ... well in my mind that is not what the good Lord intended."

"Live and let live, Charlie ... it's the song I sing every day. I belong to the Church of Later Day Hippies, and I try to love everyone and to leave everyone alone. We all have our own walk to walk."

"Got that right, Buzz."

"I am thinking that if the next preacher is as big an asshole as the last, we might be walking into a confrontation. Preacher Godly was none too happy that you squeezed him for an introduction, and if my guess is right, the name you hit him with and that number have to do with things he doesn't want us messing with. Since he doesn't believe in the plate, he must think you have all the information necessary to cause him big troubles."

"You are right, Buzz. I know how these guys can be. But I believe in the plate. We are on a holy mission and the good Lord will guide us. If not, we might as well admit what we are asked to do is impossible and go home. Our path has been set straight through the Reverend Grande and that's where I will go. I don't believe all of these guys are lost souls. Let's hope this one is for real."

"I am with you all of the way, El Cid, but we need to walk softly and keep a sharp eye out. That's all I am saying."

The meals came and the bellies were filled. The unlikely warriors exited the restaurant, climbed into the bus and drove behind the building to a small motel, "The Right Motel," that bragged, "We have clean sheets." They secured a room with two double beds and surrendered to the night.

It was April in Ohio (and I guess everywhere else, too) and with April comes weather of all descriptions. You are just as likely to get 75 degrees and sun or 30 degrees and snow. You never know. In this case, the weather edged toward the more unpleasant, as a cold front closed into north-central Ohio and the great city of Columbus. The forecast was for a mixture of rain and snow and there was a possible travel advisory due to the potential of slippery roads. This would not be enough to deter two men on a mission.

Buzz and Charlie arose early and showered for the first time in days. Actually, for Charlie it had been quite a bit longer than that. In California there was an outdoor shower near the underpass, by an outdoor pool at a hotel that had seen better times, where the good reverend was permitted to wash off a majority of his filth. It had been over a week since the last splash off. The two newly refreshed men checked out of the hotel, walked back to the Denny's and enjoyed a massive breakfast with all the coffee you could drink.

When they had finished and paid up, Charlie used the pay phone to call the good Reverend Grande. After several bounces from secretary to secretary, he was able to connect with the pastor. Horace Grande had been expecting his call and instructed the travelers to come to the church and park in the underground parking. There they would be met by church staff who would lead them up to his office.

So far, so good, thought Charlie. But Buzz was feeling a bit uneasy. Why the underground parking, he wondered. There had to be parking up top for the services. Seems they should be able to walk in the front door in bright lights, where others would be sure to be watching. Perhaps he was just being paranoid, he thought. A good bowl of herb would be sure to calm him down. They wandered out of the restaurant, climbed into the second perfect little VW bus and headed back down Highway 62, headed for the Columbus City Center where the Reverend Grande's Only True Path to Heaven church resided.

Charlie took this time to pull out the plate and get caught up with the doings in the Land of Lost Gods. He heard the beginnings of the plan and understood the danger involved. He also saw the serpent and feared the information the spy now possessed. There was no way he knew to communicate and warn them. He was only an observer and a messenger to the planet earth. He did a play by play with Buzz so he was in the loop, and when the message faded he put the plate back in his pack.

Now Buzz had even more reason for the calming effects of the holy herb. So the bowl was fired and the road was traveled, as the weather turned from cold to rain. The little bus heroically navigated the path but water at 32 degrees turns to ice and soon the roads began to glaze over. Fortunately, they were quickly approaching their destination. A long gentle hill sloped down to the underground parking beneath the church, and Buzz easily directed the little German masterpiece in that direction. As soon as he made the turn, the tires broke loose and the bus began a slowly accelerating spin to the left. Fortunately, the ramp was a wide two lanes, and the bus gracefully spun in three 360-degree loops before hitting dry pavement below the building. It was facing exactly forward as any magical bus would be, so Buzz simply directed it into an open parking space. This was easy, as there was only one other car in the parking lot, a large black limousine. Charlie and Buzz stared at each other with gaping mouths.

"Whew," said Charlie, "that was a close one! If we were out on 71 we would be toast."

"The plate be praised," said Buzz, "the plate be praised!"

Chapter 35
– Janus and a Plan

*M*ars, Mercury, Neptune, and the other Warriors of the Willing listened to each other intently, hoping to hear an idea that would bring the chance of victory closer. Their great problems were many. All agreed with Satan at the front, they were not equal in strength to the enemy. Their entire purpose in the fight was to protect the Jewish Savior from destruction. This did not mean for a minute, an hour, or a day, but for all time. To do this they would have to, in effect, destroy Satan, because to a God, they understood that for him this was a fight for all creation. He would never peacefully surrender. The Gods of Olympus were, in their nature, almost like humans. They had strengths and weaknesses. They had joy and fear. These were things that Satan did not possess. He had hate and ambition and had no known weakness. He was as complete in his evil as the simple Jesus was in his love. The plan that unfolded was full of great ideas to misdirect and slow the onslaught, but they still had nothing that even slightly resembled a killing blow. They didn't know enough about their enemy to even begin to know if there could possibly even *be a killing blow* for such a creature. He was outside of their legends and also outside of their understanding. They had lots of pretty good Gods and Goddesses and lots of pretty bad Gods and Goddesses. There was no one that came close to the purity of this one. This creature even ruled over the parts of them that fell to lust, envy, anger and all of the wicked things they did. In this sense even the good Gods were subjects, at times, to the Wicked One.

It was determined that after the initial volley of the archers, the physical battle would rage. They would not truly know until contact how this would go. They were confident they could hold their own one on one....with exceptions.

It was understood that Mars would struggle to master Hades. He was one of the three and as such, gifted with power at a greater level. That being said, there was no God that possessed the pure skill with weapons that Mars possessed. They would not know until the clash of these titans where the balance would be.

It was also unknown what would happen when Neptune clashed with Lucifer. All believed it would be no match and the noble Neptune would fall beneath the charging monster. But, they truly did not know. Neptune was one of the three and a God after all. He would bring powers that caused hurricanes and typhoons. He possessed powers that brought the tides and pushed the seas themselves in mighty currents. He wielded his trident with thunder and lightning, and was worthy of mighty respect. No one could know what would happen when these forces collided. Although he was powerful and confident, even the brave Neptune could not see an outcome where he actually destroyed the Evil One. Such an outcome was beyond his understanding.

So it was Satan that they had to focus on. If, or when, Neptune fell, it would be left to deception to keep the King of the Jews safe. Chronos could push back time as the God of the Sea fell, so that he could relive the final moments of the battle. This was very cruel for Neptune, but would allow the others to prepare for the next attack. Neptune agreed without hesitation. This the God of Time could only do once, twice, perhaps three times at the most. Then, the Wicked One would overcome his spell. The next attack must be ready at this time. Hypnos, the God of Sleep, will then hit Satan full in the face. He will bring the sleep of a million humans onto the Evil One. It is well-known that evil never sleeps, so what effect this will have is completely unknown. At best, it will slow the beast down for only moments. It was hoped it would at least confuse him so the next effort would succeed.

This was where Thetis would take on the image of the gentle Savior and redirect the monster's charge. It was hoped that the combined fighting of all the warrior Gods and with the added fog of sleep slowing his mind, he might believe the shape-shifter was Jesus and fight in his direction for some time.

This is where the strategy ends. When Lucifer finds his focus and rushes the simple Jesus, there is no next plan except to battle on. As time moves forward, hope diminishes. After this point in the strategy session, all the Gods were silent and even Elipis was losing hope.

Then, from where he had rested in the grass, Janus, the God of Doors, spoke up.

"There is one other thing we could consider."

All Gods and Goddesses turned toward the gentle God in the grass.

"My powers have been to open doors and to close doors, to allow opportunity and to deny it. I have created short cuts and detours and even opened doors to the heart....but have never considered what I will tell you now.

"In the beginning of time, as it is understood in Olympus, I was created as were you all. At this time, I was given an understanding that at the end of time I would play a part. It would be my door that creation would go through to realize oblivion. It would be through me the universe would pass to end time, and return to the great nothingness that preceded our reality. I have the power to open this door... however, I do not know if, once opened, it can be closed. It is possible it was solely created for one purpose ... to end all things. But if somehow we could push him through it....."

The Olympians considered what their brother had said. While it contained a slim thread of hope, its overall message was one of potential suicide.

Diana rose to speak.

"My brothers and sisters, this thing that our brother Janus speaks of, is again a thing beyond our comprehension. It is a potential weapon against the Evil One. It is indeed something that might actually destroy the creature. It could possibly, if directed, send him to the end of all things. It seems, if I understand our brother, the likelihood is just as great that this door could also take us and all of creation with it. It might mean the end of all Heaven and earth, the fish of the sea, the animals of the land, the humans and Gods alike. It might mean the end of Heaven and earth and a final stopping of the wheel of time. This risk seems perhaps too great...perhaps it's not a decision for mere Gods, like ourselves, to take. Can saving the gentle Savior be worth this danger?"

183

Neptune spoke. "Perhaps not, but stopping the Evil One might be worth this risk. We may lose the Complete One, but what might be left? A world dominated by all that is evil? Would Zeus return to fight at last or carve out a place where he can retain the solitude he so recently seems to have embraced. What would happen to humans or the creatures of earth as the Great Destroyer lays waste to all things? Even though I am separate from my sea and the creatures that inhabit it, I hold in my heart that it exists, and pray every day to someday return ... however unlikely that might be. If Lucifer wins, he will destroy hope, and the world will fall to torture and torment. Can the quiet of the nothingness be worse than this?"

"But, what about the 'God of All' that he is looking for," asked Mercury. "Perhaps he will make himself known and battle the Beast."

Then Mars spoke. "Can we count on the God of the Jewish Legends, to make himself known to us when to this point he never has? Do we lose to the Wicked One, then lie crushed on the battlefield listening for the sound of righteous thunder? I am a warrior and would use any weapon that might possibly stop the Dark Angel. If their God of All is to play a role, let him come in a flash and close the door of destruction, if Janus cannot. If he does exist and it is his desire to see the good triumph over evil, he will make it so ... in his own way."

"Remember," said Mercury, "we also did not personally know the little Jewish King or this Wicked One that now would destroy us. This God of All is just as likely to exist, and be just as likely to have a part to play."

"So, it is agreed," said Mars, "that we will use the power of the final door only after all else has failed, but we are agreed that to stop the Wicked One, if there is nothing left, it will be used."

The Band of the Willing Gods spoke as one ... "Agreed!"

They all looked at Janus who nodded soberly ... "Agreed."

In the grass, forever unseen, the serpent had heard enough. It looked as if the little Band of Lesser Gods had a card to play after all. How this would impact the battle was left to be seen. How the serpent would use this information was still to be decided. Silently, it slithered from the grass to the woods, and as was customary in this strange reality, with its purpose for now complete, it instantly disappeared.

Chapter 36
– The Mighty Buzz and Reverend Grande

*B*uzz and Charlie climbed out of the little bus in the parking garage of the Only True Path to Heaven church of the Reverend Horace Grande. The space was empty except for a large, black limousine that was parked by the stairs that appeared to head up toward the internals of the church complex. As they walked toward the stairs, they could not help but see two very large, very muscular gentlemen in suits that stood with their arms across their chests. They seemed to be waiting for the duo and effectively barred the stairs.

"Hey, brothers," said Buzz, "we have an appointment with Reverend Grande. Are you our escorts?"

"This is as far as you get, assholes," replied the one closest to Buzz. "The only place you're going is to the bottom of some muddy river. You have fucked with the wrong reverend, jack wad!"

Thug number two grabbed Charlie, spun him around and smacked him on the hood of the car. The first thug, the closest to Buzz, reached out to grab him by the arm.

Buzz grabbed his right hand in midair. He twisted his arm until his palm was facing straight up and bent his hand at the wrist. This palm was not straight up like your panhandle, but painfully twisted clockwise, putting his elbow pointing straight up. Buzz then brought his own elbow smashing down on thug number one's exposed, upward pointing, elbow. This had the effect of separating the upper arm from the lower arm, and pulling the elbow completely out of joint. Then, as the unfortunate thug was dropping toward the floor,

Buzz kicked him sharply in the exposed throat. He fell like a sack of cement.

The second ne'er-do-well let go of Charlie and lunged at Buzz. Buzz, with blinding speed, took his right foot (the one that had recently crushed the first evil doer's throat), and brought it up to his own left knee. He twisted sideways to the attacker, as his foot shot out, catching bad guy number two in the solar plexus. He let out a mighty "OOOFF" and slumped forward. Buzz centered to face him, kicking his falling face squarely. He also fell like a sack of cement. The parking lot was calm and quiet once again.

Charlie stood again staring at his friend. Buzz calmly walked to his bus and rummaged through a Tupperware tub in the back. He came back with some zip ties, WD40, a small, thin, plastic hose, duct tape, and some rags. While Charlie watched, he quickly zip-tied the arms behind bad guy number two, then he straightened out the arm of bad guy number one, which was at this point angling at a very unnatural 90 degrees. He gave it a slight twist as he did and it seemed to pop back into its proper position. He then zip-tied his arms behind him. Next, he quickly took the hose, sprayed it with WD40 and gently guided it down the crushed throat of the choking first attacker. When the hose was beyond the collapsed portion of his throat, a loud *hiss* was heard, and the man began to breathe through the hose. Buzz bent the hose up past his nose and duct-taped it to his head so it would not slip out. He then stuffed rags in both mouths and duct-taped them in. Both men dragged the two thugs around some piling into a dark space where they would not be noticed.

187

"OK, Buzz, OK ... I need an explanation. Let's take a short breather here and you can fill me in."

"Well, my brother, it is a long story. There may be more blockades between us and the not-so-reverend Reverend Grande that we are trying to see, so I will make it brief. I was in US Special Ops when I was in the army. You might have heard of Delta Force? I flew some missions with the Blaster over Iraq during Desert Storm. He flew with a guy named Charlie Beckwith in Nam, who put together Delta Force. The Blaster convinced me this was the best way to serve old Uncle Sam, so I figured what the hell, I served in some missions that you don't want to know about, and some I am plenty proud of. I was involved in Mogadishu ... you might have seen 'Black Hawk Down' .... and that was all I could take. I lost some amazing brothers there, which kind of crushed my desire to fight. In politics, right and wrong are just words that are a small part of the larger paradigm. Somehow the American spirit, like the teaching of the gentle Jesus, is still alive, but like religion, it's more and more being covered with a slime of twisted patriotism and phony moral posturing. So, I left the unit and began a life of love and peace. I find I can really feel what the founders were thinking when I am blissfully drifting in a cloud of the holy herb. Hooking up with you is the ultimate mission, Charlie, and I am proud you have included me. I don't feel any questions about the right or wrong of this one."

"Buzz, it's the work of the Lord that you are with me. You are a one-man guarantee for our success."

"Don't count on it, Charlie ... but there are some favors I could call in if necessary. Let's climb these stairs and find *the dick* that set these gorillas on us."

Buzz and Charlie climbed the stairs, which opened out to a large foyer with vaulted ceilings and amazing marble floors and statues. Charlie was used to the opulence of his LA Church, but this one was several times larger and twice as elegant. The place was empty, as it was a midweek morning, but the two could see that the several doors on their level went directly into a massive place of worship. They poked their heads in and saw a huge stage with giant flat screen TVs, and a pulpit that rose to the ceiling like the throne of God.

"Wow," said Buzz .... "Impressive!"

The obvious path was up a set of stairs to the second floor, which had a ring of doors that circled the foyer. As they climbed, they could see the center door was much larger than the others and had a golden crown at its top that read "The Very Reverend Horace Grande." They opened up the door and walked in.

189

As they entered the room, they could hear the soft playing of harp music. In the center of the room was a very large desk with a very beautiful young lady sitting behind it talking on her cell phone. They looked around the room, which was full of golden images of the Savior on and off the cross. The most prominent, directly behind the desk was what looked like the original picture of a very handsome, white Jesus holding a lamb in his arms.

"OK, OK, Jules, I am sorry ... you know SORRY.... What can I say? But look, I got to go, there are a couple of homeless looking dudes that just walked in. I'll call you back in five, when I get rid of them.

"Yes ... May I help you?"

"Yes," began Charlie, "we are here to see the Reverend Grande. We have an app—"

Buzz stopped Charlie and stepped forward. "Dude-ette ... did anyone ever tell you that you look like an *angel?* You are ... FINE!"

The young girl looked Buzz right in the face and smiled a smile that said yes, they have, and yes, I am.

"Look," continued Buzz, "we are here on a surprise visit to see my friend Charlie's Uncle Horace. You probably don't know it, but fifty years ago today the Reverend Grande was first baptized. Charlie was born on that very day to his favorite sister, who has since passed away. Unfortunately, Charlie was thought to have been killed in Iraq, but by the grace of God he has been found! When you open that door to surprise the Reverend, you will see a look of joy on his face like you have never seen before!"

"Well ..." The little secretary looked unsure.

"What can it hurt, my lady," continued Buzz, "and think of the wonderful moment when he sees Charlie, like Lazarus, back from the dead!"

"OK," she said with a shrug, "go right in."

She pushed a buzzer and the door swung slowly open like the Pearly Gates, and our two pilgrims, on a mission from God, walked through.

The office had a level of opulence the two travelers had never seen. The leather was rich and the wood was finely oiled. Gold and silver were in evidence everywhere. The art was original and looked to be Renaissance. The good Reverend Grande was sitting behind a massive desk talking on the phone.

"I'm sorry, Mr. President, but I will have to ... call ... you ... back."

"How the hell did you get in here? Didn't you park in the garage?"

"Oh, yeah," said Buzz, "we met your greeters ... not very Christ-like if you know what I mean."

"Listen," began Charlie, "I don't know what Abe Godly told you, but we truly mean you no harm. I have a holy pie plate that is showing me a separate place where the Lord Jesus is being forced into a great battle. I have been directed to tell the world what is happening because at some time we may be asked to play a role. I don't know many of these things, but I do know that in time I will need help to get the message across,. No one will believe a small-time preacher and his hippy friend. I am praying you will see the message and will be moved to help me tell the world. With your

191

visibility you could do this easily. I only ask that you look into the plate."

"I'll cram that plate up your deluded ass, you piece of shit, and up the asses of my worthless guards."

He pushed a button on his desk phone and barked out, "Frank, Bob, get your lousy asses up to my office and pick up this trash."

"Uh," said Buzz, "they might be a bit distracted at the moment. I don't think they will be coming up here for a while."

"What, did you bring a small army with you? It would take a small army to slow those two down."

"Nope," replied Charlie, "just us ... but we are on a mission for the Lord which makes us a bit ... more formidable."

Charlie set down his pack and pulled the pie plate out from its interior. He held it up to the preacher. "What do you see?"

"I see a pie plate, you prick, and I see two fools that will soon be seeing the bottom of a swamp." He pushed a button on his desk, which set off an alarm.

Buzz picked up a large golden cross and slid it through the massive handles on the inside of the door, effectively locking them all in.

"You think that matters?" asked the preacher with a sneer, "you will never get out of this church alive." He reached for a desk drawer but Buzz was instantly on him. Neatly tucked into the drawer was a Glock 19, 9mm pistol.

Buzz picked it up as if it were poison ivy. "Yucky," he said. He emptied it completely and dropped it in the wastebasket. "You know those things can be dangerous?"

"Look into the plate, Preacher, and try ... try to see something."

The reverend was beet red with veins standing out on his neck. He bunched his fists and considered taking the two on physically. He was a large, impressive man, in pretty good condition, but there was something in the way the hippy carried himself that held him back. Why get bruised, he thought, when there was no way out for these two and soon enough he would have his way with them.

"Very well," he said containing his rage, "I will look at this ... *holy plate*."

He stared at the plate that Charlie held aloft. He considered it for some time, then looked back at Charlie. "You are insane, you know ... a very insane, very dead, man."

Charlie took that to mean that the pastor could not see anything in the plate. He was crestfallen and went to put the plate back into the backpack.

Suddenly, a soft voice came from the plate, the voice of an old woman.

"Horace .... Horace, is that you?"

Grande stared at the plate. "What now, you two charlatans ... you will have to do better than that."

The face of a woman suddenly appeared on the plate.

"Horace," the voice continued from the plate, "you have been a very bad boy ..."

193

Chapter 37
– Evil Waits

Satan still sat beneath his golden wings. His mind was alive with the energy he was generating with thoughts of battle and conquest. He was certain that because of the fact that the God of All had created humanity, and that humanity was so obviously lacking, this God of All was fallible. The fact that he had declared them to be his crown of all creation was proof he was also delusional. Lucifer could see no weakness in his own person, which further reinforced his belief that he could crush this Yahweh and take his place as the God of All. He pictured the complete enslavement of humanity. They were no more than simple beasts of burden that would become slaves to evil. The most wicked humans on earth, whom Satan knew intimately, would become masters and leaders. Many of them actually already held such positions, but some were constrained by pathetic human laws from completely exercising their power. In Satan's world, there would be no such constraints. He could see clearly the rape and destruction of the world. An outcome it surely deserved for resisting him for so long. It had been a fun playground, but the Wicked One was ready to move on.

Outside of the evil golden tent, the willing wicked followers worked on their battle plan. As opposed to the protectors of Jesus, their only objective was to create a path between Satan and the little Jew. They did not have to hold lines, conquer individuals, or win the battle. They only had to create a path for a moment. Lucifer would easily do the rest. For this purpose, a battle wedge was devised.

On the outer edges of the wedge would be the warriors. Hades would lead the charge with Libitina, the Goddess of Death at his right hand and Pallor, the Goddess of Fear at his left.

Minerva, the Goddess of War, would be right behind him. In the inevitable confrontation with Mars himself, she would sap his spirit and break his resolve. She was a wicked warrior and capable of inflicting massive destruction. She would clean up scraps that Hades left in his wake. Vulcan, the God of Fire, would be at her side. Fire was a terrible weapon, and he wielded it to brutal effect.

Tempeste, the Goddess of Storms, would bring a mighty wind with driving rains to weaken the warriors on their way, and Trivia, the Goddess of Magic, would continuously cast spells to confuse and repel.

The rest, and there were many, would fan out like a wedge from the leaders and sweep the path clean for the drive of Satan himself. He would make short work of the little Jew and in doing so, summon Yahweh, the God of All. From that point, it was thought that the Olympians would have little impact. They would stand ready and fight as they might, but few thought they could add to Satan's onslaught. They believed it was just as likely they would be in the way and somehow hinder the Evil One. They would do as he commanded, however. With the plan fairly simple and clear, they hovered around the evil tent and discussed what the new world would look like and the awesome new powers they would possess.

It was this festival atmosphere that the snake found when he instantly returned to their presence. He slithered around the edge of the group making no comment. He listened to the plan and saw its potential. He craftily pieced together the weapons from each side and weighed his options. He curled in a giant coil, with his head to his tail, and sighed a great sigh.

He softly whispered to his tail, "This is the most fun I have had since Adam and Eve" ... and he drifted off to sleep.

Chapter 38
– Oh, Mama Grande

Charlie and Buzz also stared at the plate.

Buzz stammered "Messages, video, and now voices, and guess what, Charlie ... I *can* hear that! I can really hear that! And I can see her. The plate be praised!"

"You can see and hear it .... Thank God!" said Charlie.

"What the hell is going on," stammered the preacher. "How could you? You are dead, you motherfuckers!"

"Horace, this is no way to talk to people. You have fallen from grace, and have so very far to come back. I have watched you, and prayed you would find your soul and give up your wicked ways ... but you have fallen further and further."

"Stop that crap, you two, or I'm going to beat the living shit out of you, right here and now."

Charlie looked at Buzz and said, "I don't think I would consider that, Reverend. Buzz and I have nothing to do with any of this. It's the plate and the plate alone. If you think that looks and sounds like your mother, I would say you are right, and if you have any sense left at all, I think I would listen to her."

"Listen to these good boys, Horace. They might be the only chance you have to save your tattered soul."

"Stop this now, you bastards," screamed the preacher. "This is just bullshit and I know it. My mother is long dead and no pie plate is going to bring her back."

"Horace, dear, I still love you, even though I have seen the horrible things you have done. What happened to that young man who wanted to bring the gospel to the people? The young man who was determined to follow the footsteps of Jesus of Nazareth? Is forcing sex on six-year-old boys following in his footsteps? Are group orgies with teenaged girls following in the footsteps of your Lord? Is murder and violence the way of the gentle King of the Jews? Horace, you have been a bad boy. You have disgraced not only your name, and your father's and my name, but also the name of the Holy Father. Your disbelief and unnatural appetites have sent you to a place where you are under the spell of the Wicked One and are in danger of spending your next life in a place much worse than you can understand.'

Horace Grande was silent and stood looking at the plate. His confidence was abandoning him and his color morphed from bright red to white. His eyes were wide and seemed to be searching for a logical explanation that was becoming more and more impossible to find. "This ... is ... not ... possible," he whispered. "You're dead .... Dead is dead ...."

"Oh, Horace, if proof is what you need, then like Thomas, you may reach into the wound in my side. I will give you the proof you require and you will fall beneath its weight. Remember, Horace, you were a young boy in Wildomar. We lived in the trailer park near the railroad. You found a jar in the railroad yard ... do you remember, Horace?"

"Oh, my God...."

"Yes, you do remember, Horace ... There was a dead mouse in the jar, do you remember, Horace? You cried because you felt sorry for it, didn't you, Horace?"

"No one knows..."

"Do you remember Jill Mender from the park, Horace? She gave you your first kiss in the shed behind the wood pile at the park. Do you remember, Horace?"

"Stop it ..."

"Do you remember the boy, Billy Diamond, who you and Donnie Feller pushed into the swamp? He got so sick he almost died ... you do remember that, don't you, Horace? You prayed in the shed to God that if he lived, you would follow the Lord for the rest of your life. You prayed with all of your heart, Horace, you must remember. He got better almost at once ... it was said to be a miracle and from that day forward you wanted to serve the church. I am certain you remember that, Horace. On that day, you truly felt the spirit of the Lord. You never told me this story did you, Horace? You never told me why you made this change, but I was very proud of you ... do you remember, Horace? When your father went away you were the man of the house and took care of me ... do you remember, Horace? I died when you were still young, didn't I, Horace? Do you remember what I whispered to you, Horace, when I passed from your world? Do you, Horace?"

"Stop it .... My God, my God ..."

"I said, 'I love you, Horace. You are a man now, before your time and I will always love you.' You took my hand and cried softly over me. I still can taste your tears on my lips, Horace. I was between this life and the next then,

Horace, and had to leave you. Do you remember all of this, my Horace?"

The great Reverend Horace Grande was on his knees in the middle of the floor with his head bowed. Tears streamed down his face, which he held in his hands.

"Mama, I have been so bad. I have lost all faith. I have tortured and tormented innocence. I have made a mockery of the church and of God himself. My pride and evil spirit are beyond redemption, there is no hope .... THERE IS NO HOPE!"

"This is not so, my son. Yes, you have fallen far, and have so far to come back, but the message for you is that there is hope and, even for you, forgiveness. But you *must* surrender, Horace. Like the thieves on the cross with Jesus, it is never too late, but you must ask for forgiveness with all of your heart and soul, and you must be sincere. You can never be without sin, Horace. Your acts will haunt you and you will wear their marks for all of this life. You can never get rid of the deeds you have done, but you can be ...... forgiven."

"Oh, PLEASE ... Mama, I am so .... sorry. My heart aches, Mama...my soul is broken. I do not know if I am strong enough ... just let me die, Mama, and be done with it."

"Be done with it? No, I don't think so, Horace. Death will not end your motion ... it will not alter your momentum. You have to *change,* Horace, or suffer for so very long. It will be untold measures of time before you have another chance, Horace. You have been chosen to make a difference, Horace. The plate will lead you through the spirit of the gentle Charles and his friend, Buzz. Yes, Horace, there is hope for you and many good days ahead for you ....

Embrace them, Horace. Take this chance because as I have promised you ... I will always love you, Horace."

"Mama .... Mama" ... cried a weeping Horace Grande as he lay prone on the floor, but the image faded and the plate was silent.

Buzz and Charlie stood in silence and stared at the person they had once thought was a pillar of religion in America. Charlie understood the greed and imbalance from his experience at his former big church. He had not realized the depth of violence and perversion. He'd had no idea. Buzz was even more surprised. He had seen evil in the world that Charlie could not even imagine, but somehow his gentle image of Christian religion had held firm. He had left the military and conventional lifestyles because of a desire to escape the things he had been a part of. He was never a part of religion, and as such, did not need to look at it critically. The religion of the plate and the spiritual honesty of Charlie was his only close exposure and they were real. The corruption of the good reverend on the floor before him was a complete bursting of his existing religious bubble. How could a man of God go so wrong?

It was now very obvious to both Charlie and Buzz that the plate was totally in charge. It had become so much more than a spiritual television to another world. It had become the vehicle of change that was somehow coming because of a confrontation unfolding between ultimate good and evil. Such a conflict with its infinite magnitude could not help but shatter the foundations of the world and usher in a new reality. With the outcome undecided, the plate gave the world only the ability to be aware ... and prepare. Their confidence was growing, as was the unfolding possibilities. They looked at the quivering spiritual leader on the floor. He would be a powerful voice in the new religious revolution, but he alone would not convert the world. Charlie considered their next move and looked at Buzz.

"That was easy... let's go after the Pope!"

Chapter 39
– Charlie, Meet Jesus!

Jesus had walked for several miles on the little road when he came to a clearing with a small spring in its center. Cold, clear water flowed from its pool down a narrow path of beautiful rocks of different colors. It wound through the field and disappeared into the woods. Its bubble and splash played a soft song in the center of the perfect day.

Jesus sat on a large, flat stone next to the pool and dipped his hand for a cool drink. As he looked into the pool he was startled by a face that was swimming in the center of the pool. It was not a physical face, as we all know faces cannot live by themselves, it was an image or vision, and though the Son of Man had no way of knowing, the image was of another world, the world he had once known, and the face belonged to a person who would soon help to shape its new reality. It was Charlie.

Charlie had been watching the young Messiah wandering on the road. He saw him consider the pool and sit on the rock. He was used to watching the goings on of this alternate world, so was peacefully observing the peaceful scene. That all changed when the Lord looked into the pool. Instantly, Charlie's perspective changed and he was face to face with the Christ. He knew instantly that Jesus could also see him and they looked with amazement into one another's eyes.

Jesus spoke first. "Considering this place, nothing surprises me. And who would you be, young water man?"

"I am sorry," Charlie babbled, "but you must tell me for sure, without a doubt, you are Jesus and you can see me."

"Well, technically my name in my life was Joshua, but *Jesus* is how the Greeks spoke it, and it seems to have stuck."

"Whoa," said Charlie, "I did not know that, what then should I call you?"

"Jesus is fine. I know this is the name that is important to your heart. And what may I call you?"

"Well, sir, that is, I guess you can call me Charlie, 'cause that's my name ... I guess. Say, do you mind if I call a friend over to meet you, too?"

"Of course not," smiled Jesus, "any friend of Charlie's is a friend of mine."

"Buzz ... Hey, Buzz! Get over here. There's someone I want you to meet."

Buzz was in the kitchen making himself a tasty grilled cheese sandwich and some tomato soup. He could tell by Charlie's voice that this was important, so he dropped what he was doing and scrambled into the next room where Charlie was doing his Charlie-thing.

"Look into the plate, Buzz," said Charlie. "Jesus this is my good friend, Buzz; and Buzz, this is my Savior, Jesus."

"Whoa," ... whispered Buzz with amazement, "it's the 'DUDE' ... I mean the real DUDE! It is so cool to meet you, man! I really relate to the love thing, man. You are the Shining Light ... know what I mean? Like when you said ... 'But the greatest of these is LOVE' ... Is ... that .... TRUE?"

Jesus smiled. "Of course, Buzz. It's not only the greatest, it's the ONLY thing. If you have love in your heart, all the rest will follow."

205

"Whoa ... dude ... I'm here for you, dude. Charlie and me are here for you. We are following the plate and are your mighty new Christian army ... Charlie, me, and now the preacher dude. He was a bastard, but saw the light, and now it's all good, if you know what I mean."

"Honestly, Buzz, I have no idea what you mean. Perhaps you could fill me in?"

"Well, to be honest, Jesus, dude-Charlie is the real preacher and the chosen messenger. I'm just his wingman, so I'm just gonna kind of step out of the way now, but it was way cool to meet you, your holiness, and be assured I'm here for ya, right next to our man, Charlie."

Jesus smiled. "Your spirit shines through, Buzz, my new warrior. I feel like I am in good hands for whatever your mission might be."

Buzz stepped back, gave Charlie two mighty thumbs up and literally danced back into the kitchen, where you could faintly smell slightly over-browned grilled cheese.

"Well, I know you have no idea who we are or even where we are. It's a long story, so relax on that rock and I'll try and explain.... I used to be a preacher in a big church on the West Coast of the USA ... Oh, yeah, you probably don't have any idea where that is. I guess I need to go back a bit further....

After they nailed you to the cross....

Chapter 40
– Total Breakdown

Jesus lay flat on the large flat stone by the pool long after the image of Charlie had faded away. At first he closed his eyes as his head spun and his stomach churned. There was little he believed as a living person was true. There was no Heaven as he'd imagined in the sky above the earth. There was no Hell under the ground as he had been taught. The earth was not the center of the universe, but just one of many planets that spun around the sun. The sun did not rise and fall for the earth's pleasure, but was merely one of the specks he knew as stars in the sky. There were literally billions of them. The size and scope of it made him want to throw up, so he rolled on his stomach, arched his head off the flat stone and did. He lay in that position for several minutes with the new reality bouncing around his brain and the taste of bile in his mouth. Of all of the information Charlie had passed along, these physical realities were the most crushing to the gentle Jesus. These were piled on the mountain of other "truths," such as his coronation to God status, the millions of people who worshiped him, his "Christian Torah," the existence of the Gods of the Greeks and Romans, and the pending battle with the dark Archangel Lucifer. He was no warrior. He was no God. He was a Jew and now it seemed obvious, he was not even the Messiah as envisioned by his people. He was a failure in his mission and his message, and was convinced he would again fail in the battle being foisted upon him.

He began to weep. His mind became empty and he surrendered to despair, and from despair, he dropped the short last step downward ... to madness.

Chapter 41
– Lost Hope

*J*t was apparent, immediately, throughout the entire world of the lost Gods, that something major had happened. The skies darkened and rumbled, and a feeling of dread covered the world. The light of hope was flickering and sadness and fear approached like a storm. It was on the horizon and boiling and rolling like despair. The company of heroes in the clearing all stared at the sky and held their breath as one. This was not good.

Neptune was the first to speak. "It would appear we have a problem."

Mars softly spoke. "The Wicked One must have found the Messiah ... all is lost."

To a God, the gathering felt hopelessness like they had never felt it. This was not just sorrow or pain. This was the feeling of an end to all that was good, and a future of sorrow and emptiness. A major realization was that they were immortal and there was no escape ... not even in death.

In time, Aphrodite spoke. She was pale and shaking, but her words were steady and sure. "He is not dead."

The crowd of heroes lifted their faces to the Goddess of Love.

"I would know. I would know for sure. No, he is not dead, but as sure as life, he is in trouble. I must find him, and soon, or truly all will be lost."

In a whisper she was gone, and the company of heroes waited.

The Band of Evil reacted quite differently. They too, stared at the darkening sky and held their tongues. The suddenness of the change and the dramatic change in spirit told them plainly that nothing was the same. The tide had turned and it had turned to their favor. They looked upon the majestic cone of gold. Some thought they would see the Evil One gone. That he had brought the fight to the enemy and had snuffed out their light. This was not the case, as the evil cone of gold remained the same.

Hermes broke the silence. "The time has changed. The war is won before it has begun. What wonders have our Wicked King wrought? "

The crowd stared at Hermes and at each other in amazement. They fell on their knees in front of Lucifer's cone and chanted as one, "All hail, Satan! All hail, Satan!"

One might imagine that their praise was hollow, that the Wicked One only slept ... but one would be wrong. Since wrapping himself in golden wings, he had indeed been very busy.

Satan remained in his cone of gold, but he did not sleep. He never slept. He worked to his purpose as surely as rust.

While he could not reach the little Savior in person, flesh to flesh, he found he was able to reach out with his putrid soul and search for purity and perfection. It was obvious by its measure when he found the gentle carpenter. There was, after all, no one else here or anywhere like him. It was almost too easy. He was so much like a child ... so open ... so vulnerable. But, there was more. Satan could feel power and resolve also, and while he did not research this to its depth, he proceeded with caution and slowly sowed the seeds of doubt.

The Evil One did not know where Jesus was or what he was experiencing, but that held little matter. Doubt could be found in news both good and bad. It was just a matter of degrees that tipped a message of joy to one of hopelessness. Wealth can turn friends to thieves, food can turn the hungry to gluttons, and joy is the twin of despair only altered by perception. As for the twisting of truth, Satan was unequaled. It was his art and he was the master.

The news that Charlie gave the Lord was delivered in joy. There were great Gods that were heroically standing by Jesus's side. While there were many things that Jesus did not understand, and many new realities that staggered his world, they could have been embraced and added to the wonders of creation and the power of the God of All. Satan made sure that did not happen. He piled each new bit of information upon the back of the gentle king like stones of unimaginable weight. It was quite amazing to the Wicked One how long he maintained hope ... how many ways he found to keep his balance, but Satan had one huge advantage. The simple King of the Jews had no idea that in his mind and soul, he was not alone. He had felt the presence of the Wicked One before, in temptation and despair, but this was different. Satan knew the risk. He did not want confrontation at this moment. He would lose his path to the God of All if Jesus was defeated far from his unholy grasp. After all, it was the God of All he was after.... Yahweh, he must crush, to ascend to the most high of the most high. The little Jew was merely a door to his future kingdom, and it would be worthless to open it in a place he could not reach. So he was cautious ... he was as sly as his cunning allowed. Jesus never felt his presence and embraced the crushing load.

Satan knew about taking chances. His first attack on the God of All had failed. He would do all he could, use every resource to make sure that that did not happen this time. Bringing Jesus to ruin before the battle would deflate the unpredictable Gods, and suck the life out of the resistance. It was obvious to the Dark Angel and he moved as surely as hate toward his objectives. The collapse of the little Jew and the reaction of the enemy was evidence that he had, in truth ... dealt a crushing blow.

Chapter 42
– Next Stop, the Pope

Charlie, meanwhile, had put away the plate right after his conversation with the Lord. He was thrilled at the encounter and didn't fully realize the extent that his news had shaken the Heavenly Prince. He could tell Jesus was quiet and less radiant when the image faded, but Charlie had done the great majority of the talking and had missed the signs of agony held within the King of the Jews. He found himself reinforced and eager for his next conversion.

"Man, oh man, Charlie," beamed Buzz, "we are gonna change the world! I stand here a man amazed! We just spoke with Jesus Christ himself! How many dudes can say that honestly? I am *soooo* stoned right now, and have not had a single pull on the magic pipe."

"Buzz, between the Lord and me, we might just cure you of that habit!"

"Why in the world would you do that? You and Jesus enjoy the juice of the magical grape and me and my kind will worship communion with a bowl of the holy bud. In the end, it's the love, brother .... It's the love!"

"Sorry, Buzz," replied Charlie with a grin, "I stand corrected ... puff on!"

The good reformed Reverend Grande took this moment to enter the room. He had set the boys up in the suites adjoining his Only True Path to Heaven church. This would be mission central for their evangelical assault on the rest of the world.

"Good news, boys!" he exclaimed. "We have a meeting with the very holy Pope Peter Paul Pius at the Vatican, in a mere three days. I had to twist a few arms, but within the religious communities this is something I have become very good at!"

"I believe that Horace, my friend, we have good news for you, too ... I just got off the plate with the Lord of All, the King of the Jews, with Jesus, his sweet self! Buzz and I are just shaken from head to foot!"

"And, I just missed it ... Damn ... I mean darn it all."

"Don't worry, Reverend Grande, I have a feeling we will be in touch again. Buzz, you better get hold of the Blaster and have him rev up the mystical jet. We have a date in three short days."

"Not necessary, boys, I have the church jet filing a flight plan. That plane has been in and out of Rome so many times it flies itself. I have a pilot that was the pilot of Air force 1, under Bush junior, and a fulltime security detail...all ex-CIA. If our mission rubs folks the wrong way, it could be a rough road out of Dodge and we will need their ... er ... *talents and connections*. Believe me, I did a sermon in Iraq before the invasion, to kick up some dust for W. that was, shall we say ... effective? Folks were screaming and calling for Jihad. We made a run for the airport that was beyond belief. Full speed, no traffic, no crowds ... Now, that's what I call connections!"

"All right, Horace," said Charlie, "done and done. Buzz, you can tell the Blaster to stand down. It looks like we will be guests of the good reverend."

"OK," replied Buzz. "I feel more comfortable in my magic carpet with the Blaster at the stick, but we will do as you say my 'master of the plate.' I think there are powers even greater than the CIA at our backs, so I will quote the very wise Alfred E. Neuman ... "What, me worry?"

The three Christian soldiers plopped down on the couch and discussed the events of the day. Charlie filled in the now really good reverend on his conversation with the Christ. They had no idea what had happened since they disconnected, and that on the other side of reality, their heroes were in despair and the immortal soul of all of creation was in peril.

From the inside of Charlie's pack, a soft glow could be seen. The three apostles didn't notice, however, and so remained oblivious and, for the present, hopelessly optimistic.

Chapter 43
– Could All Be Lost?

Jesus lay on the rock and wandered aimlessly in the chaos that was his mind. It was as if he were transported to another world, yet again, where up was down, and down was up, and any effort for the good or for the bad was pointless. Even the concepts of good or bad were lost in the jumbled thoughts that had overcome the gentle Prince of Peace. What was true and constant in this anarchy of thought, was an overwhelming pain that emanated from his heart and assaulted his soul. His body on the rock simply lay face down and uttered a very soft whimper. There was little evidence of the hope for man.

This was how Aphrodite, the Goddess of Love, found him, and she instantly fell to his side and cried. She stroked his hair and kissed his lips, and gently told him of her love and of hope, but the man she had known was wandering far away from that place, and her words fell away like a song in an empty room. Her crying became more desperate as she realized the depth of his madness. She used all her powers, which were considerable, but the darkness that covered the world remained and the gentle Jesus suffered. She poured out her love from her heart to his. She filled and filled but he emptied like a rusted vessel full of holes, void of utility. She wept and wept, and fought with love and for love, until she too was empty, then she collapsed upon the gentle Savior and slept.

Time and purpose conspired and Apollo found himself at the foot of the stone. He gazed in sorrow at the two hopeless Gods, and felt the truth that cried 'the one who was complete is lost' and lost completely. The beautiful Goddess of Love lies at his side ... empty and defeated. The skies were dark and the air was becoming thick and putrid. Apollo realized at once this was a grim reality that he could not share with his brothers in war. The sight would crush them, and they would lose any sense of hope. The battle would be lost. He had no idea how he could repair the massive damage before him, but admitting complete defeat he also realized was ... premature. Time was the key here in this land with no time. If the end was to be, it would find them and be complete.

He made a decision to bring the pair to Aphrodite's tent and to allow the future to evolve as it was destined to.

He lifted them gently in his arms and was instantly gone.

Chapter 44
– Trouble in Paradise

Charlie and his plate were like a teenager and his phone. He was driven to watch the news, and the news he was watching was anything but good. It seemed he had done some real harm with his history lesson and had literally blown the Savior's mind. How could he have known? He was speaking to the Christ in "Christian." Who could be more ... stable? The message depressed Charlie in a deep way and he struggled to understand how this could be. He watched Aphrodite with hope, which turned to loss. He saw Apollo, and fought for a glimmer of hope as he delivered the two to the Goddess's tent. But from there, there was nothing. There was only the two lying together on a skin of pure white, with Apollo sitting on a pillow staring at them with a blank stare that probably focused somewhere far away.

After a time, Charlie put away the plate and sadly found his two companions. They were busy putting together things for the trip to Vatican City. They were chatting like two old friends from completely different ends of the earth when Charlie entered the room. They quickly became silent as they saw that Charlie was pale and shaking. Charlie sat on a chair and put his face in his hands. Charlie began to cry.

"Whoa, dude," said Buzz softly. "What's up man ... let's hear it, little brother. What could possibly be that bad?"

They pulled two chairs facing Charlie and the reverend placed his hand on Charlie's head and said a soft prayer for understanding and peace.

After a time Charlie lifted his tear-stained face and faced his friends. Slowly, he explained what he had seen. They all sat in silence. It all seemed so final. The plate was a vision of danger and challenge and hope, but now, after all of this, it seemed to be the story of the end times. It seemed certain the story was the story of the death of love.

Charlie spoke. "I am afraid I blew it, boys. I am the one who drove the final nail ... I am the one who pierced his side. In my zeal to tell sweet Jesus of our world and what we are doing here, I buried him in realities that were so far from his world they made him crazy. He is down and out, and it's all my fault. I am the *twenty-first-century Judas*." Charlie put his head in his hands and continued to weep.

Buzz spoke first.

"Charlie, my friend, there is as much Judas in you, as there is apple in an orange. You need to drop back, son, and look at a bigger picture. You acted with love, and when you do that, you can do no wrong. I am sure if Jesus were here he would say the same thing. Yeah, things look grim right now, but like in our mirror world over there, things happen when time and purpose align. There is a purpose for this that you and I don't know. At the very least, there is a war over there, and in war things get very ... messy. Of these things, I know. Jesus isn't just some soldier in that world. He is the ideal, the message, the love. He is the anchor that stands at the end of the tug-of-war rope. There is no way he goes in the mud first. I'd bet the rest of my lifetime stash we are only in the thick of it. Don't blame yourself for a story that had to be told, and don't count out sweet Jesus. There is no way he is going down this easy.

"Buzz is right, Charlie," said Horace. "Have faith, Charlie. Before this is over, we will need a lot of faith. We are fighting evil and we are on the right side. I have seen both sides and believe me, we are on the *right side*. I am filled with the hope of sweet Jesus, and I have not felt this good inside for thirty years. My God, I can breathe again. Charlie, it's because of you and Buzz and the holy plate, but the force behind you all is sweet Jesus. Imagine the hopelessness the apostles felt when they nailed him to the cross, when they laughed at him and pierced his side. He was three days dead ... Was he done then? Was it over? No way, Charlie! That was only the beginning."

Charlie looked at his friends and forced a slight smile. He was not so sure. The reality from the other side of the plate was as crazy as the story he told Jesus. Ancient Gods, supposedly just myths, had the future of creation in their hands. Satan crapping out Gods, and a carp that helped rule the underworld made that reality just as insane as ours must have seemed to the Lord. All that didn't drive *them* nuts. Charlie tried to figure what it was that he said that broke his back. What part of it was too much for the gentle king? He did not know, but he also did not know that it was not just *his words* that went into the Prince of Peace's ear. There was an evil worm that was in there too, that whispered lies and nurtured hopelessness. It was still there and softly and continuously it covered the gentle carpenter with a blanket of madness, with little room for reason. It was such a complete sense of surrender that the tiny light that held the core of the Savior's soul could barely hear the softest voice of reason. In the chaos of his mind, even the words when he heard them made no sense ... at first. Then, slowly, the gentle Jew began to get the message.

"Hey, Jesus ... somebody is messin' with you!"

Chapter 45
– New Morning

Jesus woke up in the pure white tent of Aphrodite. He looked as good as new, and the truth be told ... he was stronger. Being *complete* was certainly an advantage, but it left him with little understanding of the deepest confusion and despair. Oh, he knew temptation and doubt, but that was like comparing a mosquito bite to a bullet wound. What he had just experienced was the ultimate in human emotional suffering. Now, he knew the depths of both the physical and mental anguish humans experience. He also now had a deeper understanding of his enemy. He had after all spent time in his mind...and messed it up some too.

Both Aphrodite and Apollo were sound asleep when the Prince of Peace regained consciousness. He gently rolled off the pure white rug and quietly left the tent. He walked across the sand and sat cross-legged on a mound just outside. He breathed deeply and surrendered to the joy of creation. He had experienced chaos and was definitely not a fan. The sun shone and the birds sang and the vibrations of life were once again in perfect harmony. He smiled and whispered a gentle prayer of thanks to his God for deliverance.

Aphrodite was the first to awake. She saw at once that Jesus was gone.

"Apollo, wake up," she cried. "They have taken him!"

Apollo jumped to his feet and the two ran outside the tent looking for their damaged friend. The first thing they saw was a clear blue sky with air as fresh as the first day. Even the very slight feeling of the Evil One far away was ... gone. What they found also was a very much alive and obviously changed ... for the better, if that was possible .... Jesus Christ.

Jesus grinned at the two and simply said, "Are you looking for me?"

Aphrodite jumped on him and kissed him full on the mouth. "I, we, were so worried ... We thought you were lost. There was nothing I could do ... I tried EVERYTHING, and I could not reach you."

She had begun again to cry and hugged the simple carpenter around his neck, as if letting go would let him fall again to the depths.

Jesus laughed and unwrapped her arms. He looked her deep in the eyes and kissed her back ... full on the lips. "Thank you, my love ... I felt you, but could not answer or honestly even understand. I was in the wilderness ... in the darkness, until I was given the light. But, it's a bit of a long story and I would love to smell the fragrance of your most excellent coffee. What say you, Apollo?"

"Welcome back, Jesus ... just, welcome back."

The three joined arms and hugged and walked back into the pure cloud that was the home of the Goddess of Love.

In a flash, the inside of the tent was filled with the smell of coffee fit for the Gods. They rested on the pure white pillows and sipped their inky liquids in silence. Finally, Apollo spoke.

"OK, Jesus, let's hear what happened here. The entire army that assembled on your behalf has all but lost hope. The very foundation of our cause was reduced to, well, a husk of a man. You were lost and now you are found, and if I am not wrong, you seem even the better for it. Please tell us all so that, at the very least we can defend against it happening again."

"You were so far away," continued Aphrodite, "so very, very *lost*. I have never seen anyone, man or God in such a state. I could feel the vacuum of your soul."

"It is as you say," responded Jesus. "I have had quite a struggle, yet I emerged refreshed. What I have to tell you is truly beyond belief. Parts of it still make no sense to me." Jesus shook his head and smiled a small smile.

"It seems we have *watchers* in the world we once knew. There is a rabbi named Charlie, his loyal friend, Buzz, and a reformed charlatan named Horace Grande, who is the leader of the largest church that worships in my name, in a powerful country called America. I suppose you know of this place from your observations, but so much of what I was told was so far from my understandings that I became even more disillusioned and confused. I have already suffered from the perception that so much of what I believed I died for, was wrong. It is my belief that I have failed to fulfill the role I was raised to fulfill. Did you know the earth is but a small part of something called a *universe* and that there are many earths, and that the stars are suns? There is so much that obliterates my world of a Heaven in the sky and a Hell below. I suppose you have known these things, but you have had two thousand years to slowly adjust to the new truths. I believe I suffered a moment of, well, I am not sure what ... perhaps ... instability. That's when I was visited by the Evil One."

"Satan came to you ... here?" asked Apollo in disbelief. "Where has he gone?"

"He did not come in the flesh. He is after all the God of Deception and Lies. He was able to enter my mind, and he sowed the seeds of doubt and fear. I have never felt such feelings. I have dealt with this one before. He tempted me and tortured me, but this was different. In this, he took my hope. He left me without thought or reason. I was alone and afraid. But, I say unto you this ... we are never alone. There is one that is with us in the darkest hour. It was no power or reason of mine that found my way back. A voice whispered to me when all was lost, and I found a path. It was harsh and uneven at first, but slowly cleared like dawn, and I could see. I recognized the Wicked One, the most vile creature in creation. He taunted me. He whispered confusion and despair. It flowed out of him like a mighty river most putrid and foul. As in clarity I saw my tormentor, I soon realized he was unaware that I had escaped his evil grasp. So, let's just say I, well, took advantage."

Jesus smiled and looked just a bit proud of himself.

Aphrodite spoke. "This is beyond horror, for what is more valuable than your mind? What is more fragile and vulnerable than your very sense of self? To lose that is to truly be lost! It is clear to me now how I found you, and the state you were in."

"Yes," continued Jesus, "it was as far from love as I have ever been. I could not see you. But there is more. For the Wicked One to reach me over time and purpose in this place, he had to open some kind of a portal. He willed his evil spirit to me to work his mischief. A portal, however, can be traveled in both directions. Since he was unaware that I was free of his whispers I took the opportunity to pay him a visit."

"My god, Jesus," said Apollo, "you, of your own will, visited the mind and soul of the most vile Pretender? There can be no more wretched place in creation. You chose to walk this walk?"

"I had been assaulted. It is said I am destined to battle this wicked monster. Should I fear him now? It is said that all I have for weapons is the power of love. I believe with all my soul that this is the most powerful force in the universe. When I have love, what should I fear? I did venture to the heart of his being. I did walk into the depths of his depravity, but I did not attempt to battle. I did not respond to it in kind.

"I simply gave it .... love."

"You loved it?" asked Aphrodite.

"More truly, I loved in it," replied Jesus with a smile. "From the very depths of my being I loved in him. I simple stood in the middle of his being and filled my heart with love." There is no way to love any part of this creature. His thoughts and deeds are far from reason, and hate forms the walls of his being. But love exists independently, far beyond the muscle and bone of man or beast. I did not have to love it, to love. I simple stood in his soul with my head high and my arms outstretched and ... I loved."

"Jesus ... you are something!" responded Apollo with wonder.

"No, my friend, I am really nothing," said the gentle carpenter looking with authority into the eyes of his friend. Love is something!"

"What did this do to the Evil One?" asked Aphrodite.

"Well, it sort of made him uncomfortable," Jesus said with a laugh. "In fact it burned him like fire. His consciousness was still whispering lies when he felt the first sting. It took him a moment to realize how things had changed. He came to me in a fury, but I was protected by love. He meant me harm, and screamed in pain and insanity. He spun around me like a typhoon of unimaginable power and violence. I simply stood still, surrounded by the walls of love. He could not hurt me. He ripped and tore at his own soul, somehow trying to dislodge me, but I was beyond him. That is ... love put me beyond him. As he weakened, the portal he had created began to fail, and I had to escape or be doomed to remain a part of that wretched soul."

"As I think of these things, it would have probably been better to stay there. The monster would have eventually been driven mad, as I suppose I would have too ... but at least it would be over."

"Do not even think such things," said Aphrodite. "There are things in play here none of us can imagine. It is your God of All that seems to be at work here, and you and the evil one are central to his plan. I for one am very glad to see you in one piece in body and soul."

Apollo spoke. "I will echo that. I do believe that there are things to do and as we have enjoyed Aphrodite's excellent coffee, and enjoyed even more your tale of torment for the Beast, I believe we should make an effort to return to your army. They have suffered in your time of torment, and will also need some explanation. While we can't simply fly to them, I feel that time and purpose have aligned and the next bend in the road will unite us all."

"I feel it, too," said Aphrodite. The trio rose from the pillows and exited the flap of the pure white tent. As quick as a *tick*, they were gone.

Chapter 46
– Not a Battle, But a War

The army of evil was in chaos. The Wicked One was face down in the field, shaking and screeching like a howler monkey. Spit and drool flew from its mouth, and it foamed like a rabid dog. There also emanated a rancid stink, as the creature had apparently shat himself.

The Wicked Army was in disarray with several already wondering aloud how they could get back on the good side. Vulcan was explaining to Nemesis that fire could actually be used for good or evil ...Hades himself was wandering around calling for his trusted #1, Fishbone ... He ordered Trivia, a lesser God, to fetch him.

Just as they were about to leave the monster to his misery and disband, a change began to slowly take form. Lucifer began to emit a golden light. His wings and armor, which had fallen in disarray, slowly pulled themselves together like a shredded lesser God. Slowly, the giant demon pulled itself to its feet. Its bowed head and arched back slowly rose to perfect posture and its eyes began to glow with an intense ruby red. It did not appear to even notice the crowd that gathered around it. But rather focused on the horizon ... somewhere far away.

Within minutes, it had regained its majesty ... and then some. The Evil Army expected a savage rampage with unimaginable violence and fury, but there was none. The creature simply, slowly, walked back to the spot on which it had sat, and sat down. Slowly it wrapped its wings around itself to form the now familiar golden cone. At once it emanated a fearful hate that was even stronger than the aura in its past, and the air became stagnant and the clouds rolled in fearful threatening.

In a place near or far from there, the army of the gentle Savior all stood staring at the sky. They had gone from despair to joy and had been celebrating the clarity and purity since the clearing of the dread. They did not know the details, but felt that somewhere a battle had ensued and that, against all odds, the little Christ was the victor. Such assumptions were very premature. As they stared at the sickening sky, Diana spoke the words that all thought.

"It lives."

Chapter 47
– Flight to Rome

Charlie sat in front of the plane and did the play by play for his friends. While Buzz had been able to briefly see Jesus in the plate, it now returned to its original ... for Charlie's eyes only ... status.

They suffered in the apparent fall of Jesus, they rejoiced in his victory, and settled down to somewhere in the middle with the rise of the Beast. It was obvious that the battle had been joined. After it all, they were more convinced than ever that they had a role to play and the compulsion of their mission became even more intense.

The trio left the little microbus in the church's garage and jumped into the Reverend Grande's limousine. The good reverend picked up the phone in the back seat and instructed his chauffeur to take them to the airport. In moments they were boarding the corporate Lear jet that was owned and paid for by the Only True Path to Heaven church and used exclusively by its founder and senior pastor, Horace Grande.

There were two very large military looking men at the door to greet them.

"Hey Frank, Justin, these are my new friends, Charlie and Buzz. Things have changed quite a bit since our last mission, so after take-off we will brief you in the front boardroom."

The men looked briefly at Charlie, then at Buzz. They both looked hard at Buzz. Finally the taller of the two, Justin, spoke.

"Jesus Christ, it's Matt Haden. I'll be a son of a bitch. Man, you just disappeared ... I mean, *poof* GONE! Everyone thought you were probably in the mountains of Idaho living off squirrel and wild berries."

"Hey, Justin, hey, Frank! Yeah, it's been a while. Seems this will be a long flight, so we should have some time to catch up. Let's just say it's been a wild ride and it seems it is just beginning. But first and foremost, you can now call me Buzz."

The two looked at him with a thousand questions but quietly and professionally led them to their seats. Both Charlie and Horace had heard the short story of Buzz, so were not terribly surprised that the security knew him. They just shook their heads and buckled their seat belts. The plane took off with the power and precision expected of a multimillion dollar luxury jet, and all aboard settled in for the ten-hour flight to Rome.

As the plane gained altitude, a very attractive woman came forward with cups of steaming coffee.

"Hi, Horace," she smiled. "Can I get you anything?" She paused. "Anything at all?"

"Ah, no, Grace, ah, these are my friends, Charlie and Buzz. Things have changed, Grace, so at the very most I would like some water and perhaps a chocolate chip cookie. Thank you, dear."

The stewardess looked confused but continued, "Well, then, how about your, ah, friends. Would they like anything?"

Charlie said, "Hi, Grace. Is there anything to eat? I am starved!"

"Yeah," continued Buzz, "I don't suppose you have any tomato soup and grilled cheese?"

Grace looked at the three together with more questions in her eyes than she was probably permitted to ask, so she simple replied, "I'll see what I can find," and returned to the rear of the plane.

The plane settled in for the long haul. It was early evening, and as the plane flew east it left what was left of the day behind. Buzz got his tomato soup and grilled cheese ... much to his delight, while the rest of the plane enjoyed a very well-prepared Cornish game hen. There was little said and the crew ate patiently, obviously in a state of serious confusion. This was not the pompous, boisterous, demanding, mean-spirited Horace Grande they were used to. It was obvious the two with him were rubes and the reverend was, as usual, acting. This would not surprise them except his marks were usually very influential, famous power players themselves, and the two who were with Horace now were anything but.

With the completion of the meal, the entire crew, including an older gentleman who was apparently the pilot, retired to a large (for an airplane) table in a cabin to the front of the plane. When everyone was settled, Horace began:

"Well, people, it has finally happened. I have truly found the Lord!"

Charlie and Buzz smiled, and the crew simply looked sincere and nodded respectfully.

"No, guys, I know what you are thinking, but this time it is *real*. I have seen the truth and Jesus is real. While all things are not exactly like I would have thought ... no. let me correct that, absolutely nothing is as I would have thought ... the fact remains Jesus is real and, somewhere, is very much alive.

Horace looked around at the crew who maintained professional, uncommitted expressions. They were obviously used to Horace's revelations and dramatic moments created sometimes off the cuff to suit some poor, unsuspecting rube.

"OK, folks, this is complicated, so let me begin at the beginning. You see, Charlie found this magic pie plate ...."

Chapter 48
– A Serpent's Mind

A serpent is a serpent after all, and they are, if nothing else, patient. It is hard to say what this one did from creation to the present moment, but you can be sure whatever it was, it was well thought out and, well, *wicked.* In keeping with that character trait, the snake remained out of the center of activity but within hearing range of the Army of Evil. It gathered information like a squirrel gathers nuts. It stashed that information in nooks and crannies in its brain, for removal when removal was strategically called for. It was quick, quiet, and devastatingly efficient.

When Lucifer exploded from his cone and began screaming in pain, his hands squeezing his head as if his only hope was to mash its internals to paste, the serpent did not move a muscle. It would not have even batted an eye if it had a lid to bat. It merely watched and collected information. While its body remained perfectly still ... still, that is, with the exception of its forked tongue darting silently in and out, its mind was moving at lightning speed. It processed data like a machine.

Many things had changed for this evil one. Its face-to-face time with Satan had been minimal. It was only called when needed, and the Most Wicked felt he needed no one, so it was left to its own devices. It watched evil and good battle. It saw the strengths and weaknesses in both love and hate. It had come to a conclusion. They were both equal in power and neither side would ever win. This opinion was based on countless years of observation and the most extremely efficient data processing. It arrived at a statistical probability in the 99.999946% range ... give or take.

Choosing to be on the evil side was easy for it. It was created that way. Decisions on right and wrong or redemption were reserved for humans alone. The creatures in Heaven were less dimensional and were more fixed in their purpose. This was also a fact that was lost on most, but derived from countless bits of information processed carefully and precisely by a creature with the innate ability to do so, and lots of time to kill. Being evil was its nature and it was comfortable with that.

With Satan's display of pain, the snake had learned something new. The intensity of the attack proved there was something in the universe, outside of the God of All, that could harm this creature. The data did not support a theory that included the God of All. The serpent felt that meeting was still a ways away. He again was certain the residents of this world, even though they were in fact Gods, were not capable of inflicting the pain he had witnessed. That only left the little carpenter. He did not know how the Messiah struck, but legend supported a theory that the two would battle, and battle takes two. If the little Jew was powerless the legend would be that he was crushed. That is not how it went, so the only entity that had the power to possibly do what he had seen done to the Devil was the gentle Jesus. The Christ could inflict pain but continuing its theory of parity, the serpent doubted even he could kill the Dark Angel.

The snake now gave Jesus more credit than before. This changed the dynamics of the battle and complicated how Satan would get before the God of All to realize his final demise. If there was true parity, the battle could go on literally forever. This was not to the snake's advantage. Its whole purpose was and is to rule over evil on earth. There was no room for both Satan and the serpent in its happily ever after. Satan had to go.

There were several scenarios it could imagine that would accomplish its purpose. With the power and magic of the lesser Gods, yes, it could be accomplished. There is no way they could seriously damage the Most Wicked, but they could surely jack him around.

The snake only needed to make sure they jacked him to the God of All.

Chapter 49
– More Travel and Lost Gods

*T*he conference in the Only Truth Path to Heaven Lear jet broke up, and the groups separated to go to their seats and reflect. The security staff had only one question. "Is the compensation plan changing?" The answer was not at all. This seemed to satisfy them, and without a whisper of emotion they agreed to continue their employ and returned to their seats.

The pilot was also unimpressed and retired to the cockpit.

The only one who seemed altered was the stewardess, Grace. It became obvious that she and Horace had a "thing" that somehow she thought was significant. In spite of all the evidence of the reverend's infidelity, she had felt she was special. Of course, making his victims feel "special" was one of Horace Grande's gifts, and he slathered it on especially thick to sexual objects within his employ. He always enjoyed having *sure things* strategically situated, to ensure his considerable sexual appetite was easily sated. He flew often and Grace was absolutely essential. Of course, now that had changed. Horace had truly found the Lord and his heart was overflowing with remorse. Somehow, his tearful confessions to Grace did not receive the heartfelt forgiveness he longed for. He did receive a pitcher full of ice water, full in the face, and a sincere, "Fuck you, Horace," response from poor Gracie. She retired in tears to the back of the plane.

That left Charlie, Buzz, and Horace. And Buzz was the first to speak.

"Get used to it, Horace. It seems obvious you have been quite a dick. There is going to be a lot of folks looking for paybacks, now that you have lost your fangs."

"True enough, Buzz," replied the preacher. "I have it coming, too. I just hope I can dodge enough bullets to keep effective for the cause."

"We all have our weaknesses, Horace," replied Buzz. "Lord knows I have done some wicked things. A word like *sorry* just doesn't seem very big but, when it is meant from the heart, it's about the best we earthlings have. After all of my repentance, I have found a tiny bit of the bud gets the vibrations back in sync for a while, to allow me the peace to plan my better deeds."

Buzz took his ever-present pipe from his pocket and stuffed it with a very potent smelling bud. He lit it, took a deep puff, smiled with his eyes closed, then passed it with reverence to the repentant preacher. Grande looked at it skeptically, shrugged his shoulders, and took a mighty pull. Charlie and Buzz expected Horace to cough and choke like most novices, but the reverend simply closed his eyes and held it in. Slowly he released the smoke and gazed through half-closed eyes at Buzz. He smiled a sad smile and softly said, "I am afraid it is going to take a lot of this to clear my heart."

Buzz reached out and held his hand. "I know, brother ... and I can help you out with that."

Charlie, Buzz, and Horace sat at the table for the better part of an hour. Horace filled them in regarding procedure at the Vatican and what they could expect. He warned them that it would take a huge miracle from the plate to turn a ship as massive as the Catholic Church, and the pope was the living representative body of that church. Nothing gets to the church without first going through the current Pope Peter Paul Pious, and his actions as pope had proven him to be a strict follower of all things Catholic. There would be no changes while he was in charge. He even was making moves to return to a Latin service, much to the dismay of the great majority of his followers. That being said, from a distance the conversion of Horace Grande would have seemed impossible. Charlie was convinced the plate would come through. Horace and Buzz were not so sure.

Finally, the three were talked out. Horace went to the back of the plane to try and comfort Grace ... to try and explain. Charlie went to his seat and pulled out the plate. Buzz went to sit next to his old friends who had been working sleazy security for the Reverend Grande.

"Well ... Buzz, is it?" asked Justin. "This is the absolute last place I expected to run into you."

"Yeah, well you just never know, do you, Big Dog. I am a man with many surprises."

The three old acquaintances chatted for a while and it quickly became apparent that whatever history they had had, their paths today were very different. The two were hired guns. They couldn't care less about the plate, or if Grande was good or evil, or for Jesus Christ himself for that matter. They were hired muscle and Buzz knew better than anyone that they were very good at what they did. After a bit, Buzz left the two and wandered back to his seat. He tilted it back and closed his eyes. Those two were very dangerous, but as long as the pay was right ... and Buzz figured that Grande paid them very well indeed ... they would be dangerous for someone else. He hoped there would be no need for such men, but after his welcome to Reverend Grande's church, he could not be sure. If there was trouble, Buzz took comfort in the fact that Justin and Frank were there, and that these two were capable of doing the job they were paid to do. His mind began to relax and he drifted off to sleep.

Charlie was resting in his seat with the plate in his lap. A lot was going on in the World of Lost Gods and he tried to piece it all together in a way that made sense. It was not easy. Charlie finally did a mental shrug and concluded that it didn't matter. He had faith in Jesus, in the plate, and in the truth of his mission.

The plate was showing the army of the gentle Jew milling around and trying to come to terms with the rebirth of the Dark Angel. Charlie imagined correctly that they were considerably more concerned with events and what their future might bring. It seemed certain that would include a physical fight with Satan. Now *that* would keep you up at night.

Suddenly Diana yelled, "They're back!"

The crowd turned to see where she was looking and saw the trio rounding a curve on the little dirt road between here and there

The first thing the crowd noticed was that they were smiling. It would be hard to imagine one single act that might have lifted the entire army's spirits more effectively.

The three were swallowed by the throng. They stood mostly in silence, as for many this was the first time they had even seen the Christian God. He was surely smaller than most had thought but none the less impressive. That he was "complete" seemed obvious, and the halo was surely something.

Jesus looked around. The army had by this time swelled to several hundred. There were huge giants and tiny sprites. He looked around for Sing and Song, but did not see them. Truly, this would not be a place for his little friends. There were Gods that were half-animal and animals that were half-Gods. It was beyond anything the gentle human could have possibly dreamed could be true. They were all staring at him with a mixture of love and curiosity. The little carpenter was greatly moved. He understood the danger they were in and the risk they were taking for him. Tears filled his eyes. He lifted his head and simply said softly but clearly, "Thank you."

That seemed to break the spell, and pretty soon everyone was hugging and crying, and all were fortified in the knowledge that the army was now more or less complete. Mars, Neptune, and Diana came forward and expressed the need to fill in, and to be filled in. This seemed logical, so the six retired to a grassy spot off to one side, away from the godly clutter.

They explained how the army had evolved, and what they were thinking as a strategy in the battle sure to come. They explained to Jesus the strengths and weaknesses of their army and their plan, completely and honestly. It was plain to see that this, like every battle, would have to evolve on the battlefield. There would be no way to depend on the enemy's actions one way or another. They would clearly have to have plans A through Z.

Jesus told them of his travels and of Charlie and the plate. He told them of his experience with the Devil and of his own vulnerability and of Satan's. Gods are Gods after all, and a Gods' world is about as strange as anything in creation, so for much of Jesus's tale they simply nodded and understood. As for Charlie and his plate, however, this was beyond Godly odd. None could imagine what purpose this might serve, but all took some comfort in the fact that the little earthly army of three was on their side. It was agreed they must surely have a part to play.

When everyone was up to date on actions and realities, they rose from the grassy spot and began to introduce Jesus to his army. The little Christian God was keenly aware of everyone's danger and courage. He was moved by their sacrifice in fighting a fight that was, honestly, not theirs. Theye did not feel any animosity in spite of the fact that the followers of Jesus had most certainly thrown them from their Heaven. They, like Jesus, were grounded in love and goodness. He was extremely thankful and overwhelmingly proud to be a part of such an army. He was committed in his heart and mind to wield the power of love, to fight as well as he was able and to keep them as safe as possible.

On the other side of somewhere, the Dark Angel sat wrapped in his wings. His mind was running full out. His hate was tuned to a completely new, much more potent key. He, too, was completely committed ... but to something altogether different.

Chapter 50
– Satan's Revelation

*E*ven after the original expulsion from Heaven, Satan's fury had been less than at this moment. Yeah, he had been beaten. He had been bested along with his army and cast out of Heaven. It was a real bummer. But he was bested by the best. He was vanquished by the army and power of the God of All. This was different. While he had not been conquered, he had been reduced to feeling fear. This had never happened to him before. He did not believe he was capable of experiencing this feeling. This he felt was for inferior creatures. He, deep within himself, suspected that in the final confrontation with the God of All there might be some ... uncomfortable moments, but it would be when he was toe to toe battling for the control of all creation.

That he had experienced the searing agony at the hands of the puny Jew was beyond his comprehension.

That he had embarrassed himself in front of his army when he had squealed like a ... *human*, that he had shat himself and flopped on the ground, did not concern him. These lesser Gods were merely simple tools to achieve an objective. They had no value to the Evil One. His own army of demons on earth would maintain their positions of power when he was through with the God of All and these ... creatures would be free to suffer in Hell with the rest of humanity. Truly, how he appeared to them had no value.

But, he seethed. For an unknown time after his ... experience ... he was incapable or unwilling to even form words in his mind. There was only fury. It was beyond any hate even the Prince of Darkness had ever generated. It was an entity unto itself that resided within and without him. He stood apart and watched it swirl in malevolence around him. He centered at its core and allowed it to rotate around him like the whole of creation itself. He watched in awe at the purity and power of his own self. He was filled and refilled with the truth in his completeness and power in the incredible depth and finality of his weapon of hate, hate that existed externally even from the majesty of himself. It was like the *love* that the Jew had controlled while in his mind.

This revelation was new to the creature. His limitless pride and hubris allowed him to believe he was the source of all hate. That he alone created its awesome power. Now it occurred to him that he was not actually hate itself, but rather its master. You might think that this was in some way a disappointment to the Dark One, but you would be wrong. In an instant he knew he had far more power than the simple lies and deception, much more than lust and fear, so much more than pain and suffering .... Oh yes, so much more.

In his minds' eye, his confrontation with the God of All would have been like an All Star Wrestling match. He would have grabbed him and strangled him and crushed him with the weight of his hate. Truly his plan did not really go much further than that. He felt that with the many mistakes the God of All had made, it was obvious he was not infallible, and with this knowledge, Satan had lost his fear. He was sure he could beat him. He believed now he had only experienced the smallest portion of his own magnificence. In truth, the little Jew had taught him this. Jesus had not ripped at his flesh. He had not pounded on the matter of his mind. He had not tried to rip his mind to shreds. He had simply loved and now for the first time, Lucifer realized this would be how he would defeat the God of All. He could wield the same power.

He could simply *hate*.

Chapter 51
– The Pope

The private jet landed softly and smoothly at the Aeroporto di Roma Ciampino, just southeast of Rome. This was the airport preferred by Reverend Grande, and a sizeable detachment of well-dressed suck-ups were there to greet them.

In the past, the attention would have been devoured by Horace Grande, and obscene gratuities would have been slathered on the grovelers for their efforts, but those days were obviously gone. Grande was embarrassed by the attention and repulsed by the insincerity of the participants. The little group pushed by them in silence and quickly entered a waiting limousine.

Grande began, "I am sorry, my new friends, but I am afraid you will experience many things that reflect the excess and perversions of the life I have now left behind. I cannot change those things and cannot explain to all involved that I am no longer that man. As you might imagine, some will be thrilled at my transformation ... others will be furious. We will have to plan accordingly, and for our own safety at times keep the new me and our mission to ourselves. Please let me take the lead on this."

"You got it, Horace," said Buzz. "At the beginning this should be only for those that need to know. We will operate in *stealth* mode!"

"I agree," added Charlie. "This will be difficult enough without ruffling feathers unnecessarily."

The security staff was silent as they understood their responsibilities, regardless of the mission. They were, as always, ready for anything.

The limo pulled onto the Grande Raccordo Anulare, the GRA, that encircled Rome and headed northwest toward Vatican City. It was only about thirty miles from the airport to Holy Ground, and soon the luxury vehicle was pulling into a parking lot near the Passetto, the entrance at the south end of the complex.

Vatican City is only .17 square miles, and as such is the world's smallest independent state. It is about half buildings and half open lands, which are primarily lush, well-tended gardens. Approaching the complex, it was easy to feel the history held within.

As the small group neared the building, a serious looking man opened the door and held it as they entered. He was dressed in a blue uniform with a frilly white collar. He had white gloves and black boots, with a sporty black beret. Horace explained he was one of the elite Swiss Guard that was charged with the protection of the Holy Father.

They had been expected and were led down a massive hall to a small, by Vatican standards, office just off Saint Peter's Basilica. Judging by the size of the room and its lack of papal splendor, this was not the usual meeting place for the pope. Reverend Grande had personally spoken to Pope Peter Paul Pius and asked for a low profile meeting, with a minimum of scrutiny. The small contingency was led into the room by their Swiss escort. The door that closed behind them was flanked by two more of these elite, if mostly ceremonial, soldiers.

The pope was sitting to the rear of the room in a large, high-backed chair that had obviously been brought in for this meeting. It looked completely out of place in this otherwise spartan office. He was a wizened old man dressed in his white *zuchetto* or skull cap, and his white *mozetta*, which was a short, hooded cape. He accessorized with a large pectoral gold cross and red shoes. Horace Grande approached the Holy Father, fell on his knees and kissed the ring of the leader of the Catholic Church. The pope put his hands on his head, looked closely at each of his visitors and softly spoke, "My dear son, Horace, may God bless you and your company and may the Holy Mother keep you in the bosom of her love. You have asked me here with great urgency and I have responded. Please confess your sins, make clear your soul, and then express your heart's desire.

The reverend stood before the pope, looked around with a large smile, leaned over and spoke softly to the pontiff. "I have sinned, Father, as you well know. I am changed forever, however, and the Lord Jesus lives!"

"Well said, my son," ... began the shriveled old man...

"No, you don't understand, your holiness. He really does *live* .... This is no puffed-up dogma. This is no sideshow for the gullible. I have seen proof, and we are here today to show you as well."

"Do you think, sweet Horace, that the true voice of God needs proof that his manifestation on earth lives? You speak such foolishness to me, whose connection is indisputable and whose word is infallible."

Horace suddenly looked much more serious. "OK, Antonio (the pope's name before rising to pope-dom), time to cut the crap. I mean you no harm here, and we both know how this game is played. Remember it was me who removed obstacles which allowed you to rise to your present position. I will not, and need not, go through the list. We both know way too much about each other."

The pope's visage changed from one of gentle love and acceptance, to something between fear and hate. "Be very careful, Grande. You know all too well the power of the church, and you and your ... followers are now in *my* world!"

"OK, OK, calm down. As I said, we mean you no harm. In fact, we mean you and the church great joy. The Savior does live and is at this very minute preparing for a great battle with Satan himself. It is impossible to believe, but, your holiness, he is fighting alongside ancient Gods of the Greeks and Romans. I would not utter such insanities but for the fact that it is *undeniably true.*"

"You are insane, Grande, and I have had enough ... Guards, remove these fools and prepare my way back to the sanctuary."

The guards moved to do as the pontiff asked but hesitated when Frank, Justin, and Buzz stepped in their path. It was obvious this would not be easy and they knew such a confrontation would risk injury to Pope Peter Paul Pius.

Horace stepped forward. "No, no, no .... This is so unnecessary. Antonio, my brother from so long ago, I do not ask for anything that would endanger you or the church. Please allow us to show you what we have seen, and then you be the judge. When you have spent these few minutes, we will leave and you will be done with us. On this you have my word."

Even a man's word among thieves has value, so the ancient crust of a man elevated to splendor slowly nodded his head. "Proceed, but be quick about it. My time is precious and you have wasted enough of it."

"Come up here, Charlie," said Horace, "and bring the plate."

Charlie fished the plate out of his pack and set it on the pontiff's lap. He lifted it and looked at it with disbelief. He turned it over and looked at its well-worn surface. It could truly be nothing but as it appeared. It was an old pie plate.

"Is this some kind of a joke? Why would you bring this to me?" Suddenly he truly looked afraid. "I trusted you, Horace. You must ... there is no other ... do you ... mean me true harm?"

"No, sir," spoke Charlie. "I know it's hard to imagine, and believe me, I didn't believe my own eyes at first. I thought I had lost my mind. Not everyone can see the story, but you are holy and powerful and to you the plate has brought us. It must mean something. Please look into the surface of the plate."

The pope, wishing only to be done with this unpleasant episode, turned his gaze to the surface of the simple pie plate.

At first, there was nothing. It was just what he expected to see, a flat surface of an old pie plate. Then, the image began to appear. It swirled at first, then slowly came into focus. There was a large group of what looked like ancient Gods and Goddesses. At their center was a smallish man in white robes and sandals with what was unmistakably a golden halo. It wasn't just the picture he saw but the aura and feeling that emoted from the simple plate. His heart could not deny he was indeed looking at the foundation of his very church, the Messiah, the Savior, the Lord Jesus Christ himself. The pontiff gave out a little squeal and threw the plate with all of his might.

Now, this pope was certainly no Nolan Ryan, so the plate landed about ten feet away. Charlie picked it up and reset it on the Holy Father's lap. It was obvious to the group that their mission had been accomplished. The plate seemed to have the perfect message to deliver, a message that removed all doubt from the one who needed to be persuaded. The pope was obviously persuaded. He did, however, refuse to look back at the plate. He covered his eyes and whimpered. Slowly he controlled himself and simply said to Charlie, "Young man, would you please remove this thing from my lap?"

Charlie did as he was asked, and the group stood in silence around the seated pope. They knew that he knew that Jesus lived and now would surely help in their mission to tell the world. After a time the pope raised his head and spoke.

"There is nothing I can do for you," was all he said.

"You can't be serious!" said Horace. "Antonio, this means that we have another chance. We can move past the past, and this time get things right. Believe me, I am redeemed and you can be too!"

The little old pope looked even smaller and, if possible, older. He slowly nodded his head. "Yes, Horace, you are probably right. This could be a new beginning, not just for me, but for the entire holy Catholic Church. But this will not be. I will not let it be. The church is my life and family, and the life and family of millions of believers. Will they all stare into the plate at once and believe? Will there be a cloud that envelops the world, and in an instant all will change? I don't think so, and what would become of mother church? There will be great loss and suffering as in all great change in this world. With your birth comes our death and I will not allow it. The church exists perfectly without this new Jesus Christ. Our '*Jesus Christ*' has taken us two thousand years to perfect. Our Mother Mary, the virgin, has evolved as his equal and equal to God Almighty. It has taken TWO THOUSAND YEARS! We have all of the saints and Gods we need. Take your new truth and your old plate, and leave this place, but know this ... I, and through me the holy Catholic Church, will fight you for every inch of this world and for every soul upon it. Now leave this place, Horace Grande. Take your friends and that holy plate with you. I have more important things to do in service of the holy church. I thank you for showing me your new truth and am satisfied it will help me to prepare for the confrontation to come. Yes, thank you .... Now leave."

He waved his hand and the three Swiss Guards led the stunned missionaries out of the room and out of the Vatican. They climbed into their waiting limousine, drove out of the parking lot, and were gone.

Chapter 52
– Satan, Worse Than Ever?

𝒥t did not take long for Jesus to understand the strengths and weaknesses of his Olympian army. The largest obstacle was that of the Evil One himself. All others balanced out, but the Devil was the tipping point. Somehow, Jesus knew it was up to him to counter this. He knew in his heart that in a war he was no match for Lucifer. He could not possibly fight him power for power. He had already faced evil as was manifest in his earthly existence. It had nailed him to a cross and killed him dead. At that time those were only Satan's surrogates, this time it would be the creature himself. Jesus was not created for that kind of a battle. He would most surely lose.

It was easy to see that it would be up to others to fill the gap. The door at the end of creation was perhaps the most promising. Jesus felt strongly that the decision for the end of times would rest with the God of All, with no disrespect for Janus. If this was a battle God was creating, and if the end times were nigh ... so be it. Jesus would never support a plan that left humanity at the mercy of the Dark Angel ... never. The plan as envisioned was a good one. It held honor and hope. The warrior Gods were in place and all were ready. There was really nothing more to do but wait.

On the other side of somewhere, Satan was in a grand mood after his recent revelations. A grand mood for him was a mood honed to a razor's edge with hate and violence. He emerged from his golden cone, lifting his wings to the sky and flexing his muscles like a bodybuilder cubed.

His army was startled by his sudden emergence and fell to their knees in awe. The wicked aura that he emitted was blood red in color and heavily burdened in its unholy stench.

His army was not as focused as the army of the Christ, and after his display of weakness, they were somewhat less assured than they had been. It was true that the level of hate in the air had risen dramatically, and the feeling of power displayed by the Beast was many times greater than before, but many could not clear their minds of the image of the creature flat on its face, covered in its own shat. Oh yeah, he looked glorious now, but ...

Lucifer could feel their minds and it infuriated him. His new realization of power made him suspect he didn't need them at all. He was about to rip them all apart for sport, when a familiar *hiss* reached his ears.

"Great Lord...Mighty Omega, please ... a moment's counsel."

The monster's eyes slowly turned to the serpent. They were afire with an intense ruby glow. They pierced the serpent's defenses and froze his heart with icy fear. There was nothing like this in the snake's past. He had never felt such terror. It was pure. It had no words. It was nothing except the full force of the creature's hate. It was beyond words and the serpent writhed in pain, its eyes pleading for the mercy it knew its tormenter lacked. It was only time that saved it, if not from death then from insanity. Madness would have been the only escape from its hold ... probably not to a better place but to any other place.

The serpent fell to the ground with a sickening thump.

Beelzebub looked back on his quivering army and reconsidered their total destruction. But, he had time. He was complete in his new realization of power. He did not need anything and could possess everything. He looked again at his one-time lieutenant.

The snake was slowly regaining consciousness. It sat upon its coils with its massive head swaying back and forth. A stream of saliva drained from its gaping mouth. As it recalled its most recent descent into Hell, it bolted straight up in the air and screamed a shrill, silent, snake scream. When it landed, it made a break for the tall grass in a futile attempt at escape. The demon grabbed it by the tail and forced its face into its own. The snake's unseeing eyes were filled with terror. The Wicked One whispered in the serpent's ear ... "Calm yourself, fool. I am realized and without equal. I have one purpose and you may still be of value, or you would not exist. Speak to me now and make it *please me* ... you will not get a second chance."

The snake was ancient beyond memory. In its countless centuries, it had many times experienced things outside of its information. While this was terrible in its core, it was experience, and the snake folded it into its store of knowledge and centered itself.

"Please, master," began the snake, "I only wished to consult and to suggest, for your own glory. I only strive on your behalf, and while you were meditating, I have gathered information to your advantage. This information might alter your strategy and further solidify your guaranteed success."

Lucifer knew this to be a lie, as this was the Great Deceiver with no other purpose. But there was no other

256

creature more suitable to serve Satan than this one. Truth is truth, whether evil or good, and this was true. What it gleaned from the snake's ramblings was that it had information. That was true.

"Continue."

"I have been to your enemies' camp and know their thoughts. Hear me Wicked One as it will assure victory. Even for the God of All, in their story there is peril. I sensed your will was to destroy our pathetic army, as well you should, but wait for my story and for the battle. Will you listen to my meager message, Wicked One?"

"I do not need you or them any longer, serpent. I am realized and more powerful than even I supposed, but I will listen. Time has become nothing to me, and in this place it means even less."

The snake told his story of spying on the Army of the Good. He recounted many things that he heard and the methods they would use. The mighty Dark Prince nodded and heard what was said, but saw little of value and less to fear.

The snake finished his tale and the two stood. They walked and slithered through the Evil Army as they moaned and wailed and praised the God of Evil. When he passed Hades, he reached down and grabbed the loyal Fishbone by the neck. He smashed it between his two fists and turned it instantly to mush. It did not have time for a single "Slop, slop," and it did not have the ability to regenerate. Hades stood in horror with a generous splatter of his loyal friend dripping down his face. The Devil did not even look down.

Satan was satisfied. He had heard his spy's tale and saw wisdom in letting the miserable little Gods suffer for him. He still had only one purpose, and that was to get before the God of All, and the little Jew was the key. One of his many new revelations was that the carpenter too had great power. He had given him the only physical pain, outside of Heaven, he had ever known. If it was not necessary, he had decided he would not even touch the Prince of Peace. Let these fools do it. He would simply wait for his opening and spring through to face the God of All for the confrontation that had been building since God's creation of man. He thought with a wicked smile, "My will be done!"

The serpent slithered behind the giant Demon. It had said its piece, and was content with its result. Had it told the Beast everything? It had not. The snake had counted on Satan's arrogance to keep him from a solid search for truth. Satan did not believe after his show of new power that the serpent would hide anything, and if it did, the Demon believed in its continued arrogance that it did not matter. The truth is the truth, however, and the truth is, the serpent was created for deception and deceive it would. In truth, all it did was keep a closed door ... closed.

For both sides, the good and the bad, the left and the right, the up and the down, in this place of Lost Gods there was nothing much left to do. There would be a moment when time and purpose conspired, and the battle would begin ... no one doubted this, but for now, the only action they could take was to wait.

Chapter 53
– Sister Mary and a Grand Plan

It was quiet in the limo as the tiny earthly Army of the Lost Gods collected their thoughts. They had thought the truth of the plate would move the Vatican to their side, and the entire world would prepare for the battle to come and its aftermath. To be rejected so entirely was a surprise ... at least to most of them.

Upon returning to Aeroporto di Roma Campino they found to their dismay the corporate jet was completely wrapped up in red tape. It seems Horace did not just stiff a few baggage handlers when they landed, but also a complement of airport management and local politicians. His disinterest had earned them what was evolving into a bureaucratic nightmare.

After lengthy conversations between Horace and the local government, and after copious amounts of local tender was dispersed, it seemed a path was greased to their escape. What would have taken days or weeks to manage for a normal mortal, Horace cleaned up in a couple of hours. As they were preparing for their final boarding, a tiny Fiat drove onto the tarmac and a small woman exited. She was dressed in a simple black dress with a white collar. The simple white headscarf and the golden cross on her chest were the only indications that this was a nun, and she walked to the small group with purpose.

"It is said that my Jesus lives ... I have come to join you, and to do what I may simply do to help. I have felt in my soul that this time was near, and I am ready. My name is

Sister Mary Madeline, and I am responsible for the activities of all men and women in religious orders ... worldwide. I think I may be of some assistance."

The little group of holy warriors stared at the tiny nun.

Buzz spoke. "The plate be praised!"

The group huddled around the nun with smiles and hugs. Charlie said to her with a grin, "There is so much to tell ... we are so glad you have come."

They all climbed up to the church's Lear jet, which was finally cleared for takeoff. The fact was not lost on anyone that if they had not been delayed, they would have left without Sister Mary. They felt the miracle, and were buoyed in the certainty of their mission and direction.

"I should have known," said Horace, when they had returned to the jet's conference table. "It should have been obvious to me. I guess I was so excited about my second chance and a true new religion that I would actually be a part of. I guess I wasn't thinking. I have known Antonio for thirty years. I have known him for years before he was made pope. He, for all his personal excesses, is truly married to the church, not to Jesus or Mary or the God of All, but to the church. It is all he has ever known, and to just walk in and say ... Guess what, Antonio ... you got it all wrong. Close the church and walk into the sun ... Well, that would be a bit much. Perhaps he will truly pray. Perhaps the God of All will move him. I should have known it would be more than a street minister, an old hippy and a repentant, sinning, huckster preacher could accomplish. But now we have Sister Mary. It is not necessary to turn our backs on our Catholic family, and the war that Antonio will wage will be blunted by the good sister's presence. Antonio, even as the pope, is only one man, and like Jesus said, 'My Father's house has many rooms.' Now, let's visit a few more rooms and see what we can find. I have a feeling that a rabbi or perhaps the Dali Lama might be more receptive. I am confident we can bring some more TV preachers to the table."

"What I propose is a worldwide, multi-faith conference. We'll do it big ... Vegas! We'll invite representatives from every religion in the world. We'll buy broadcast rights and blast it out on TV all over the world. We'll create a website and use every digital media available. Believe me friends, this is what I do ... and, I do it well!"

Charlie was sitting up against a window with the plate in his lap, with Sister Mary Madeline at his side. He was going over the history as he knew it, and recounting the amazing adventure they had been on. The little nun was mesmerized, and took time to silently pray and to lovingly kiss the cross that hung around her neck. Her unbridled joy mixed with fear and apprehension for the little Savior's battle to come was apparent. After a time, Charlie looked up at the little meeting and said, "Well, brothers, we better do this quickly. It looks like most of the pieces for the battle beyond are in place. It could begin at any time and if I am not mistaken, whatever is going to happen will happen *fast*. Whatever opportunity we might have to play a part will be over just as quickly."

"I hear you, bud," said Buzz. "I don't believe the plate brought us this far to fail. How long do you think it will take to put this together, Horace?"

261

"Well, I would guess at least a month."

The entire party looked at him with disappointment.

"Well ... I have an entire empire trained at these things, and if I push and shove and we all pray like crazy ... maybe ... two weeks."

"So be it," said Charlie. "Who knows how time works in the place where this battle will rage. It is surely very different from here. We will move full speed ahead, with a focused purpose and a joyful heart. And above all, we will have faith!"

"Amen!" said their newest member, the gentle Sister Mary Madeline.

Chapter 54
– Viva Las Vegas

Charlie was truly amazed at the amount of <u>things</u> that could be accomplished in a very short time. It had been a week since the church jet had landed back in Columbus, and the little team turned into a whirlwind of action.

While Las Vegas wouldn't be the choice for your average spiritual retreat, the size and timing and the good reverend's connections made it one of only a few possible locations.

Once again, Buzz amazed Charlie by being the most efficient, stoned-out hippy he had ever seen. He made calls and pulled in favors. It was left to him to organize the physical event including hotels, the event center, meals, and transportation. The Reverend Grande put all of the sizable staff of the Only True Path to Heaven church at Buzz's command. But the incredible empire that was Buzz's own URSU materialized with the most resources. It seemed one of the enterprises was a huge fleet of mobile taco trucks that catered to parking lot cuisine outside blue-collar factories. This crew provided not only motivated loyal labor, but fantastic cooks and kitchen help.

One of the first things Buzz did was to put in a call to the Fly Away Café and ask the lovely Mandy if she would manage the morning fare for the gathering. The combination of a trip to Vegas and another chance to see Charlie (whom she had been quietly dreaming of) made the choice easy. She was also thrilled when Buzz sent his legendary jet and the Blaster to pick her up.

Horace had a very strong contact at the Mandalay Bay Casino on the Strip, so that was the choice for the evolving conference. It was and is a site built for anything ... anything with money that is, and a beautiful destination if you're going to Las Vegas.

All of Charlie's labor at URSU worked through labor unions, so the friction that might have been was quickly resolved with the existing Vegas unions. For whatever impressions the powers of America have created regarding labor unions, when the rubber hits the road there is not another group of individuals that can operate with such blinding efficiency. The South Sea Ballroom at the Mandalay was *Ground Zero* and this man/woman machine went to work. Lovely tables and decorations were set up, all with a South Seas motif. Huge flat screens were attached to the walls with every seat a great seat, and at the center of the room was raised seating for the speakers and their guests. Buzz was amazed at Horace's contacts, and Horace was amazed at the old hippie's talents. Charlie was amazed at everything.

Horace and Sister Mary Madeline were responsible for gathering the guests. Their target number was around two thousand. The idea was to try to bring folks with authority in the religious community, and to expose them to the plate. What would happen after that was up to the plate, and surely for the little group of believers, a matter of faith. The message was, "Things have changed, Jesus is alive, and there is proof ... all creation is in peril and all persons of good will are needed. All of your expenses will be paid."

While the message was loud and clear, the free trip to Las Vegas probably clinched the deal. Horace Grande seemed to know every popular, visible holy person in the world. He also was a gifted pitchman and preacher in his own right. That he had created the largest born-again church in America was evidence. Now, he had a genuine mission in the service of the Lord, and his passion was redoubled. The leaders of churches of all descriptions bowed to the preacher's persuasion, and began their pilgrimage to Vegas and Mandalay Bay.

Sister Mary Madeline was also on the march. Her job with the Catholic Church made her the most powerful woman in the church, with an outreach that covered the globe. She knew the meek and the powerful, and leaders of many faiths. A nun's message of love and service, and her many years in that practice gave her credibility with the truly righteous that the good Reverend Grande lacked. If some wavered for Grande, he sent Sister Mary Madeline to them. There were very few that refused this truly righteous little nun.

Within the Catholic Church she had some problems. The pope was not one to sit by and watch the work of fifteen hundred years crumble, so he promptly excommunicated the gentle nun. This was difficult for her, as she loved the church almost as much as she loved the Lord, but that was almost. She knew the conflicting actions of her church and the patchwork history of good and evil. She also knew of the many mistakes within the church and of its inability to admit error. She focused on her overpowering love for the Lord and marshaled on. The male hierarchy of the church basically ignored her. She tried to witness to them. She asked them to look into their hearts, but few responded. A very small number truly heard her and made their way to the conference. They too were excommunicated.

The females with authority within the church reacted much differently. Their hearts were more open and they heard the message of the little nun. They made their way en mass to the Mandalay Bay ... to the promise of a living Savior. They were also all excommunicated.

The word was beginning to get out to the general public, and small groups of folks from Key West to Fairbanks were beginning to slowly make their way to the deserts of Nevada.

Chapter 55
– More Mandy

Charlie was there when the Blaster landed Buzz's Grateful Dead Gulfstream at the North Las Vegas Airport. Oh sure, it would have been closer to touch down at McCarran Airport, but a low profile was important to the Blaster and to Buzz as well, so the less traveled NLV was chosen.

There had only been the one meeting for Mandy and Charlie, so Charlie was plenty nervous when Mandy stepped off the plane. That one and only meeting at the tiny Fly Away Café in California was electric for Charlie, but he was far from certain Mandy had felt the same, or would even remember him for that matter. Mandy did not know that Charlie would be there to get her, so when she saw him, her face lit up like a casino with a grin from lovely little ear to lovely little ear. Charlie beamed back with relief, and took her hand to help her down the steps from the jet. He had come in one of the church's limos at Horace's insistence, so the chauffer opened the rear door and Mandy slid in. Charlie went back for her bags, which the Blaster struggled with coming down the narrow steps.

"Well, she sure has plenty of gear," mumbled the Blaster. "It looks like she intends to hang around for a while."

"Well, I sure hope so," replied Charlie. "Are you coming into Vegas, Blaster? You must have a vice or two."

"No thanks, Preacher …. I have all the vice I need right up there. It's only filled with noise of my making and I only have to speak with myself ... whose company I can stand. No, you go into the belly of the beast ... I have had all I need of that. I will have this baby gassed up and pointing up the runway, should we need to make an escape. If you do come to the plane and you ain't with Buzz, first rap on the bottom of the plane and shout out. It'd be better for both of us if you did."

"OK. Thanks, Blaster, I will."

Charlie ran around to the far side of the limo where the chauffer was holding open the door. He was swallowed by the shiny black whale, which slowly pulled away from the plane and headed toward Las Vegas.

Blaster walked back up the stairs, itchin' his ass and mumbling. He took one last look at the retreating limo and ran his hand through his chaotic jungle of hair. He shook his head and turned to close the door with one comment:

"Fuck'n'A."

So now Charlie and Mandy were, for all intents and purposes, alone with each other in the rear of the limo. There was a tinted glass partition between the driver and the passengers. This was essential in the reverend's past, when what he said and with whom he was speaking, were strictly classified. The driver was ex-CIA as were most of Grande's personal employees, but secrecy and evil deeds were conjoined twins, and even his close staff had only need-to-know status. There was a phone for necessary communication between driver and passengers. There was no need for that phone now.

"I am so glad you are here, Mandy," said Charlie. "I have been swallowed by a world and events that are light-years beyond belief, but every day at some time or another, I found myself thinking about you ... and no matter how bad those moments were, that thinking of you made me feel a little better."

"That is so sweet, Charlie Pilgrim. You certainly are a charmer." Mandy sat still, a ways from Charlie with her arms folded across her not at all small but not too big bosoms. Not that Charlie noticed. (He did.) As smitten as she was, she was not a girl at this point and certainly not ready to jump off the pier into any man's arms. She wilted a little under Charlie's bashful stare, so began conversation that was of the less dangerous kind.

"So, do you know what my responsibilities are for this party? This is way beyond anything I have done, but I will not let you and Buzz down. I will work my ass ... er ... butt ... er tail off!"

"I am sure you will, Mandy. This is a big deal but I am sure you will be excellent at it. I don't know the spec_fics, but we will have about two thousand guests. You will be responsible for the breakfast meal and for making sure there are donuts, sweets, and coffee at all times."

"Two... thousand... people! Are you out of your mind? I start to fumble when I have eight or nine people stacked up in my station at the café!"

"Relax, Mandy, you will only have to manage Buzz's crew, who are all professionals accustomed to this type of affair. Quite honestly, you will be part of the small group of us that are putting this thing together. While there will be times when you will be needed and your talents will be tested, you are here because I really wanted you to be here and Buzz knew you had what it is going to take ... and, also, he thought it would be cool. Trust trumps experience in this one, Mandy, and we need a core of folks that we can turn our backs on. Quite honestly, none of us knows what we are doing or what is going to happen. We are servants of the plate, and the world of Gods it represents."

"Plate? ... world of Gods? Charlie, I know this is important, and I know Buzz well enough to know he isn't nuts ... well, not too nuts ... but I need some explanation."

"Oh, Blaster didn't tell you anything?"

"He put his headphones on and we said exactly nothing. He is not exactly a social butterfly."

"No, I guess not. I am sorry to dump this on you, and I would rather just kind of court you, but you will see this is beyond us. God willing, there will be time. First things first .... I have something to show you."

Charlie pulled the plate out of his ever present backpack.

"Can you see anything in the plate?"

"No, not really ... sorry, Charlie."

Charlie and Mandy pulled into the Mandalay Bay with a whisper in the large, black limo. Employees rushed to the vehicle looking for some little thing to do that would earn them a generous tip from the obviously well-heeled occupants. Charlie, at this point, had no money whatsoever. Buzz seemed to always have a roll of bills and it is certain Horace was well used to spreading the wealth, but Charlie hadn't tipped since his days at the mega-church in Seattle. It took him a bit by surprise. Fortunately, the chauffer was used to occupants that could not be bothered with lesser humans, and generously took care of the folks with their hands out. Charlie and Mandy escaped into the casino hotel.

While two thousand guests were a huge number of folks for Mandy, it was small by mega casino standards. Folks were checking in at the long desk, and behind them gamblers were pulling slots that rang like reindeer bells at Christmas. Charlie led Mandy to the desk, and she checked into her room. She was shaken and thrilled at the same time over the story Charlie had told her. While she could not see anything in the pie plate, it had begun to cast off an aura of feeling that could not be denied. That, combined with the story, was enough to convince the most skeptical observer. Mandy was not skeptical. She could not deny the huge event that was evolving. She was thrilled, and secretly very proud of her gentle suitor.

When she had checked in, Charlie carried her bags to her room and stopped at the door. "After you have freshened up, find your way to the South Seas Ballroom on the third floor. We can see how things are going and take it from there."

"OK, Charlie ... and Charlie ... thanks for coming to get me." She leaned over and kissed him quickly on the lips.

Charlie smiled a big smile and wandered down the hall.

The South Seas Ballroom was a flurry of activity. Union workers were buzzing in and out with wiring, carpets, tables, and boxes of every description. They seemed to be a picture of efficiency. From across the room Charlie could see Buzz, surrounded by a group of much better groomed business people. In this impressive group of professionals, it was still easy to see who was in charge. Buzz was responding to a question regarding communications when Charlie arrived on the scene.

"Look, Bill, you are the techno-genius, that's why I love you. Let's be prepared for anything. We don't know at this time how this is going to play out. Create a website, start a blog, do it all ... we need to be wired for anything."

"No problem, Buzz ... naturally to be prepared for 'anything' will be pricey. I know, I know, money is not a problem, but I am just say'n'."

Buzz noticed Charlie standing respectfully outside of the little group.

"Hey, Charlie ... come on over here. I want you to meet some people." Buzz introduced his senior management team at URSU. Each of these individuals had impressive titles with impressive histories. It was obvious Buzz hired only the best. After introductions the team dispersed and went to work. Buzz and Charlie walked to one side of the room and sat in a couple of gray folding chairs.

Buzz began, "Any news from the plate, Charlie?"

"Not a thing, the plate is ... silent. I think that is good news from our position, and honestly, I have this feeling that whatever is going to happen over there is ... waiting for us."

"Well, we are peddling as fast as we can. I just got off the phone with Horace and he is doing better than we could have hoped. The honest preachers seem to be genuinely inspired, and the rascals love the idea of a free trip to Vegas. Seems like this project has something for everyone."

"Have you heard anything from Sister Mary?" asked Charlie.

"Not a word *amigo*, but I am sure she is knocking 'em down. I am stoked on that little nun. Hey, did you find Mandy? Did you rekindle the magic?"

"Yeah, the Blaster delivered on time and well. I surely do feel some magic ... er ... a lot of magic. I have trouble talking to her with my heart in my mouth. I just don't want to blow it."

"Not a chance, Charlie. You are just too much, Charlie, to wander too far off track. Mandy is a sucker for the real thing and you more than fit the bill. Relax my brother and enjoy the ride!"

Mandy took that moment to appear and the subject changed.

"Let me give you two the tour and get your feelings about the direction we are taking," said Buzz.

He showed the two the evolving room, complete with controlled local Wi-Fi and multiple huge flat screen monitors. They were being wired for computers, Internet, and cable with every technical advantage possible. They really had no idea what was to happen but were convinced in the correctness of their direction. It was faith and it was palpable. The tables were to be large and round, with each seat to have a keyboard with access to the monitors. This would allow every participant to have a voice in the ever-changing realities.

"I have no idea where this is going," said Charlie, "but I feel in my heart that this meeting will be the time when the message of the plate will be universally realized. How the plate handles this I cannot say. Without a doubt, being prepared is the key. You are more than amazing, Buzz."

"Yeah," piped up Mandy, "who knew?"

"My mama," said Buzz with a grin. "Now, let's try and look at seating strategy. I think you can be a big help on this one, Mandy."

They walked to the center of the room where a big table sat, and plopped down in front of a large seating chart. They began to figure out some kind of a plan.

In the rest of America, little bands of people were getting larger and they were all headed for the desert. There was a powerful feeling on earth and the word was getting out. Jesus had had his second coming ... he just didn't come *here*.

Chapter 56
– More Preparations

Sister Mary Madeline had found herself a small office for hotel guests and was contacting holy people from every religion in the world. Her story, even as strange as it was, seemed to resonate with Christians and Jews all over the world. Most had known her personally or if only by reputation and they knew she was a very dedicated woman of God. To some she made her plea personal and to that, few could refuse. The women of the Catholic Church as said before were more receptive. While most of the men were of the church, most of the women were of the people, and their practice was much closer to the practices of the gentle Savior himself. The gentle sister kept her message simple, with really no detail. Jesus was alive and a great battle was brewing. All who loved him would be needed.

Other religions seemed to be immune to the power of the plate. It had to be recognized that without some holy spirit flowing from the story, the story itself was, well, ridiculous. The Gods of Olympus real and alive, and fighting with the King of the Jews? The words fell off them like water off wax. In this the gentle sister was dismayed and prayed with all her might that they too could hear the new message. It was of no use, however, so she directed her energies elsewhere.

Jews and Christians of power were making their way to America's center of sin. From all over the world they came. The driving hope was that they would hear the message of the plate and bring the news back to the world. The list tallied around two thousand invited, combining Sister Mary Madeline's folks and the Reverend Grande's group. After rejection by most of the world's religions, the number settled around eight hundred. Their invitations became public quickly, however, with mass media and the Internet, and the story began to spread. The message of hope and peril resonated with the Judeo-Christian masses and their interest grew. If folks had the means or were close enough, they began to make their way to Vegas. Others scanned the net for information. It wasn't words, however, that seemed to have power, but the spirit that possessed and persuaded.

Mary finished her calls and checked her final box. Even the Dali Lama, whom she loved and respected, rejected her message. He listened respectfully and suggested that love in all forms was valid, and she should probably take some time off. She did not understand, but there was so much of this that was beyond human understanding. She made her way to the South Seas Ballroom to find the rest of the gang and to report. In many ways, she felt she had failed.

"Don't even think that way, little sister," said Buzz. "So much of this is beyond us. We are just simple tools for whatever power drives the plate. We are simply doing the work. We have never had a single instruction ... never one in *words*, anyway ... we simply put a foot out and away we go. I totally believe we are a world of one people ... the differences are all an illusion. I believe that as strongly as I believe in the plate, but I can tell you this .... Those of us who truly believe that are like a flea on the ass of an elephant. Talking to most folks is like talking to an entirely different creature. Yes is no, and black is white .... When the details get too much for me, I just disappear into a cloud of the righteous bud and flow with the universe. Why there are such differences, I don't need to know. For now, the plate tells us what we need to know. Do what you can and keep pressing forward. If I have faith in anything, I have faith that when the dust settles, no one will be left behind. Not one single person.

Sister Mary Madeline smiled at the aging hippy. "Thanks, Buzz, I am sure you are right ... It's just this is so important ... I do not understand."

Buzz pulled a small pipe out of his pocket and quickly fired it up. He was so good at this that a person five feet away would never notice or even smell anything. He looked deeply into the sister's eyes and smiled. He held out a closed hand, in offering to the gentle nun.

Sister Mary smiled back and softly said, "Thank you, Buzz, for your holy offering, but I have my own that also packs a punch!" She held up her rosary and gently kissed it.

"Go with the flow, sweet sister," whispered Buzz. "Go with the flow."

Chapter 57
– To Vegas from All Directions

*T*he strategy for the launch of this program was to not really tell anyone very much. There was a connection to Jesus and a battle with Satan was imminent. It would happen in another place but "technology" would perhaps let us participate. Without the power of the plate no one in their right mind would believe such a thing, but a growing energy presence was undeniable. They all believed something was happening.

The truly righteous simply gathered in small groups to discuss the possibilities and to pray. Many of the Reverend Grande's guests simply gambled or availed themselves of the many other diversions available to them in Las Vegas. Their numbers swelled and the South Seas Ballroom transformed.

Aside from the invited guests, others began to pack the Mandalay. Soon every room was full, in fact, every room on the Strip was full, and hotels in Old Town and elsewhere were beginning to reach their limits. Vegas can get that way, so it was a while before folks began to ask themselves, "What the heck is going on?" Most of the folks that came had a simple story with no details, and a vague notion they needed to be there.

Another group of folks were also making themselves visible. People without the resources to spend on a hotel room, but felt the pull, began to appear in mass on the streets of Las Vegas. Soup kitchens and housing for the poor were beginning to reach capacity. People in authority were beginning to notice.

Vegas being Vegas, there was no shortage of hucksters willing to claim responsibility for the amassing of the masses. There were fortunetellers, magicians, and the simply insane that walked the streets telling tales and claiming claims, in an attempt to fleece the already terminally fleeced. In truth, they made little headway. The crowd was focused on something very real just over the horizon and had little time for flimflam.

These folks did catch the attention of the local authorities that were desperately trying to make sense of what was happening in their town. They held few answers, but the mumblings of the masses, and following the obvious, led them eventually to the Mandalay Bay and a small convention on the third floor.

Horace, Charlie, Buzz, and Sister Mary were at the seating table putting the finishing touches on the who-goes-with-who project, when the mayor of Las Vegas and the chief of police walked up to the table.

"Can someone tell me who is in charge here?" asked Mayor Jim Dodge.

The little group looked up to see a tall, thin, extremely handsome man who was the mayor of Las Vegas. He was flanked by a shorter, somewhat husky man in a rumpled suit, who scanned the room with his eyes and seemed ready for anything. They were visually complete opposites, but had come with a singular purpose: they wanted to know what was going on.

"Well, who is exactly in charge would be difficult to explain, but my name is Charlie Pilgrim and I will help you all I can." Charlie made introductions around and the mayor continued:

"Well, Charlie Pilgrim, it seems you have created quite a ruckus in a town that was created for ruckus. Can you let us know what is going on? What are all of these folks coming to town for? We are not here to discourage your choice of Las Vegas for your 'event' but, we are beginning to have some issues with managing things that we don't understand. We have several thousand new homeless folks in town, and it appears there are thousands more on their way. Whatever their reasons are, this seems to be tied to your event here. How about helping me out some with this, Charlie?"

"Well, Mayor, I can say in all honestly we have had nothing to do with the folks outside. I also have heard that almost every room in town is filled with good paying customers. Something slightly mysterious with that too, wouldn't you say? The truth of the matter is, we are having a spiritual gathering here, and I have to imagine it's the *spirit* in *spiritual* that is bringing these people here. Our meeting is set for tomorrow, and is scheduled for one day. After that time, I will not promise that things will be back to normal, but I would guess the folks following our efforts will be leaving town."

Buzz joined in, "Look, Mayor, from what I can see, these are simple, honest folks and I would bet there is very little additional crime going on. With the windfall of money that has hit this town, I imagine you could afford to take care of the extra homeless folks for a couple of days."

Charlie continued, "We are wrapping up the majority of our setup, so we can add some manpower to your efforts. What do you say, Mayor?"

Charlie stuck out his hand.

280

The mayor looked at the chief ... "What do you think?"

The chief of police made a small nod.

He took Charlie's hand. "Very well, folks ... then it is done. Send your people to the courthouse and we'll organize from there."

Chapter 58
– Charlie and Mandy's First Date

*A*ll of the setup was complete for whatever was in store from the plate.

The tables were set, the electronics were in place and every guest had a table assigned. The folks without a place to stay had been made comfortable in tents hastily erected by the city, with help from URSU. The Mandalay was generous in allowing the large majority to occupy the green spaces around the complex.

For a few short hours, the small band of believers could relax. They had done all that they were able.

Charlie took this opportunity to ask Mandy for a date. They had enjoyed cold pizza while putting on the finishing touches, so Charlie simply asked her to join him for a drink. This was Vegas, and it also was their first date, so they made their way to the sixty-fourth floor and the Mix Lounge.

As they entered the bar they were assaulted by pinks and purples. The low light had all the appeal of a cross-dresser's finest. It was so over-the-top Vegas, and the view was amazing. They settled at a small, round, white table by a window that screamed *vertigo*.

It seemed that all the help at the hotel knew who they were as the word was out regarding the mysterious attraction of the third floor. Their service was prompt and the drinks were complimentary.

"If there is anything we can do, please just look my way," said the manager. "We are having the best week at the hotel that anyone can remember, so my bar, tonight, belongs to you."

Buzz had given Charlie cash for stuff, so he offered the manager a twenty. "No, no sir. As I said, your money is not needed here."

Charlie nodded his thanks and Mandy just smiled and looked at her hands folded on the table. Charlie ordered a light beer and Mandy went for a Sloe Gin Fizz. The beer came in a stemmed goblet with a golden rim and the Fizz came long and tall with etchings of palm trees in the glass.

"Boy, you really know how to treat a girl, Charlie Pilgrim!" said Mandy.

At his first church and in his first marriage he had had some experience with the excesses reserved for the very wealthy. Mandy, on the other hand, was blue collar through and through. Oh, she had had some fancy dates, but not enough to get real comfortable there, and certainly not recently. She lifted her glass.

"Bottoms up, cowboy."

Charlie clinked glasses with her and sipped his beer. Mandy took a sip and they both sat in awkward silence.

Mandy was the first to speak. "Geez, Charlie, you would think we had never been on a date before. What is it about you that makes me feel like I'm fourteen again and scared of my own shadow?"

"I'm not sure," replied Charlie, "but I've got it, too. It's ridiculous. I think if I can speak for myself that I now believe in *love at first sight*. When I looked into your eyes at the café, I felt weak all over. Now, I'm no playboy, but I have been around, and I can say in all truth I never felt that before.

I think I am nervous because I really want you to like me, too. I might feel a bit too ... desperate."

Mandy reached over and took Charlie's hand. "I think you just said exactly what I am feeling, too. I was no tramp, but I have been to a dance or two and you make me feel ... well, it's kind of corny but .... it's like I have finally come home after being lost a long time. I am just going to come right out and say it. I think I might love you, Charlie Pilgrim. There, it's said. Whatever happens tomorrow or the day after that, I don't want to waste a single moment. This may be all the time we have and I want it to be with you."

Mandy started to softly cry and Charlie realized she was not just in love, but also very scared.

"Please know I feel the same way, Mandy. You can feel it and by now you know, when it comes to women, I am not exactly a *sweet talker*. If nothing else, I am an honest man and I mean exactly what I say. I also believe this, truth and love conquers all. There is no Devil that can stand up to the force of it. The God of All would never let Satan devour the earth ... NEVER! I am going to spend a good long life making you happy and in being happy. I think this is the *real thing*, and why we might even have to have a kid or two."

"Geez, Charlie, I am no spring chicken. If you want kids we are going to have to get to it!"

Charlie was smiling about as happy as he could smile, and so was Mandy. They held hands and looked more into each other's eyes than out the window. The beautiful view was out there still and the glass was a two-way mirror that reflected just how really good life can be. After two drinks and small talk, they left the bar hand in hand. They went

284

down the hall, and where they went after that was their business alone.

Chapter 59
– War

$\mathcal{T}$here was no turn in the road. There was no opening door or window. What happened in the world so far from here was a complete shift of terrain. One minute both armies were simply waiting, the next they were on opposite sides of a great plain. There were hills on each side with each army poised and prepared. They went instantly from sitting on the ground unarmed, to being poised in formation, in full armor. Each position was correct for the battle plans that had evolved. Even for Gods, this was startling.

There was one difference in the armies. Hades was standing next to his brother, Poseidon. He had had enough of the Wicked One and its cruelty, even to its own. He saw no upside there. Both Gods smiled grimly at each other, then turned to face an enemy they both greatly feared.

Jesus had agreed to stay at the rear. He was the unknown factor, and although it was difficult for him to allow others to suffer for him, he understood that they were, in fact, immortal and if they could somehow defeat the Beast, this might avert a confrontation of ... well ... biblical proportions.

The serpent and the Devil were at the back of their army on a small rise with a complete view of the battlefield. The snake *hissed* loudly and the Beast whispered, "Finally."

At about four a.m., the plate began to glow. Charlie and Mandy were in deep sleep and did not notice the change. After a few minutes of unresponsive glowing, the plate began to ring like a cheap alarm clock. Both Charlie and Mandy sprang out of bed looking in vain for the erupting timepiece.

Finally, they followed the noise to the still glowing backpack. Charlie pulled it out and looked at the scene it displayed. He looked at Mandy with a mixture of fright and resolve ... "It's started," was all he said. They both dressed quickly and made it to the ballroom to alert and mobilize.

When they arrived at Mission Central, there was already a small group of believers in attendance. Buzz was there sitting in a gray folding chair, feet up on a round table, staring up at a big flat screen that had somehow replicated the scene from the plate. The two armies were still on the two hills preparing for the confrontation, which would obviously be soon. Sister Mary was on her cell phone making calls to gather the invited. Reverend Grande was doing the same. They both nodded as the couple walked in and continued with their business. Buzz jumped up and greeted the two.

"My room alarm took off at about four a.m. though I didn't set it, so I figured something was rocking. Same happened to Sister Mary and Horace and we landed here about the same time. Looks like your plate has gone public." Buzz pointed to the flat screen, "I am told that media all over is showing the same thing. Online, broadcast TV, cable, it's all the same. I wasn't sure how this was going to roll, but it looks like the plate knew what it was doing. Nothing left for us to do except to sit back and relax." With that, he pulled out his ever-present pipe and took a long pull. He slowly let the smoke wrap around his head and muttered, "Oh, mama."

In minutes, the room began to fill and in very little time, every table was occupied with guests of every description, all of whom stared at the flat screens and the story unfolding.

Mandy and her crew had set to work so every table had hot coffee and pastries. The entire room was a controlled bustle. While, to an outside observer, the picture on the monitors could have been any movie, to the people there it was so much more than the image displayed. There was an overwhelming feeling that turned the image into something entirely different. There was not a soul involved who did not believe completely that what they were watching was real, and its outcome would dramatically change the world. Not one person doubted. Every soul jumped from their seat when the image suddenly changed, and the War at the End of the World began.

A wave of evil descended from the dark army led by Libitina, the Goddess of Death. Her position was more symbolic than powerful because these Gods had never known the possibility of death. They had never known an enemy like the Dark Angel, either, so this new possibility was, in their minds, very real. She was followed closely by Tempest, the Goddess of Storms and Fury, casting wind and thunderbolts. Vulcan, the God of Fire, was at her side blasting streams of flaming destruction, rolling flames that engulfed the Army of the Righteous. The defending warriors stooped behind their massive shields.

Pietus, the Goddess of Duty, flung herself over the all too human Jesus and took the brunt of the blast. The pain of her burning flesh must have been excruciating, but she said not a word and helped the stunned Jesus to his feet. In moments, her body was restored, and she returned her attention to the battle.

Mars led the charge behind his shield to meet the enemy in the center of the plain. This would be the line of protection and he was determined they would not give an inch. He collided with Vulcan, knocking him to the ground, and smothered his fire. Before the Fire God could regain his feet, he swung his mighty sword and cut Vulcan in half, from the top of his head to his groin. Mars lifted one bloody half of the Fire God over his head and threw it with all his might to the rear of the Army of Good. The second half would have a difficult time uniting through this battle line.

Fortuna, the Goddess of Fortune, wrapped her angelic arms around Libitina, and made certain that death was once again controlled by one's own fortune. It was a brilliant tactic, suggested by Mars, and it worked perfectly. Jesus was the only truly vulnerable one at this point, but the battle was in fact all about the little Jew and protection was the objective.

Mercury had talents in all forms of weaponry, which served him in his assault on Tempest. He used a chain mall net to completely cover the Goddess, which subdued the crushing storm.

The first wave was stopped and the two armies paused in silence in the middle of the plain. The warriors stood face to face, God to God, breasts heaving, and there was a moment when their histories and intertwined families made them regret the position they were in. They regretted that it came to this with God against God. This moment lasted the shortest of time as the Wicked Demon recognized the hesitation, and covered his army with a putrid green cloud of hate that fortified their evil natures. He screamed a primal scream, which bolstered their resolve and terrified all decent defenders. It consisted of only one legible word ... "ATTACK!"

Both armies, now numbering in the hundreds, came crashing into the plain. Bellona, Mar's sister and a mighty War Goddess, clashed with Minerva, also a War Goddess and terrible in her might. Hercules once again fought the horrible, three-headed, fire-breathing monster, Cacus, whom he had once defeated, but whom Hades had returned to life. Pietus, the Goddess of Duty, stood ground against Pallor, the Goddess of Fear. Honos, the God of Honor, faced Pavor, the God of Alarm, while Diana loosed arrow after arrow, bringing down huge numbers of the lesser evil masses.

The battle swayed back and forth with no real progress and little to suggest any would be quickly coming. Satan and the serpent watched the evolving scene from the hilltop. Poseidon and Hades watched from the top of their hill, with a special eye for Lucifer and any move he might make.

Jesus was with Aphrodite and Apollo in the center of the hill. Satan could clearly see the halo of the gentle Christ, which softly lit the hill above the fray. He would wait. He would see if in time the Evil Army would prevail and smite the fragile human. If not, he was as sure as his own existence that he could go through the Army of Gods like a hot knife through goat cheese. They would melt before him, and he would face the King of the Jews. Truth be told, he was not as sure that in this confrontation he would have as easy a time. The pain he had experienced had given him new respect for the little human. He was surely *complete* and it seemed that

that matters. It would be preferable to have his army crush the Jew, as it had in Jerusalem. Jesus was flesh, and flesh would fail.

For Jesus, the scene was beyond anything he had experienced. He understood war, and with this understanding he had rejected Judas's call to fight the Romans. He had chosen his own demise in the most horrifying of manners. He chose the cross over the mass suffering of his people, for his sake. War was no solution, but here he was enmeshed in one with the most fearful of consequences. He watched the pain and torment for the warriors that could not even end with the peace brought by death. It was beyond description and ripped at the gentle Savior's heart.

Every person back on earth had settled in their seats to watch events unfold. They, to a person, were transfixed by the images on the big screens. They were actually watching the Gods of the Greeks and Romans and it was an experience beyond anything anyone could have ever imagined. Then, kick that up another ten-fold and that would be their feelings at actually seeing Jesus Christ, and on the other end of morality, Satan. They were stunned.

Charlie, Buzz, Sister Mary, Horace Grande, and Mandy were somewhat more prepared. They had all had some kind of exposure to the unfolding realities. Charlie more and Mary less, but they all knew what was about to unfold. The actual images were beyond what anyone could imagine. It was one thing to hear Gods speaking and interacting with each other, but an entirely different thing to see them wielding their astonishing powers to the absolute edge of their capacities. The images in the plate were striking, but to see the story unfold in giant HD digital flat screen technology was something altogether different. It was an assault on their consciousness, and many in the room were weeping in personal anguish. Charlie and Mandy held each other's hands tightly as they immersed in the war that they had somehow become a part of.

The battle continued with each side effectively neutralized by the other. It seemed the forces of good and evil were mirror images of each other, with powers equally offsetting. There were massive casualties with gruesome results. The immortality factor, however, soon repaired their bodies and all quickly returned to the fray. Satan watched from his hill.

"Can you feel it?" asked the Demon. "Can you feel the delicious agony? In this is my greatest creation....*War*. Oh yes, it has sprung from my loins like a pup from his bitch. It belongs to me and is perfect in its design. There are never any winners and multitudes of losers. The instigators are, without exception, tormented and wicked and in my command. I thought that humans were the perfect pawns for this machine of horror, but behold, these so called 'Gods' rent and smash and bleed and suffer, then find no rest. They knit and heal and begin again. Can you feel it? The agony is ... delicious!"

"*Yessss*, O master, your design is beyond the imaginations of creation. Soon may the God of All suffer in captivity for eternity, as you reshape the cosmos. I can feel its inevitability closing in on us like a vise. Soon, O master ... it will be soon. The tiny human Jew will fall before you. Drink your fill of the hopelessness below, then claim your reward and the inevitable confrontation you rightfully seek."

The Wicked One watched the carnage from his perch and rolled his eyes in delight at the suffering. His muscles slightly twitched and his mighty hands clinched and unclenched. He laid his head back on his massive shoulders and his tongue lolled out, dripping with streams of saliva. In the center of his putrid soul, the suffering was causing such an orgasm of perversion and twisted joy that even this Evil One had rarely experienced. The destruction was that great. It was at that moment that the great trident of Neptune pierced his massive chest and shredded the internals of the Wicked Beast. He fell to his knees with a look of tortured surprise.

As much as Lucifer reveled in the misery, the Gods of Good despised it. Neptune could not bear to allow it to continue and chose that moment to make his move.

The rent in the Beast's chest created an opening for Hades, who commanded the Legions of the Dead. Countless souls eternally tortured by the Evil Demon were thrust into his chest, intent on revenge. The monster's entire being was flooded by Legions of the Dead. They swirled within him like millions of maggots in a carcass. He writhed and twisted on the ground, screaming like a hurricane. Neptune and Hades were on him in a heartbeat. They hacked at his flesh with sword and mallet. The warrior brothers never hesitated for a second, and continued a fearful barrage.

The serpent quietly retreated to the tall grass.

Back on earth, the crowd was on their feet. They did not cheer, as everyone knew this was more than a football game, and that creation hung in the balance. They simply held their collective breaths and hoped against hope. Satan had been dealt a vicious blow and the gentle Jesus remained untouched. Somewhere deep within each of them they questioned if it could be that simple. They could feel the depth of evil and prayed the powers of the two could equal the power of sin and deception.

The cloud of hate that had engulfed the Army of Evil slowly lifted. Once again, the two enemy armies looked at each other's faces and recognized what it was that bound them through family, and time before time. They stopped their battle in mid-stroke and stared across the field with looks of confusion.

Of course, we all know this could never end here. This is a battle at the edge of creation, between good and evil. As good as Neptune and Hades were, at this moment, they were nowhere near the depth of evil of the Dark Angel. Although Satan was momentarily confused, and the onslaught was demanding most of his attention at the core of his being, that place where he was complete and in total oneness with evil was intact. He centered his soul on hate and it emanated from him. The hate of the countless dead was absorbed within him and made him all the more powerful. The wicked cosmos whirled around him like a universe sucking everything and everyone near him into its vortex. Neptune and Hades were like leaves in a typhoon and soon helpless in its grasp. The world could now see Lucifer in his glory, on his feet with his massive arms held above him, spinning the powerful Gods of the Gods like so much dust. His voice boomed above the field.

"Behold! I am time .... I am the beginning and the ending ... No God shall stand before me. I will not destroy when I can torture, I will not end suffering when I can enjoy it for eternity. Go now, not to that pathetic afterlife you retained beyond the Styx but to my home, to the reflection of my perfect hate and anguish. Do not die, you Gods of eternal life, but live forever in perpetual suffering."

With that, he simply *absorbed* the two Gods that were once great rulers of the Gods, the mighty two of the three. Now they were gone, and to where they had been sent, all who had witnessed trembled to think.

A scream could be heard from the rear of the Army of Good as Neverita fell to her knees in hopelessness and loss.

The cloud slowly lowered upon the Evil Army. and the war without death continued.

Slowly, Satan began to advance, moving as a sphere of agony down the hill to the plain below. It left in its path scorched earth, devoid of life or expectation. Behind it was ruin and void as it absorbed every last remnant of hope. Even those in its own army who ventured too close, were sucked into the creature's gravity and absorbed within its hell.

The Army of Good retreated to form a wall between the Beast and the gentle carpenter. The hill would be their point of last defense.   Diana, Mars, Mercury, Bellona, and Hercules were at the front. Apollo and Aphrodite were at his side, with Fortuna and Pietus, for luck and duty, close by. Others fanned out from either side hoping to find a way to help. Janus, the God of Doors, stood in front of the Messiah, ready to call forth the door that would either cast the Demon to the end of time or would end time for all creation. His mission would be the last and most desperate choice.

Slowly, Satan began his ascent of the hill from the plain. He had barely begun this final advance when a wall of flames erupted from behind the defenders. Vulcan, in the confusion, had penetrated the Army of Good to recover his discarded half. In moments, he was whole and found himself behind the battle, gazing at the exposed rear of the Army of Good. The one closest was the gentle Savior himself and Vulcan released a mighty blast. It devoured all it touched; all Gods, both good and evil, stood in silence.

The Gods of Good slowly regained their selves and turned to face their assailant. Vulcan stood in silence, staring ahead. All eyes followed his and centered on the body of the fallen Christ. He had been blown to the ground and lay face down. His back was burned clear of robes and all flesh, to his exposed bones. His vital organs including his heart could be seen, charred but still softly beating. All on the field, both good and evil including Satan himself stood silent, trying to absorb the dramatic change of events.

Apollo and Aphrodite's bodies quickly knitted, and they stooped over the fallen Savior. They laid a robe on the ground and gently turned Jesus over. Aphrodite held his head, cradled in her arms. Soft sobbing could be heard throughout the Army of Good. In time Jesus spoke.

"I am lost."

"It is not so, Lord," whispered Aphrodite, "All is not as in earth, in this World of Lost Gods. It is possible this is just another trial ... another challenge to be met."

Jesus smiled softly at the beautiful Goddess, as she tried not to lose control and fall to despair.

"It is not for me to question the true God or his will. This would not be if not for his desire. Understanding from us is hardly ... necessary. I ... can't ... believe ... this is worse than the cross. The pain ... I need to be free of it."

Aphrodite could feel the back of Jesus's head. It was void of hair and beginning to ooze and bleed.

Satan slowly moved to the fallen Messiah. Apollo moved to block him, and was thrown many meters away with a wave of his hand. Aphrodite buried her face in the face of the gentle Lord, but she too was thrown meters away with a slight wave of the monster's hand. An impenetrable ring surrounded the Dark Angel and the fallen King of the Jews. He gazed down at the broken human and smiled a wicked smile. The creature's eyes bulged and his tongue lolled to his chin. Saliva dripped off it and landed on the face of the fallen Christ. His hands clinched into fists and his body trembled in anticipation. Slowly, he lowered his right hand down, pointing his crooked finger with its massive claw, to touch the face of the pinnacle of the God of All's creation. Within inches he stopped. His face turned thoughtful as he considered the still bright aura around the Christian God's head. His chest heaved and he spoke.

"I feel your pain, Jew. I ... love your pain, Jew. It flows off you and over me like the very base juices of perversion. It fills me, and I am pleased. There is no hurry, I have felt your sting. It is preferable that I simply drink your agony and wait. Surely, the so-called God of All will deliver you. Yahweh would never leave you in my hands ... would he,

O Great Savior? Would he forsake you again and let me dispatch you to my living Hell for eternity? It is he I would crush, but tormenting you in Hell would be a worthy second prize. In time, he will have to face me or allow his 'complete' human to suffer beyond understanding."

"Woe, to one so devoid of love," responded Jesus. "I do not have the power to forgive you ... but I pity you."

"Save your pity, carpenter. You will have time to learn to pity yourself after eternity as my guest."

Jesus drew a ragged breath. His chest heaved and every breath brought wrenching pain of the flesh. His spirit became weak and his halo began to dim.

The watching Gods cried for the gentle human. They cried for love and hope and the dimming of its standard bearer.

Satan smiled as he drank in the new measure of hopelessness. He laid his head back on his shoulders and rolled his eyes in ecstasy. Slobber covered his chin and his body shook with perverse pleasure. He rolled his head back and forth and moaned.

Satan surrendered himself to his bliss, and did not notice a glow that brightened in the sky as the gentle Savior's aura dimmed. When he opened his eyes he stared into the pure white light of Heaven. Its brilliance was beyond the limits of the Demon's eyes, so he shaded them with his giant right hand.

THIS is what his effort was about, he thought. His plan had worked and the time had come for the final confrontation. He centered himself and prepared for the battle he was convinced he had evolved to win.

Slowly a descending image began to appear in the blinding perfect light. Lucifer began to gather in his power. He began to create the new creation by simply emitting evil. He understood this was the power that would overcome the God of All, and it pulsed from him like the independent universe it was. He was about to commit fully to an attack on the light, when the image became clear. It was golden and beautiful beyond description with long white hair and massive pure white wings. It emitted an aura of power and purity. Satan stared into the face of the familiar.

"Gabriel .... What ... No ... Now I must fight you? You are nothing to me ... merely a lapdog for Yahweh. I am newly realized and beyond even the imagination of Heaven itself."

"Well, aren't we full of ourselves!" the archangel replied. "Your revelations are interesting but meaningless to me. No, I do not come as a warrior to do battle, my dark brother. I come rather as a thief to steal from you what you desire most. Perhaps at the end of time we will once again meet, but for now I must bid you farewell."

With that, the golden angel lifted Jesus and ascended into the perfect white light. Before he could react or even think a thought, Satan blinked and the light was gone. So too was the little human Savior.

Chapter 60
– Satan's Fury

*T*he South Seas Ballroom in Las Vegas watched in a state of shock. The power emitting from the plate and by extension from the flat screens, together with the images and the story itself, created an event that was beyond human experience. The only historical equivalents might be Old Testament in nature, the burning bush, Moses and the Ten Commandments, the parting of the Red Sea ... The impact was so severe, the participants were nearly comatose. They watched with complete attention, which for humans ... is impossible. As the battle raged, they gasped and sighed at the right places. They hung on every deed as if their very life depended on the outcome ... which, of course it did. They flexed and jumped and cried. They prayed. Sister Mary Madeline worked her rosary until her fingers bled. The intensity of the reactions was the same for everyone in the room. The truly pious and the faux preachers were moved beyond their experience. It can be assumed that some were fortified by the ascension of Christ, while others quietly wondered how what they were watching was going to affect their lives, and if there was going to be a price to be paid. Satan was very real and very much alive. Who now would defeat him? Certainly not the small group of defenders left on the battlefield with no one to defend. For them this could not be good.

Satan stood motionless for what seemed like eternity. No one moved or uttered a word. Finally Nodutus, the little God of Tying Knots in Wheat smiled and whispered, "Sweet."

Satan reached out and grabbed the little God by the throat. He held him in one hand, extended to the length of his mighty arms.

"Today you will all be in Hell with the hosts of the damned. This is my present to you. You will live in death and agony for the immortality you possess. I will confront the God of All ... he cannot hide for eternity. Let him for the moment live with his cowardice. I will feed on your suffering and absorb your rotting souls. For the moment it is necessary that I feed my rage, and you all will be my bread."

With that he simultaneously crushed Nodutus, and absorbed him into the realms of Hell. The monster's eyes next fell on Aphrodite, the Goddess of Love and beautiful beyond words.

"You are next, O Love Goddess," ... he hissed, "but first you will be ravaged like no creature in creation. He loved you ... I hate you ... he was gentle ... I am not. Your friends will watch and will have no power. If your Jesus sits with the God of All, let him, too, watch ... Prepare your loins ... as if you could."

Aphrodite was instantly naked and in the monster's hand. He lifted her womanhood to his lips and licked a gentle lick .... "Delicious!"

"Careful," said Apate from near the back of the Evil Army, "he's a biter."

The Goddess in the beast's hands was not as she appeared and suddenly the beautiful Goddess transformed into a grotesque ogre, with its asshole presented to the Dark Prince's lips. The ogre turned his less than handsome face to Lucifer, and purred ... "Delicious? Why, thank you!"

Lucifer spat and threw the creature to the ground where it abruptly changed into a frog and hopped away. It was in fact Thetis, the shape-shifter who, in the confusion of the ascension had replaced Aphrodite, fearing what the enraged Beast might do.

Mars immediately jumped in front of the Devil, and with a mighty swing of his broadsword sliced off his right arm. He spun in a quick circle and chopped off the left, then jumped back in preparation for the counterattack.

Satan slowly smiled. His arms reappeared in an instant, and he flexed his massive fists.

"Mars, ah, I face a warrior ... a true warrior. And what is a WARRIOR?" he spat the word out like a foul taste. "So full of feelings like 'honor' and 'truth' and 'loyalty,' so full of these things of such value for the good and righteous, and then what can you do with such things? You train and practice and train some more. You perfect your craft of killing and search for a place where your efforts shall be worthy, and this is where I command. This is the joke on you, Mars. It is I who created war, and I who command all who instigate and commit such deeds. I own all who would send your kind to the killing fields. Their purposes are, without exception, twisted and wicked. Their outcomes are the feasts that I feed on, the suffering and anguish that enriches me. Yes, Mars, you serve me well."

Mars replied, "Honor, truth, and loyalty are for me and mine. Your dismissal of their import only reinforces me. Come, O monster ... feel my sword and suffer the sting of the true God of War."

Mars attacked with renewed purpose. The Evil Angel grabbed the Warrior God like a small child, and instantly absorbed him into his being. He stood and rolled his eyes in pleasure.

"Rot in Hell, O mighty War God."

Diana loosed her arrows and sent a mighty flurry. She too, was instantly absorbed. Hercules grabbed the creature by the back of his wings and lifted him into the air. He too, was gone in a heartbeat.

Satan stood and smiled. He fed on the fear and hatred he was generating in the Gods. He closed his eyes and raised his arms to the Heavens.

"See, you God of All ... see the suffering you allow in your cowardice."

Softly, a familiar voice whispered in the ear of the Beast.

"My unholy God ... there issss a door, it is here and it will lead you to the one you seek." The serpent spoke quickly, as he knew too well the Devil knew no patience.

Lucifer grabbed the snake by its neck and lifted it to his face. He hissed.

"Speak ... what do you know?"

"There is a God here, O Wicked One, who is the God of Doors. It is said in his time he opened the door to the mornings and closed the door to the night. He was most revered and has the power you seek ... he controls the door to the Almighty, and was to use it to save the little Jew. Events were too quick for him, and now that door remains closed. Twist him to your will, O Mighty One, and walk through the

door to the God of All ... Thisss God ... he is known as ....
Janus."

The Devil stared into the eyes of the snake.

"You kept this from me ... You knew of this door and
you kept it from me."

"Oh no, master, I only heard of this since your charge
... I was hiding there ... over there .... in the grass and I heard
these things. I hurried as soon as I could to tell you, master, I
only work for your glory ... I only exist to pleasssse you,
glorious Lucifer, and live for your glory to come!"

The serpent was the perfect Deceiver. He had been
created to bring the fall of what was said to be God's greatest
creation ... man. It turns out, deceiving man was a very
simple thing, but through the centuries, the snake had grown
in envy and ambition. It was its overwhelming desire to
replace Satan as the Master of Hell, to rule the wicked on
earth. This was his one and only chance. This was the
moment he had prepared for.

"We shall see," spat the Demon. "I have eternity to
deal with you."

With that, he threw the snake aside and looked
around at the remaining Gods that had resisted him.
Nemesis, the Goddess of Revenge, came to his side and
pointed. "He is there, master."

Satan walked and stood facing the God, Janus. He
towered over him like an All-Star wrestler, looking down at a
five-year-old child. He stared into the eyes of the lesser God,
and considered in silence. Janus looked into the eyes of the
Wicked One, and showed no fear. He was a God, after all.

"Is it true that you control this *door*?"

Janus was silent.

"So, it is true ... It appears that both time and purpose have aligned in this piss-hole of a world. Show me this door ..."

"I will not," was all the lesser God said.

"But, I have the key," replied the monster. With that he jumped into the crowd and emerged with the real Goddess of Love, Aphrodite. He held her upside down by her ankle. Her clothes fell from her, exposing her perfect body to all. "Do you understand what I am capable of?" he asked the God, Janus. "Can you feel how I will enjoy not only the door that you control, but the turning of this ... delicious ... *key*. She was with him, who I hate ... Her defilement will fill many purposes.

"I'll give you a moment."

Janus was silent and stared at the vicious Beast.

"Very well," it spoke. "You will change your mind."

With focused perversion, it attacked the Goddess and she cried out in pain. It was a perfect combination of suffering and indignity.

"ENOUGH," yelled Janus. "Put her down ... I will do as you wish."

"No," whispered Aphrodite, heroically playing her part, "all will be in vain."

"This was never our fight," cried Janus. "Let the God of All deal with this ... if he can. I will not see you suffer for another God who has done nothing for us."

"Wisely spoken, puny God, now show me your door and I will leave this ungodly cage."

"When I do this, be quick, as I cannot hold this door open for long, and this cannot be repeated."

With that, Janus held his arms in the air ... he knew the dangers of opening the door to the end of time, but to put an end to the Beast, he chose to ignore the risk. He was hopeful that the deception was complete, and that the Wicked One would not hesitate. He spoke words of incantation, and images rolled between his fingertips. History of creation beyond even the memory of the Beast blasted in circles between his outstretched arms. Soon, a glowing ball was pulsating like a living thing, high in the air above the God of Doors. This was truly the portal to eternity, Satan thought, and he wasted no time. He threw Aphrodite to the ground, lifted on his mighty golden wings and flew directly into the ball of light.

In an instant, the World of Lost Gods was swallowed by darkness and silence.

Chapter 61
– A Welcome Reunion

*T*he flat screens went black. Silence filled the ballroom. Charlie looked to the plate, which had suddenly become, well, a pie plate.

People began to talk, talk turned to shouts and shouts turned to cheers. It would appear that Jesus had truly ascended and Satan had been cast to the end of time. The ancient Gods of the Greeks and Romans had been heroic in their defense of the Christian God. The wicked Gods had done their best to support Lucifer, but the truly heroic were the mighty Gods who fought a hopeless battle against all odds and prevailed. They were real, and would never be forgotten for the deeds they had done.

As the people in the ballroom began to focus, it became apparent to them that they were not alone. Walking about and around them were the very Gods that they had feared were condemned to Satan's Hell. In fact, many of the Gods they had just been watching were walking among them.

They were dressed as they were in the World of Lost Gods. They were not armed, but were magnificent in their appearance. They emitted auras of energy and halos of light. The humans on one side and the Gods on the other had one major thing in common. They were all totally confused.

Mars approached the head table with Charlie, Mandy, Sister Mary, Buzz, and Horace. In spite of his glory, the War God looked decidedly pale.

"Is this the Hell of which the Demon spoke? It does not feel like Hell."

Charlie stood up.

"No, Sir, this is not Hell. This is earth. This is the place you left so many years ago. It would appear that you are no longer fit for a World of Lost Gods. You see, your memory is no longer twisted and there are many now that believe."

"Welcome home!"

Mars slowly fell to his knees and wept. Soon the entire ballroom was full of humans and Gods laughing and crying. There were hugs and handshakes. It was clear to them that this meeting had been the reason that people believed in them, and that Charlie and his group were responsible. While they did not yet know the details, they understood the big picture. They owed these few so much.

Buzz took a mighty pull on his pipe and confided to a laughing Mercury, "Dude, my mind is totally BLOWN!"

Charlie was thrilled to meet Nodutus, the little God who made knots in stalks of wheat. He had felt a simple connection with him from his first appearance in the plate. They would have a friendship that would sustain Charlie and his descendants for generations to come. Even though he was only the God who made knots in wheat, he was a God after all.

Aphrodite came up to a shy Mandy and hugged her tightly. She cried and looked deeply into Mandy's eyes. "You and I have much in common, sweet one," she said, "your love is strong."

"Oh my," said Mandy with a slight, uncomfortable curtsy, "you are a Goddess, what could we have in common?"

"I am not a soothsayer, but there is some of the future that is clear. You see, my love, we are both with child, I from the Christ, and you from your Charlie."

"Oh, no," stammered Mandy, "you see Charlie and I only did ... er ... just once, last night; it is way too early tc ..."

"Mandy ... believe me, in this I am certain. I am a Goddess, after all."

Mandy held her hands over her mouth and stared at the Goddess of Love.

Aphrodite continued, "They will both be fine men and in truth, best friends. There is still evil in the world with pain and ignorance. There will be challenges on the path that our two will meet. I have lost the love of my life, but he is in his Heaven and his spirit lives on, both in hearts and in my son. There will be many songs sung and stories told. She looked around the room at the windows, at the lights. What kind of world is this that we have returned to?"

But Mandy could not keep it in.

"CHARLIE," she screamed and went running across the room to his somewhat confused arms. "You are going to be ... a DADDY!"

Chapter 62
– Evil, Too

Somewhere else in the world, in a giant swamp, the evil Gods and Goddesses sat. They were totally confused, with no real idea of where they were. In time, a familiar creature appeared, rising from the stinking muck with first a forked tongue, followed by the snake itself.

"Welcome home," it said. "Oh yesssss, you are back on earth. It is an earth much like you have known but so much different. There will be time for you to learn, as it is for all immortals. One thing is for certain, I am ruler of hell on earth, and the Master of All That Is Evil. You will bow before me."

The serpent rose on its body to its full height, twenty meters of pure silver, and flared its head in glory.

The group of evil Gods stared at the Master of Deception, and after a respectful time broke out in laughter.

Eris, the Goddess of Discord, responded, "You do not know us, Serpent. We follow no one. We spread our evil for our own pleasure and no other. Perhaps you can master the humans ... this will only be known in time. We do as we please, with respect or honor to no one."

The Gods all shook their heads and wandered away, leaving the snake alone in the center of the swamp, a swamp much like the one where we had first found it. It pondered at what had just happened, but having seen many things and knowing many things, it was soon clear considering the recent events. These evil Gods did wicked things for pleasure. Humans were their puppets that they made dance. There was no end game for them. Generations of humans came and went and it meant nothing to them. For the serpent, things were different. It battled for souls. One deed or two would not satisfy. It needed to possess for eternity. The battle was not the war. The war was for all time. In spite of their insolence, these Gods would serve its purpose and serve it well. Each temptation they created led simple humans closer to it. The serpent had no need for loyalty. It even laughed at itself for considering it. It was the *souls of man* that it coveted. It was, in fact, the "new Satan" and the Master of the Destruction of man. Man, who was weak and imperfect. It occurred to the serpent, that what Lucifer had said had some truth in it. How could the God of All be perfect in the creation of such imperfect creatures. Perhaps he WAS vulnerable. Perhaps he COULD be replaced. In truth, the snake had in effect killed the Dark Angel himself, by tricking him into jumping through the door to the end of time. Could the God of All be much more difficult? It would consider this. It did have eternity to plan and *yesss*, why not? It liked the thought of the possibility of becoming the God of All. It began to feel like this might be its destiny.

On the beach of southeast Florida, near the city of Boca Raton, Neptune and Neverita were watching the sunrise. One human walked by but had headphones on and a metal detector. He was so intense in his search that he did not even notice he was in the presence of Gods. Neverita looked up at her massive Sea God and shook her head, smiling ... humans never change. She laid her head on his shoulder, and breathed the breath of freedom and of being a spirit reborn.

311

"We failed so miserably," said Neptune. "We became involved in our own miserable stories and neglected our sole purpose. We did not maintain the nobility of Gods, but surrendered to the foibles of humans. We left them without reason to believe in us. We became no different than they are, and they turned away. After meeting the Christian God, it is no wonder they chose him. He did not forget his purpose. While his followers did twist his memory, his words survived. We must make it part of our own story, to rebuild his memory, and take within ourselves the message he brought ... a message of love.

He looked deeply into the beautiful Goddess's eyes. "We will not fail again. This, I swear!"

The two lifted themselves from the sand and walked to the surf and into the sea beyond. Neptune was freely crying with great joy. His sea, his glorious sea ... how he had missed her!

Chapter 63
– Heaven's Gate

Zeus sat upon his rickety throne, still somewhere between here and there. He was looking at his fingernails, which were in need of a good cleaning, when Gabriel dropped the gentle Savior at the foot of his throne.

"Thanks, Gabe, thank you ... you are the best thief ... EVER!"

Gabriel smiled and replied, "Believe me, that was MY pleasure!" and in a wink he was gone.

Zeus waved his hand and the little human was instantly healed. Jesus rose to his feet and looked up at the King of the Olympiads. He fell to the ground and stammered, "My God, my God, I fall before your glory, an unworthy servant."

Zeus looked down at Jesus and said, "I knew I could not fool you, Jesus. You always see with your heart. Get up now, and settle yourself. You have been through much."

Jesus got up and shook the dirt off his robes. The pain from his burns was gone, and his flesh was healed. The fear in his heart was also gone, but his confusion remained. He looked up at his God, and at the rickety throne of Zeus.

"But why, my Father, why pretend to be a Greek God?"

"Pretend? ... I am the God Almighty, and I do not pretend. Of course I am the God of the Gods, just as I am the God of the angels in Heaven, and the God of man. I am the God of All. All is *all*, and it is that simple."

"But, the Torah," stammered Jesus ... "The beginning, in Genesis ... Is the book of the Jews as false as the book of the Christians?"

"False? False? Oh, how you speak so lightly of such things. So you think these things cannot be true? Because of your perceived conflicts, you think these things cannot be true? Can green and blue both be true? Can hope and loss both be true? Can black and white be true? What exactly are the limits of truth? Man says I am the God of All, and that my powers are without limit. Then they judge what I can and cannot do. Verily, I say everything is true because it is true, I have no limits ... Well, that is not exactly correct, I have one thing that I cannot alter. I cannot change what I am, what *IS*."

Jesus sat cross-legged at the foot of the God of All, as he did before the wise men of his age. His mind was racing, and as in his life, hungry for truth.

"How about a little refresher?" asked God the Father. Instantly, there were two mugs of bubbly golden liquid, one in front of the little Savior and one in the mighty fist of God.

"What is this?" asked the little Savior.

"Why, it is the perfect truth of my love for man. It is called 'beer.'"

Jesus lifted the mug to his lips and took a long drink.

"PHEWWW..." He spat on the ground.

God bellowed a huge laugh and sayeth, "Well, it does take some getting used to, but when you do ...." He took a long draught, "Oh, *YES!*"

316

Jesus smiled and said, "If it is possible, I would enjoy a bit of red wine."

Instantly there was the finest wine in creation (of course) in his hand.

"I like wine, too," replied God, "but I *LOVE* beer!"

After a few moments Jesus began, "Please, Father, explain all I am capable of understanding."

God looked down at his "complete" human. "Lesson one ... do you think I am not capable of teaching you all of creation? I do not have the power to make you equal to me? What is the power you think I do not have?"

"I, uh, was just ..."

"Relax, Jesus, I am only making a point. This has been at the root of many of the problems in humanity. They define by their own limitations. Even in their Gods they build in limits, yet they say out loud that they have none. They say I am without limits, that I am 'Eternal,' 'Almighty,' that I am the 'Creator,' but then they turn around and create religions that divide me and challenge me. It is as if after my Creation things went very wrong. Nonsense, I am perfect as are all things.

"It is very odd, I must say. Humans are so tribal. My side is correct, but not yours. Can it be that a God that has limitless powers can have limits? Is it not possible to be Yahweh *and* Vishnu? Could I not be Zeus *and* Buddha? Is it impossible that I might be Allah and also be Oden? How about this, is it impossible that I am the God of Jesus, and too, the God of Satan? No, it is all true. I am the alpha and the omega, the beginning and the end. I am the reason and the source. Without me, there is nothing. The God of All is exactly that, THE GOD OF ALL!"

"I have known Satan, and I do not believe you could be this creature."

"What you believe is nothing to me. I am independent of belief. Before, I said the only thing I cannot change is what 'is.' Evil is. And though it is hard to deal with, it too, is part of the perfection. It is beyond beautiful. It is 'PERFECT.'"

"But the hate, the suffering, the deception and the murder, there is no sense in this. What purpose could it possibly hold?"

"Balance...."

Jesus was clearly confused. "I do not understand."

"It is the force that is the universe, and without it all motion would cease. Without this force, we would return to the void. When it is finished, it will. But I see I must go slowly. In the beginning there was the void and as in all things it too had, for lack of a better word, purpose. I am that purpose. In the beginning, there was only one choice, as all things have a half and the two sides of the void was and is 'do, or not do.'

"I did."

"You did?"

"I did, and now creation 'is.' Think hard, I am only capable of perfection. This fits your mythology. I am perfect. As a perfect being, my creations must as a result, be perfect. There is no this way or that. There is only ... 'perfect' and now it 'is.' I can report to you some of the features of what is, if that would help."

"Please, Father, I am still confused."

"OK, think of all that you know. There is up and down, left and right, in and out, right and wrong. There is the physical and the spiritual, and it is all the same. Without balance, one side falls down. There is the yin and the yang, there is hate and love, there is pain and pleasure, there is Jesus and there is Satan. There is infinite hope and infinite despair ... balanced and perfect.

"This 'is' the balance that 'is,' simple and perfect."

"How can there be the Gods of the Far East, the God Shiva and you, my God, and our stories, and have them *all* be true? It seems to me that you are truth, and then they would all be false."

"But here I sit before you as Zeus. What of your new friends? What of Aphrodite? Are their stories false? Did they not happen? Do you believe I am not capable of making two realities true? Is the story of David the King true?"

"Of course."

"And the story of Moses?"

"Of course."

"So, two stories can be true ... of course. But humans need to protect their own stories, to include and exclude. I am right and you are wrong. My tribe is better than your tribe. Again, this shows the balance. You see this is the reason humans are the finest creation in creation. They have the ability to generate hate. There are other generators of hate in the cosmos. You have known Satan, who is my 'complete' being of hate, and is absolutely necessary to exist or you, my perfect being of love, would not exist. This is also something that makes a human the greatest of what 'is,' humans are very good at generating love. They are perfect engines of balance in the universe. Also, in all things there, by necessity must be extremes. You and Satan both are extreme. If there were not extremes, if you follow this strain of consciousness to its end, there would only be two masses in perfect balance which, to be honest, would not, in fact be perfect. What 'is,' is perfect."

"Why would the masses not be 'perfect'?"

"Where is the love, the hate? I know that this is too much. To explain every detail of creation would take all of eternity, literally, because everything is also changing. Change is a foundation of what 'is': evolution, devolution, growth, loss ... balance. Modern human science is beginning to see, but this is not of your world and I will not confuse you, and what they see is like a drop of rain in the ocean, but nonetheless they see. Let it be known that everything is there for all to see, and in the end everything leads back to me."

"My Father, what are you?"

"I am ... what 'is.'"

Jesus questioned, "I am not made in your image, as it is written?"

"I am everything that 'is.' What is it that might not be in my image? If I am all things, then you have to be an image of 'me'... if that is important to you. Try not to consider what is written on parchment, but rather what is written in your heart."

"There are those that say you do not exist..."

"There are those that say a creature that decides what happens day to day, and judges man, and considers and creates the engines that run the universe does not exist. In

320

this they are right ... and wrong. If you asked them if the universe exists, if it truly 'is,' they would mostly say 'yes.' And they are right. I am what 'is.' Again, the only thing I cannot alter is what 'is.' It is perfect and exists without intelligent design, perfect does not have variables. I am here with you because it is an unfolding of what is. It is necessary and perfect. In order to be 'perfect' it is necessary. I am a reflection of what you might think of as 'desire.' In this I am able ... because again, I am without limits ... to make you 'complete,' to make Satan, 'complete.' I can shuffle and I can move, I can inspire religions, and become Gods of all descriptions. In this, I am the energy that 'is,' and a manifestation of the spirit of man. Am I a creature that decides day to day what happens? Do I judge man, and did I create the universe by intelligent design? The universe is what is, I am what 'is.' I did do all of these things, but more clearly, I *am* those things and so much more. Do I judge gravity? Do I judge sunlight? Like man's deeds, they are cause and effect. They are exact as is the judgment of man. They are judged by what 'is.' I am the alpha and the omega, the beginning and the end. Do remember that what 'is,' boils down to 'do,' or 'do not' ... I did. Also, those that swear I do not exist would never believe in a creature like a 'human,' if they did not know they do exist. Imagine all of the tubes, pipes, flesh, and a heart that pumps for no reason. Birth and the miracle there would fall below the wheels of their intelligence. Not possible!"

"I am sorry, Father, but this is much for me."

"Only because much of what you have in your life has been *taught*. You more than understand my words. Ask the question that is biggest in your heart. Go ahead ... ask it."

"What is death, then, Father, if I cannot consider the words of the Torah."

"Ah yes ... this is the real question, isn't it. Life itself! This is the mystery that directs the lives of all who understand the concept of death. It is what makes man the crown of creation. It is the greatest generator of *fear* in creation. Death, a constant humming, fear-generating machine! It is also a great generator of love and peace. Who would easily sacrifice something as precious as life? It gives life itself value. There is no other phenomenon that produces so much emotional energy, energy necessary for the existence of creation: happy, sad, fear, courage, joy, despair, and on and on. The question you really ask is what happens to you when you die."

Jesus nodded.

"Please remember that I am speaking to your understanding. It is so much bigger. You will change, and in time there will be more.

"Life itself is energy, and even man's present science realizes that this cannot be created or destroyed. You see it goes back to being perfect, as it is ... funny to be constrained by *perfection*, huh?" God smiled and shook his head. "So, what happens when the flesh fails? What happens when eyes close for the final time and man breathes his final breath? Here it comes ... wait for it ....

"He exists."

He continues. "Oh yes, it's true, he continues. There are two things that are basic in what 'is,' balance and momentum. In creation there is motion. Energy is always in motion. In out, up down, round and round. It is the same for all things in creation including man's energy, or his soul if you prefer. In this you might think of good as up and evil as down when, in fact, for what truly 'is' it does not matter at all. When a man is a good man and trying to always be a better man, he would be going up. When a man is a bad man and getting worse, his soul is going down. Of course, the big question is, where is up or down? This again is complicated to infinity. I will explain within your truths. You are reborn. Every other expression of energy in the universe has ... consequences. If you hit a ball with a stick, it flies. If you crush a frog with a rock, it dies. Heat water, it turns to vapor; cool it down, it turns to ice ... consequences. The same goes for emotional energy. If you are hateful to someone, they are hurt. If you love someone, they feel love. This is way simplified, but you get the idea. Emotional action creates reactions, just like any other expression of energy. All the things you do exist in creation. All of these actions create momentum. When your body drops, there is still momentum. The deeds you have done propel you to what is next for you. There are some religions that have some of this correct, but the entire mystery of creation is energy of all that is beyond any one creation. Does a camel's tail understand a camel? I don't think so. But for you, my Son, of whom I am very proud, I explain what will fulfill you."

"Maybe I understand some. Please continue, Father."

"Well, when I say 'deeds' it is really deeper than that. Deeds create emotion, and these emotions boil down to dimensions of love and hate. Deeds generate sadness, joy, hate, and love and countless levels in between. When I say deeds, it is the fruit of these deeds that I truly mean, and this propels man through death to the rightful level in his momentum projection. There is no judgment, it is not necessary. If you push a cart down a hill, it will go to exactly the same place if you again push it down the exact same hill with the exact same force. The same goes for the soul of man. If acts in life are on a certain projection, this will continue until there are more acts, which will either continue or change the momentum and the direction. Forgiveness is not necessary, as going up or down fulfills man's, and creation's, ultimate purpose. And no single act determines a man or woman's ultimate projection. It is simple and it is perfect. It is what 'is.' Now, consider balance. In all of creation there is exactly the same amount of hate as love. It is the perfect balance in the universe. This is why man is so magnificent. He is capable of generating massive quantities of each. Here there is peace, there there is war; here there is creation, there there is destruction; here hate and over there love. This is what 'is.'"

Jesus was visibly shaken. "So, for every act of love I inspired, there was a REQUIRED amount of hate generated? This is a nightmare! I, in effect, am responsible for great suffering through my acts of love. This is madness."

"This is what 'is,' my Son. Without balance the universe would cease to exist. It is what modern man might call physics, extended to the spirit, which they might deny."

324

"So there will never be a Heaven on earth," continued Jesus. "Man is cursed to go into and out of wars and hate for eternity? To understand this, would bring madness and despair."

"Well, hold on, Junior ... who said that earth can never become a Heaven, as you imagine one? It most certainly can!"

"How can that be if it must be 'balanced'?"

"Oh yeah, I guess I did not mention ... there are countless earths in creation. There are numbers beyond imagination. There are earths beyond your ability to imagine on the head of a pin! Oh my, yes ... and they are places where the soul might go. If a human is good and trying to be better every day, he or she might go to another 'earth,' where the entire world is better. If he or she is bad, they might well go to a world where things are much worse, as you can imagine. The earth you have known is exactly in the middle, and its momentum is to be determined, but yes, in time, it could become your *Heaven* ...or a *Hell*. The self-determination is the true engine of human emotion and an essential part of me ... of what 'is' and of course ... it is perfect. Humans alone will determine earth's future, and as for the side of love you should be proud, you have played an important part."

"But, what now, will I go back? I need to fight this fight and defeat the Monster. I am not done."

"Oh, you are done, my Son. You have said what needed to be said, and you have done what you needed to do. You created great momentum. More of the same words would not make much difference over time. And the Wicked One is done, too. But be not afraid. There are others that

325

take up your sword. Earth has witnessed your final battle, and again believes in your recent Godly friends. Man once again believes in them. They are renewed and will have another chance to serve in directing earth through good and evil."

Jesus smiled and nodded, "Thank you, Father, they will do well, I am sure."

"They will be 'perfect,'" replied the God of All.

At that moment there was a great ball of light and Satan crashed into the little throne of Zeus.

The God of All looked over at Jesus and smiled ... "Ah, once again PERFECT!"

Chapter 64
– Perfect!

Satan flew from the ball of pure white light. His strategy might have been to center and evolve into pure hate before attacking, but his raging emotions propelled him directly into the God of All. The image of Zeus didn't fool him, and he hit Yahweh like a freight train. The true God's eyes were as big as saucers as he struggled with the furious Dark Angel. Their arms wrapped around each other and it was then that Lucifer began to center. He pulled all evil into his heart. He focused all hate on the living God. He surrendered to the void of all destruction. The two began to spin within the void. The world around the new Mt. Olympus began to take on a wicked hue. The balance shifted as the face of the God of All took on a look of terror.

It was then that the little Jew rose to stand. With a grim look, he charged the wicked Demon and knocked God from his grasp. The two rolled on the sand and began to transform. Satan's face became more Christ-like and Jesus took on a visage that can only be called ... evil. The two champions exchanged physical and spiritual attributes several times and settled somewhere in between, neither was particularly good, neither was particularly bad. Throughout the entire struggle, peals of laughter could be heard coming from the image of Zeus, from the God of All, rolling in the sand.

When they had each become part of the other, the two stood, and looked at each other in amazement. They were in fact identical images.

It was then that the God of All spoke.

"Enough!" he said, and the two returned to their original selves. Again, the two looked at each other in amazement, and then they turned their eyes on the true God.

Finally, Satan spoke, "You are cruel beyond words ... In this division of energy I have been the loser. Love and joy are strangers to me, and now I am cursed to exist in misery and loss. I hate you even more."

God smiled, "Good, Go and hate some more!" With that God pursed his lips and sucked the Devil into his mouth. He chewed and chewed and swallowed. Then, he turned and looked at the amazed Jesus.

"Tastes just like chicken!"

Jesus finally began to speak. "I have felt evil. I now know hatred and perversion at its most vile depth. This is half of you ... Now, whom do I worship? When I pray, when I ask for guidance, who will answer me? Now, there is no one I can trust. Not even myself."

"Oh, Jesus, you are so dramatic. This was simply a gift to you. Now you know what humans experience, and now you will battle evil with your eyes wide open. Like in physics you need effort to throw a ball into the air ... it falls on its own. It takes effort to create love. With no effort, things fall into evil. For balance, at times my help is required and prayers are answered. Your mission on earth was simple and pure. You will go into a place that is much more complicated. Fear not, know that I love you, and as in all things ... you are 'perfect.'"

With that, God pursed his lips and sucked Jesus into his mouth. He chewed and chewed and swallowed. A big smile crossed his face, and he said to no one in particular: "Tastes just like chicken."

If anyone was there to witness it, the scene was again about to change. The God of All got a look on his face that suggested an idea. Quicker than a thought, He was suddenly transformed into a beautiful pure white Chanticleer rooster, a truly amazing looking bird. It jumped down from the throne of the New Olympus and scooted out to the little dirt road. It turned its head sideways and eyed a tiny pebble. It pecked with precision and grabbed the little rock in its beak. It seemed to be surprised and dropped the little stone. Then, it wandered down the tiny dirt road, meandering back and forth in typical chicken fashion. Its typical rooster strut was only interrupted once with a jump high into the air, where it clicked its rooster heels together. The mighty God of All then continued, like any really happy chicken would, down the exceptionally lovely little road, somewhere between the beginning and the end, exactly in the middle of here and there, with the blue sky and puffy white clouds of another perfect day.

Epilogue

In another part of this place of endless possibilities, along the very same lovely little dirt road, there was a scene not exactly unfamiliar. As far as healthy eyes could see down this road, it ended in a cloud on the ground, which you or I might call a *fog*. Just inside of this cloud, one could barely make out the form of a person who seemed to be moving onto the road. Naturally, as whoever it was came further down the road, they went further from the cloud and so became clear as the day itself. The person was in soft brown robes with a white turban and white cloth scarf around his neck. He wore fancy slippers of all colors on his feet, and sported a full brown moustache and beard. Even from far away, it became clear to any who might observe, that this was obviously Shafi, the Healer, Ahmad, Most Commendable, Faith Conqueror and Opener, Bashir, the bringer of good things, the Messenger of God, it was indeed none other than the Prophet Muhammad himself.

...and he had no idea where he was.

About the Author

Gary Belschner was born on May 1, 1950 in New Haven, Connecticut. His family moved to Edina, Minnesota, in 1964. In 1966 Gary went to Shattuck Military School in Faribault, Minnesota, where he attained such distinguished designations as "Captain of the Work Squad" and "President of the Privates Club." He was also captain of his Varsity Soccer team and was the recipient of the excellent education offered at this fine school.

Gary attended college in several locations, before heading north in 1972 to Alaska for adventure and riches working on the Alaskan Pipeline. He spent thirteen years working as a surveyor on construction sites and in many remote native villages across Alaska. In Valdez, while working construction, he met his wife and soul mate, Rosemarie. They were married in Anchorage in 1977 on the day they first sent oil down the Trans-Alaska Pipeline.

After enough adventures to write several books, they moved in 1985 to a small farm in Polk County, Wisconsin. They were blessed with two perfect daughters, Jennifer Rose and Rachel Marie, who both continue to warm their hearts to this day. Jennifer and her man, Nathan, have created the perfect granddaughter, Rosalie Danger, who now adds to the love. A second grandbaby promises even more to love.

Gary continued to do surveying, but a very poor local economy limited the possible income, and other strategies were set in motion. Being very conservative and blessed with a strong business sense, Gary decided raising thoroughbred racehorses would be a sure source of steady income. Again, after enough stories to write several books, the horses were all sold at auction (at a considerable loss), and Gary began selling real estate.

Through all of this, the patient Rosemarie was working as a facilities maintenance engineer for a plastics company in Stillwater, Minnesota, about forty miles from the farm. The family funding fell to Rose as the real estate market produced riches about as quickly as a the horse venture. In 1992 Gary went to work as a Direct Salesman for a company that manufactured the finest surveying instruments in the world, WILD. In the mid-1990s, WILD went corporate and changed its name to Leica Geosystems.

Gary had found his working *home* and was very successful working in this excellent company. He went back to school and earned a better-late-than- never degree from Western Governors University, in Marketing Management. He was made part of a Senior Management team and was promoted to Vice President. The company was promptly gobbled up in a hostile takeover, which involved replacement of management. Gary excelled, with his neck under the boot of the new regime, until Oct 1, 2010 when he decided to follow a different brick road.

Gary's first novel was *River Jim: A World Class Piscator*." He also has a CD, "Katie Stares at the Moon," under his musical name, Gary Earl.